Daniel

TEACH THE TEXT COMMENTARY SERIES

John H. Walton
Old Testament General Editor

Mark L. Strauss
New Testament General Editor

When complete, the TEACH THE TEXT COMMENTARY SERIES *will include the following volumes:*

Old Testament Volumes

Genesis .... Richard S. Hess

Exodus .... T. Desmond Alexander

Leviticus and Numbers .... Joe M. Sprinkle

Deuteronomy .... Michael A. Grisanti

Joshua .... Kenneth A. Mathews

Judges and Ruth .... Kenneth C. Way

1 & 2 Samuel .... Robert B. Chisholm Jr.

1 & 2 Kings .... David W. Baker

1 & 2 Chronicles .... Robert R. Duke

Ezra, Nehemiah, and Esther .... Douglas J. E. Nykolaishen and Andrew J. Schmutzer

Job .... Daniel J. Estes

Psalms, two volumes .... C. Hassell Bullock

Proverbs .... Richard L. Schultz

Ecclesiastes and Song of Songs .... Edward M. Curtis

Isaiah .... Frederick J. Mabie

Jeremiah and Lamentations .. J. Daniel Hays

Ezekiel .... John W. Hilber

Daniel .... Ronald W. Pierce

The Minor Prophets .... Douglas Stuart

New Testament Volumes

Matthew .... Jeannine K. Brown

Mark .... Grant R. Osborne

Luke .... R. T. France

John and 1–3 John .... David L. Turner

Acts .... David E. Garland

Romans .... C. Marvin Pate

1 Corinthians .... Preben Vang

2 Corinthians .... Moyer V. Hubbard

Galatians and Ephesians ...... Roy E. Ciampa

Philippians, Colossians, and Philemon .... Linda L. Belleville

1 & 2 Thessalonians, 1 & 2 Timothy, and Titus .... Philip H. Towner

Hebrews .... Jon C. Laansma

James, 1 & 2 Peter, and Jude .... Jim Samra

1–3 John .... (see *John*)

Revelation .... J. Scott Duvall

To see which titles are available, visit the series website at www.teachthetextseries.com.

TEACH the TEXT
COMMENTARY SERIES

Daniel

Ronald W. Pierce

Mark L. Strauss and John H. Walton
GENERAL EDITORS

ILLUSTRATING THE TEXT

Kevin and Sherry Harney
ASSOCIATE EDITORS

BakerBooks
a division of Baker Publishing Group
Grand Rapids, Michigan

© 2015 by Ronald W. Pierce
Captions and Illustrating the Text sections © 2015 by Baker Publishing Group

Published by Baker Books
a division of Baker Publishing Group
PO Box 6287, Grand Rapids, MI 49516-6287
www.bakerbooks.com

Casebound edition published 2021
ISBN 978-1-5409-0235-1

Printed in the United States of America

The Library of Congress has cataloged the original edition as follows:
Pierce, Ronald W., 1946–
    Daniel / Ronald W. Pierce; Mark L. Strauss and John H. Walton, general
editors.
        pages cm — (Teach the text commentary)
    Includes bibliographical references and index.
    ISBN 978-0-8010-9213-8 (cloth)
    1. Bible. Daniel—Commentaries. I. Strauss, Mark L., 1959– editor. II.
Walton, John H., 1952– editor. III. Title.
    BS1555.3.P54 2015
    224′.507—dc23   2015003269

21   22   23   24   25   26   27   7   6   5   4   3   2   1

This commentary is dedicated to my students at Biola University who, for nearly four decades, have partnered with me in a close reading of Daniel. From their widely varied disciplines, rich experiences, and maturing knowledge of the faith, they have helped to shape my ever-growing understanding of this literary and theological masterpiece of sacred Scripture. More importantly, we have grown together in understanding the person and work of the Most High God of Daniel, Hananiah, Mishael, and Azariah.

A special word of gratitude is due to Patrick B. Flynn, my teaching assistant for several years at Biola University and primary research assistant throughout this project during his graduate studies at Talbot School of Theology. His academic skills, insightful critiques, and rigorous labor in the Lord proved vital to bringing this commentary to publication. Appreciation is also in order for my current teaching assistant, Kayle J. Curley, a Torrey Honors student at Biola, who thoughtfully and carefully crafted the index for the volume. Finally, I am indebted to Talbot for providing me with research leave to work on this project.

Contents

List of Sidebars and Tables

Welcome to the Teach the Text Commentary Series

Why another commentary series? That was the question the general editors posed when Baker Books asked us to produce this series. Is there something that we can offer to pastors and teachers that is not currently being offered by other commentary series, or that can be offered in a more helpful way? After carefully researching the needs of pastors who teach the text on a weekly basis, we concluded that yes, more can be done; this commentary is carefully designed to fill an important gap.

The technicality of modern commentaries often overwhelms readers with details that are tangential to the main purpose of the text. Discussions of source and redaction criticism, as well as detailed surveys of secondary literature, seem far removed from preaching and teaching the Word. Rather than wade through technical discussions, pastors often turn to devotional commentaries, which may contain exegetical weaknesses, misuse the Greek and Hebrew languages, and lack hermeneutical sophistication. There is a need for a commentary that utilizes the best of biblical scholarship but also presents the material in a clear, concise, attractive, and user-friendly format.

This commentary is designed for that purpose—to provide a ready reference for the exposition of the biblical text, giving easy access to information that a pastor needs to communicate the text effectively. To that end, the commentary is divided into carefully selected preaching units, each covered in six pages (with carefully regulated word counts both in the passage as a whole and in each subsection). Pastors and teachers engaged in weekly preparation thus know that they will be reading approximately the same amount of material on a week-by-week basis.

Each passage begins with a concise summary of the central message, or "Big Idea," of the passage and a list of its main themes. This is followed by a more detailed interpretation of the text, including the literary context of the passage, historical background material, and interpretive insights. While drawing on the best of biblical scholarship, this material is clear, concise, and to the point. Technical material is kept to a minimum, with endnotes pointing the reader to more detailed discussion and additional resources.

A second major focus of this commentary is on the preaching and teaching process itself. Few commentaries today help the pastor/teacher move from the meaning of the text to its effective communication. Our goal is to bridge this gap. In addition to interpreting the text in the "Understanding the Text" section, each six-page unit contains a "Teaching the Text" section and an "Illustrating the Text" section. The teaching section points to the key theological themes of the passage and ways to communicate these themes to today's audiences. The illustration section provides ideas and examples for retaining the interest of hearers and connecting the message to daily life.

The creative format of this commentary arises from our belief that the Bible is not just a record of God's dealings in the past but is the living Word of God, "alive and active" and "sharper than any double-edged sword" (Heb. 4:12). Our prayer is that this commentary will help to unleash that transforming power for the glory of God.

The General Editors

Introduction to the Teach the Text Commentary Series

This series is designed to provide a ready reference for teaching the biblical text, giving easy access to information that is needed to communicate a passage effectively. To that end, the commentary is carefully divided into units that are faithful to the biblical authors' ideas and of an appropriate length for teaching or preaching.

The following standard sections are offered in each unit.

1. *Big Idea.* For each unit the commentary identifies the primary theme, or "Big Idea," that drives both the passage and the commentary.
2. *Key Themes.* Together with the Big Idea, the commentary addresses in bullet-point fashion the key ideas presented in the passage.
3. *Understanding the Text.* This section focuses on the exegesis of the text and includes several sections.
   a. The Text in Context. Here the author gives a brief explanation of how the unit fits into the flow of the text around it, including reference to the rhetorical strategy of the book and the unit's contribution to the purpose of the book.
   b. Outline/Structure. For some literary genres (e.g., epistles), a brief exegetical outline may be provided to guide the reader through the structure and flow of the passage.
   c. Historical and Cultural Background. This section addresses historical and cultural background information that may illuminate a verse or passage.
   d. Interpretive Insights. This section provides information needed for a clear understanding of the passage. The intention of the author is to be highly selective and concise rather than exhaustive and expansive.
   e. Theological Insights. In this very brief section the commentary identifies a few carefully selected theological insights about the passage.

4. *Teaching the Text*. Under this second main heading the commentary offers guidance for teaching the text. In this section the author lays out the main themes and applications of the passage. These are linked carefully to the Big Idea and are represented in the Key Themes.

5. *Illustrating the Text*. At this point in the commentary the writers partner with a team of pastor/teachers to provide suggestions for relevant and contemporary illustrations from current culture, entertainment, history, the Bible, news, literature, ethics, biography, daily life, medicine, and over forty other categories. They are designed to spark creative thinking for preachers and teachers and to help them design illustrations that bring alive the passage's key themes and message.

Abbreviations

Old Testament

Gen.	Genesis	2 Chron.	2 Chronicles	Dan.	Daniel
Exod.	Exodus	Ezra	Ezra	Hosea	Hosea
Lev.	Leviticus	Neh.	Nehemiah	Joel	Joel
Num.	Numbers	Esther	Esther	Amos	Amos
Deut.	Deuteronomy	Job	Job	Obad.	Obadiah
Josh.	Joshua	Ps(s).	Psalm(s)	Jon.	Jonah
Judg.	Judges	Prov.	Proverbs	Mic.	Micah
Ruth	Ruth	Eccles.	Ecclesiastes	Nah.	Nahum
1 Sam.	1 Samuel	Song	Song of Songs	Hab.	Habakkuk
2 Sam.	2 Samuel	Isa.	Isaiah	Zeph.	Zephaniah
1 Kings	1 Kings	Jer.	Jeremiah	Hag.	Haggai
2 Kings	2 Kings	Lam.	Lamentations	Zech.	Zechariah
1 Chron.	1 Chronicles	Ezek.	Ezekiel	Mal.	Malachi

New Testament

Matt.	Matthew	Eph.	Ephesians	Heb.	Hebrews
Mark	Mark	Phil.	Philippians	James	James
Luke	Luke	Col.	Colossians	1 Pet.	1 Peter
John	John	1 Thess.	1 Thessalonians	2 Pet.	2 Peter
Acts	Acts	2 Thess.	2 Thessalonians	1 John	1 John
Rom.	Romans	1 Tim.	1 Timothy	2 John	2 John
1 Cor.	1 Corinthians	2 Tim.	2 Timothy	3 John	3 John
2 Cor.	2 Corinthians	Titus	Titus	Jude	Jude
Gal.	Galatians	Philem.	Philemon	Rev.	Revelation

General

//	parallel	esp.	especially
ad loc.	*ad locum*, at the place	fig.	figure
ANE	ancient Near East	n(n).	note(s)
cf.	*confer*, compare	no(s).	number(s)
chap(s).	chapter(s)	NT	New Testament
contra	against	OT	Old Testament
e.g.	*exempli gratia*, for example	v(v).	verse(s)

Ancient Text Types and Versions

LXX	Septuagint (ancient Greek version of the OT)
MT	Masoretic Text
OG	Old Greek (earliest translation of Daniel in the LXX)

Apocrypha and Septuagint

Bel	Bel and the Dragon
1–2 Esd.	1–2 Esdras
Jdt.	Judith
1–4 Macc.	1–4 Maccabees
Wis.	Wisdom of Solomon

Modern Versions

ESV	English Standard Version
KJV	King James Version
NASB	New American Standard Bible
NIV	New International Version, 2011
NJPS	New Jewish Publication Society, Tanakh Translation
NKJV	New King James Version
NLT	New Living Translation
NRSV	New Revised Standard Version

Greek and Latin Works

Arrian

Anab.	*Anabasis*

Diodorus Siculus

Bib. hist.	*Library of History (Bibliotheca historica)*

Herodotus

Hist.	*Histories*

Josephus

Ant.	*Jewish Antiquities (Antiquitates Judaicae)*
Ag. Ap.	*Against Apion*

Polybius

Hist.	*Histories*

Xenophon

Cyr.	*Cyropaedia*

Secondary Sources

ANEHST	Mark W. Chavalas, ed. *The Ancient Near East: Historical Sources in Translation.* Malden, MA: Blackwell, 2006
ANETP	James B. Pritchard, ed. *The Ancient Near East: An Anthology of Texts and Pictures.* Princeton: Princeton University Press, 2011
BDB	Francis Brown, S. R. Driver, and Charles A. Briggs. *The New Brown, Driver, Briggs, Gesenius Hebrew and English Lexicon.* Peabody, MA: Hendrickson, 1979
HALOT	Ludwig Koehler and Walter Baumgartner. *The Hebrew and Aramaic Lexicon of the Old Testament.* Revised by W. Baumgartner and J. J. Stamm. Translated and edited by M. E. J. Richardson. 2 vols. Boston: Brill, 2001
IVPBBCOT	John H. Walton, Victor H. Matthews, and Mark W. Chavalas. *The IVP Bible Background Commentary: Old Testament.* Downers Grove, IL: InterVarsity, 2000
NBD	D. R. W. Wood, ed. *New Bible Dictionary.* 3rd ed. Downers Grove, IL: InterVarsity, 1996
ZIBBCOT	John H. Walton, ed. *Zondervan Illustrated Bible Backgrounds Commentary: Old Testament.* 5 vols. Grand Rapids: Zondervan, 2009

Introduction to Daniel

Five introductory matters are foundational to teaching the book of Daniel: its authorship and composition, its twofold historical emphasis, its twofold literary structure, its use of an apocalyptic style of writing, and its canonical theology. These considerations guide us in interpreting Daniel on its own terms as the author intended.

Authorship and Composition

The book of Daniel never explicitly reveals its author or time of composition. In some places Daniel is described in third-person narrative (1:8; 6:1), while elsewhere he writes in the form of a first-person dream/vision report (7:2; 10:2). The complex arrangement of the book suggests that a single author and/or editor oversaw its final composition. There is no reason why Daniel could not have completed this manuscript in his mideighties, around the time of Cyrus's third year, 536–535 BC (cf. 10:1), as Daniel possessed unusual gifts and abilities in literature and language (1:4, 17).

A scroll containing a large portion of the book of Daniel was discovered in cave 4 (shown here) at Qumran. Other fragments containing the text from Daniel have been identified from at least eight other scrolls that are part of the Dead Sea Scrolls materials. Dating from the second century BC to the first century AD, these manuscripts give support for an early composition date for the book of Daniel.

Such a view has been the long-standing tradition of Jews (Josephus, *Ant*. 10.11.7, first century AD) and Christians (Jerome, *Commentary on Daniel*, fifth century AD), although the internal and external evidence does not allow for a rigid dogmatism. Moreover, nothing would be lost exegetically or theologically if Daniel were not the last, inspired editor.

The pagan philosopher Porphyry (third century AD; see Jerome, *Commentary on Daniel*) foreshadowed the modern critical assessment of the date and authorship of Daniel. He argued that any writer who knew second-century events with the detail found in Daniel 11 must have lived at the time of the persecutions of Antiochus IV Epiphanes (171–164 BC). This so-called Maccabean thesis reemerged in the nineteenth century. The heated and polarizing polemic of modernists versus fundamentalists continued into the next century. By this time, most liberal-critical scholars agreed that an unknown second-century BC author created this book in the name of Daniel. To be fair, most of them were not arguing that the intent of such an author was to deceive his readers, for pseudepigraphic literature from that time is common. Some even would speak of a God-inspired, Maccabean author who wrote in the name of the sixth-century BC Daniel. Yet they argued that this multistage process began in the third century BC with the writing of an Aramaic book of "court tales" (Dan. 1–6), to which the "vision" of chapter 7 was added. Daniel 8–12, then, originated in the Maccabean era (around 164 BC), when the entire book was completed and reworked.

In addition to challenging the idea of a genuine, distant-future, apocalyptic vision, skeptics today cite other objections to Danielic authorship. First, they point out that the book contains a small number of Persian and Greek loanwords. In response, one can argue that Daniel lived into the Persian era, when ancient Greece existed; furthermore, scribes who copied the early manuscripts may have updated these terms.[1] Second, skeptics assert that some questionable historical references to the sixth century exist, such as Darius the Mede (who cannot be verified outside of Daniel). In response, the existence of Belshazzar as king was denied until confirming Babylonian documents containing his name were discovered in the 1860s. Third, certain theological concepts, such as resurrection, angels, and messiah, are better known in the Greek era. In response, this argument assumes a late dating of Daniel, as well as other Old Testament books that mention or allude to such ideas. Fourth, Daniel appears in the last of the three sections of the Hebrew Bible—Law, Prophets, and Writings—suggesting the "Prophets" section is closed by 164 BC.[2] In response, the book's placement may result from its narrative and apocalyptic style and the minimal traditional "prophetic" work of Daniel (chaps. 4–5). In final response, fragments of Daniel appear among the Dead Sea Scrolls from the second century BC—remarkably quick for a writing to be recognized as sacred Scripture.[3]

In contrast to seeking resolution for the question of date and authorship—which is not essential to understanding the book's message—this commentary proceeds from four convictions. First, as part of sacred Scripture this book is fully inspired and authoritative. Second, the narratives are historically accurate. Third, Daniel saw

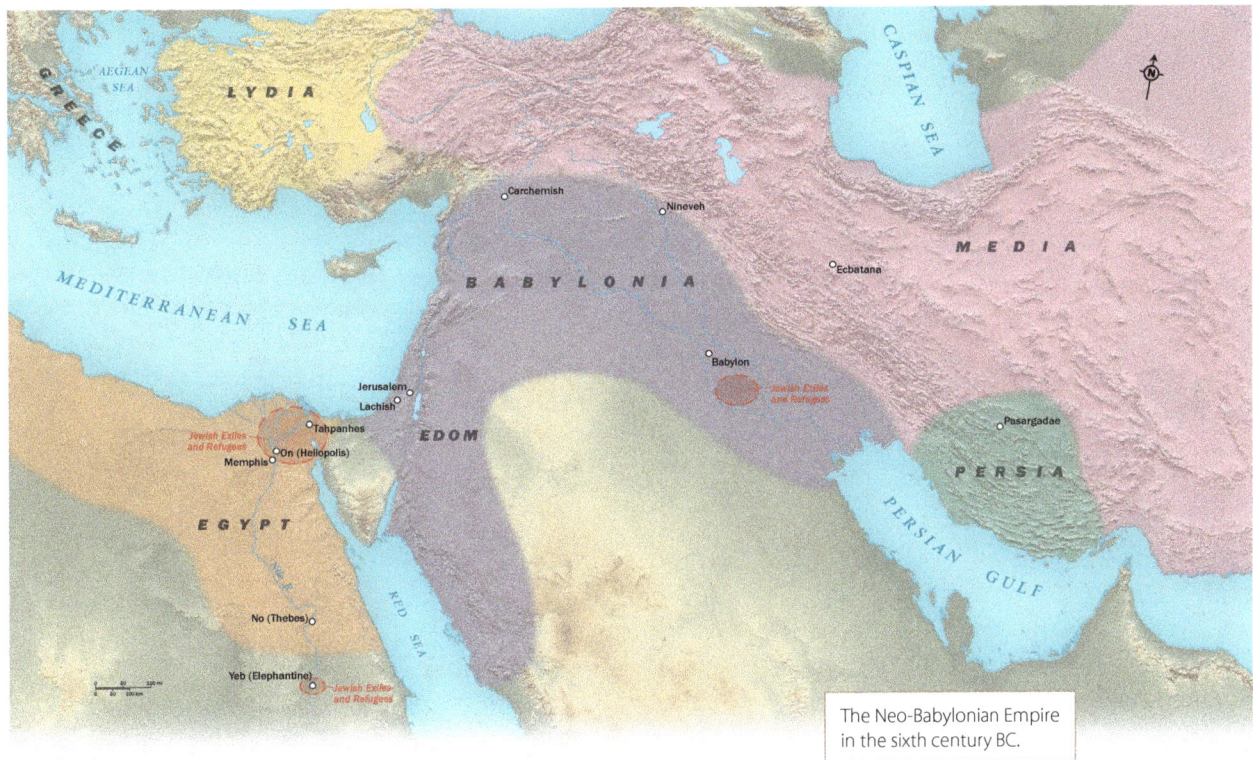

The Neo-Babylonian Empire in the sixth century BC.

and recorded summaries of his own visions. Fourth, the book's literary-structural intricacies point to one final editor—who likely is Daniel.

Twofold Historical Emphasis

Daniel explicitly names four kingdoms that dominate Judah for nearly five centuries (with an emphasis on the first and fourth): Babylon, Media, Persia, and Greece. He highlights Judah's exile under Babylon (sixth century BC) in the narratives of chapters 1–6. Then, in contrast, the apocalyptic visions in chapters 7–12 focus on Jewish persecution in a partially restored Judean province under the Greeks (second century BC).

Babylon

Daniel 1–6 spans the rise and fall of Neo-Babylonia (605–539 BC), including its conquest by Media and Persia. Chapters 1–4 reflect the reign of its first king, Nebuchadnezzar II (605–562 BC), whose unparalleled forty-three-year rule followed the conquest of Assyria (with the help of Media) by his father, Nabopolassar. Assyria had conquered the northern kingdom of Israel in 722 BC, scattering its people around the Fertile Crescent. As crowned prince, Nebuchadnezzar helped his father capture Nineveh (612 BC) and Carchemish (605 BC), dividing the Assyrian Empire between the Medes to the north and the Babylonians (or Chaldeans) to the south. After Nabopolassar's death, Nebuchadnezzar conquered and exiled the southern kingdom of Judah in three deportations, which occurred in 605, 597, and 586 BC. Daniel 1 recounts his subjugation of the Davidic king Jehoiakim in 605 BC, while chapters 2–4 reflect settings later in his rule.

Ignoring the reigns of lesser kings, Daniel 5–6 brings the reader to Babylon's fall under Belshazzar (553–539 BC), who was coruling with his father, Nabonidus, until their defeat by the Persians. This event ended the approximately "seventy-year" exile of Judah (Jer. 25:11–12; 29:10) and was followed by the Jews' return to Jerusalem during the spring of the first year of Cyrus the Persian (539–538 BC; cf. 2 Chron. 36:22–23).

Greece

Although Daniel receives his apocalyptic visions (chaps. 7–12) in the days of Belshazzar of Babylon (7:1; 8:1), Darius the Mede (9:1), and Cyrus the Persian (10:1), these visions consistently focus on the domination of Judea by Greece (333–164 BC)—the book's second historical emphasis. After brief references to the rulers of Media and Persia, the text transitions to

The narratives in Daniel span the seventy-year Babylonian exile of the inhabitants of Judah. Nebuchadnezzar ordered three deportations, which occurred in 605, 597, and 586 BC, during his military campaigns against Jerusalem. This Assyrian palace relief shows an even earlier deportation when Israelite families were sent into exile after their city, Lachish, was conquered by the armies of the Assyrian king Sennacherib (700–692 BC).

Greece's Alexander the Great, who defeated Persia, extending his empire east to India and south to Ethiopia. After his premature death (323 BC), his four generals divided the land into successor kingdoms: Greece and Macedon, Thrace and Asia Minor, Egypt and Judea, and Syria and Babylon. Two quickly became warring factions: the Ptolemies in Egypt (south of Judea; dominant 323–146 BC) and the Seleucids in Syria (north of Judea; dominant 312–164 BC). Rulers from these divisions appear unnamed, although identifiable, in

Daniel 11 as the kings of the "South" and the "North."

The visions in Daniel 7–12 focus on Jewish persecution in Jerusalem under the Seleucid ruler Antiochus IV Epiphanes (175–164 BC). While traveling through Judea to and from his campaigns against the Ptolemies in Egypt (169–167 BC), Antiochus attacked Jerusalem, desecrated the temple, and Hellenized many Jews by force (1 Macc. 1; 2 Macc. 5–6; Dan. 8:11; 11:31). His actions caused a family of pious Jews to instigate the Maccabean Revolts (167–164 BC), which led to the Hasmonean Kingdom (104–64 BC) in the ancient homeland of Israel, from Dan to Beersheba on both sides of the Jordan River (1 Macc. 2–5; 2 Macc. 8–15). This was the most significant Israelite occupation of this land since David and Solomon's extensive kingdom from the Wadi of Egypt to the great river, Euphrates (cf. Gen. 15:18; 1 Kings 8:65 ["Lebo Hamath" is on the way to the Euphrates]). Judean possession of that kingdom was lost after Solomon's death in the tenth century BC. Daniel only alludes to the rise of Rome as "the western coastlands" (11:30) and the Jewish revolts that would begin in 167 BC, giving "a little help" to the persecuted (11:34).

A few passages in Daniel reach beyond these two historical contexts—such as the final establishment of God's kingdom (2:44; 7:27) and the final resurrection (12:2). Nevertheless, understanding the majority of Daniel is enriched by a basic knowledge of Babylonian and Greek history.

Twofold Literary Structure

Understanding Daniel's literary structure is important for teaching and preaching because the author shapes his essential message through it.[4] Similar to its twofold historical emphasis, the book's structure is also twofold, and at the same time, slightly overlapping to form a tightly woven unity. It includes a two-part chronological arrangement, reflecting different literary styles (narratives in chaps. 1–6 and visions

Table 1: Chronological and Stylistic Literary Structure of Daniel

Daniel 1–6: Paired Third-Person Prose Narratives about Daniel and His Friends

1: Judean exile to Babylon (Nebuchadnezzar's first year, 605–604 BC)	Dated narratives
2: Fourfold statue/kingdoms (Nebuchadnezzar's second year, 603 BC)	
3: Blazing furnace (after Nebuchadnezzar's dream but early in his reign)	Undated narratives
4: King's illness (at or shortly after the height of Nebuchadnezzar's reign)	
5: Handwriting on the wall (Belshazzar's last year, 539 BC)	Dated narratives
6: Lions' den (Darius/Cyrus's first year, 539–538 BC)	

Daniel 7–12: Paired First-Person Apocalyptic Visions Reported by Daniel

7: Four beasts/kingdoms (Belshazzar's first year, 553 BC)	Symbolic visions
8: Media, Persia, and Greece (Belshazzar's third year, 550 BC)	
9: Seventy sevens (Darius/Cyrus's first year, 539–538 BC)	Appearance visions
10–12: Persia, Greece, end of days (Cyrus's third year, 536–535 BC)	

in chaps. 7–12), as well as a three-part concentric ("chiastic") arrangement distinguished by language shifts (Hebrew in chap. 1, Aramaic in chaps. 2–7, and Hebrew in chaps. 8–12). Both encompass the same ten literary units that parallel the book's chapter divisions (with the exception of the single literary unit of chaps. 10–12).

Chronological and Stylistic Structure

The book of Daniel may be viewed through two contrasting literary styles: prose narratives and apocalyptic visions. Within each is a linear progression, with the second section reaching slightly beyond the first (see table 1).

These narratives span Judah's approximately seventy years of exile under Babylon. Chapters 1–4 focus on the first king of Babylon, while chapters 5–6 mark the transfer of power from its last king to the mysterious character Darius the Mede. Daniel's interpretation of Nebuchadnezzar's dream in 2:36–45 is an intentional exception to this style, in that it incorporates "vision" terminology (2:19, 28)—identical to that in 7:1 and 8:1—which reveals three kingdoms that will follow his rule of Babylon. Although Daniel's vision in chapter 2 is seen first by a pagan king, it serves to preview the apocalyptic visions that are solely Daniel's in chapters 7–12.

Daniel 7–12 is set in a tightly focused context (553–535 BC)[5] that witnesses a diminished Babylonian influence and an increased Median threat, which later combines with a dominant Persian power. This second chronological unit transitions the reader to the late fourth century BC, when Greece becomes the next world power. Judah's domination by one foreign kingdom (Babylon) extends to three more (chap. 7; most likely Media, Persia, and Greece named in chap. 8). Visions of the last kingdom focus on Jewish suffering under Greece (chaps. 8–11) and into the distant future, "the time of the end" (12:4).

Concentric and Linguistic Structure

Daniel also has a concentric or "chiastic" structure (A-B-A′ pattern). This is discernible in two Hebrew sections that frame the central Aramaic section. At the same time, the element of forward movement is preserved as the first Hebrew section (chap. 1) introduces the Aramaic section (chaps. 2–7), while the last chapter in the Aramaic section introduces the final Hebrew section (chaps. 8–12). In this arrangement, Daniel 7 connects the two overlaid structures by ending the concentric Aramaic section and beginning the second chronological section. This feature highlights the chapter's essential messianic role in the book's intentional structuring.[6]

A **Hebrew prologue: Judean exile to Babylon (Dan. 1)**

  B **Aramaic center section: Focus on God's kingdom**

    C Four kingdoms, then God's kingdom: Statue (Dan. 2)

      D Servants faithful to God: Shadrach, Meshach, and Abednego (Dan. 3)

        E King opposing God: Nebuchadnezzar (Dan. 4)

        E′ King opposing God: Belshazzar (Dan. 5)

      D′ Servant faithful to God: Daniel (Dan. 6)

C′ Four kingdoms, then God's
   kingdom: Beasts (Dan. 7)

**A′ Hebrew final section: Focus on Ju-
dean oppression and persecution**

   F Opposing God and his people:
      Media, Persia, and Greece
      (Dan. 8)

      G "Seventy 'sevens'" of ex-
         tended exile for God's
         people (Dan. 9)

   F′ Opposing God and his people:
      Persia, Greece, and the end
      (Dan. 10–12)

Both of the concentric sections contain
paired and parallel subsections. The Aramaic section (chaps. 2–7) focuses on the
triumph of God's kingdom over earthly
kingdoms (C, C′), deliverance of faithful
servants (D, D′), and judgment of pagan
kings opposing God (E, E′). The final Hebrew section frames the extension of Judah's exile (G) with the gentile oppression
of postexilic Judea, most intensely under
Greece (F, F′). Then, in order to connect the
two concentric sections, the writer parallels
the outside pair of the Aramaic section (C,
C′) with the single center of the Hebrew
section (G) and, in reverse, parallels the
outside pair of the last Hebrew section (F,
F′) with the dual center of the Aramaic section (E, E′). This creative, literary artistry
tightly weaves the entire book of Daniel
into a unified tapestry.

The "symbolic" nature of the visions in
Daniel 7 and 8 links their content, whereas
the "appearance" nature of the visions of
chapters 9 and 10–12 links theirs. Also, the
clearer identifications of the last two kingdoms in chapters 8 and 10–12 inform the
less-clear revelations in chapters 7 and 9.

Therefore, Daniel 2, 7, and 9 announce that
seventy years of foreign domination under
Babylon has been extended to "seventy
'sevens'" (units of time) under Babylon,
Media, Persia, and Greece, after which
God's kingdom is to be reestablished. The
significant theological questions that this
last point raises are discussed throughout
the commentary.

By so structuring his book, the writer/
editor emphasizes the establishment of
God's kingdom in the climactic Aramaic
center section of the book (cf. 2:44; 4:3,
34; 6:26; 7:14, 18, 22, 27), while setting
Judea's suffering in a secondary position
in the final Hebrew section, where God's
kingdom is not mentioned. To place this
historically, God establishes his kingdom
sometime after the time of the Greeks, but
until then Judea suffers persecution.[7]

Apocalyptic Style of Writing

The genre of Daniel 7–12 is "apocalyptic."
The Greek *apokalypsis* means "revelation,"
but not in the sense of a straightforward description (like the narratives of chaps. 1–6)
or a traditional prophetic utterance (like
Daniel's confrontations of Nebuchadnezzar and Belshazzar in chaps. 4–5). Rather,
apocalyptic literature employs mysterious
dreams and visions with highly figurative
metaphors, similes, and periods of time.
Even Daniel, as a skilled sage who is spe-
cially gifted by God, does not understand
their messages. A brief moment of unexpected clarity appears with the use of the
names Media, Persia, and Greece later
in the book (8:20–21; 10:1, 13, 20; 11:2),
which focuses most of these visions on a
specific event within history (10:1–11:35),
while other sections seem to transition to

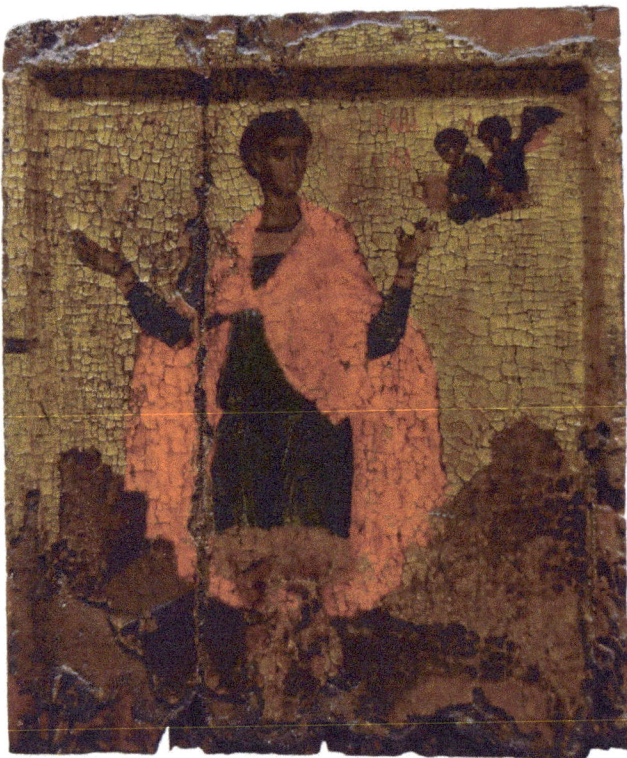

One of the major themes in the book of Daniel is that God is able to rescue and reward faithful servants. This is illustrated through the experiences of Daniel and his friends. Shown here is an icon of Daniel from the fourteenth century AD.

two centuries, speculations about the end times have become the primary focus of many conservative Protestants. This has led to a debate about whether the kingdom of God is to be viewed mostly as a spiritual rule in the hearts of human beings, starting at Jesus's first coming (Reformed or covenant theology), or as a literal rule focused on a revived national Israel at the end of the age (dispensational theology). Not surprisingly, these systematic eschatologies (studies of the end times) are brought to bear on opposing interpretations of Daniel's visions. Regretfully, this often leads to interpreters reading as much into the book ("eisegesis") as out of it ("exegesis").

During this same era a different approach to Christian theology developed known as biblical or canonical theology—the latter is used here. Canonical theology focuses on contextual exegesis, which looks primarily for what a given text "meant" to its original writer and readers within its historical and literary contexts. It is a limited, narrowly focused discipline that often leaves unanswered questions that do not arise directly from the text at hand. With such a method, a theology of Daniel can be developed on its own terms, which then can contribute to a larger Old Testament theology, and eventually to a broader and more inclusive Christian, canonical theology (including the NT). Yet at any of these stages, the principles one learns through this approach can be applied on a practical level, or they can inform a broader (although often more speculative) systematic theology.

the culmination of history as we know it (11:36–12:13). It is important to remember that apocalyptic literature differs from prophetic—the former envisioning the distant future, the latter predicting it.[8]

Canonical Theology

The more essential church doctrines achieved some degree of consensus in the ecumenical councils (AD 325–787), which were followed by the great schisms of the Orthodox and Catholic, then Protestant, factions (AD 1054, 1517). During the past

The writing of this commentary is guided primarily by a canonical-theology approach to Daniel. Taken together, the book's historical emphases and literary structures inform this theology, speaking clearly to the book's central idea: God's sovereign control over humanity, from exiles to kings to kingdoms.[9] This big idea is expressed more specifically in three key themes that recur throughout Daniel: God is able to rescue and reward faithful servants; God holds accountable people and kings who oppose him; and, in the end, God will replace all earthly kingdoms with his eternal kingdom. Although this idea and these themes must be applied carefully in different times, cultures, and situations, the essential principles that lie behind them remain relevant across these divides. From Daniel's easily accessible Sunday school stories to its dark and difficult apocalyptic visions, the central message of Daniel is available to all who would seek it.

God Subjugates Judah under Babylon

Big Idea *The incomparable Lord is sovereign over all earthly kingdoms, holding rulers and subjects alike accountable for sin and challenging believers to spiritual fidelity.*

Understanding the Text

The Text in Context

Daniel 1:1–21 introduces the narratives of chapters 1–6, which reflect the writer's perspective on the approximately seventy years of Judean exile (605–538 BC) alluded to in verses 1 and 21 and throughout the book. It also serves as the Hebrew prologue to the book's concentric Aramaic and Hebrew sections (chaps. 2–7 and 8–12). Daniel 1:1–7 is the first of three pericopes within the chapter marked by someone or something God "gives" (*natan* in 1:2, 9, 17). Here, it is Judah's King Jehoiakim, some temple vessels, and selected Judean youths who are exiled to Babylon. This judgment of an ungodly Jewish ruler foreshadows later judgments of Nebuchadnezzar and Belshazzar (first and last Babylonian kings) in the parallel narratives of Daniel 4–5 (in the latter, Belshazzar desecrates these same vessels). It also anticipates Antiochus IV Epiphanes in the more distant future (Dan. 7–12), a contemptible Greek ruler who persecutes God's people (175–164 BC).

Within this framework, 1:1–7 divides into three parts: the subjugation of Judah (1:1–2), the selection of the Jewish youths (1:3–5), and the renaming of the youths (1:6–7). The Lord alone is the supreme active agent in this public display of his sovereignty over earthly monarchs, as well as in the gifting and honoring of the Jewish youths in 1:17–21. The indoctrination program leads to the interplay between Daniel and God at the chapter's center regarding a struggle that is resolved in its conclusion.

Historical and Cultural Background

Assyria ruled the Mesopotamian Valley from about 900 to 600 BC, until it fell to the combined forces of Media and Babylon under Nabopolassar (Nineveh, 612; Carchemish, 605). After his death, his son Nebuchadnezzar established Babylon as the capital. Within the year he subjugated Jehoiakim, making him a vassal and Judah a province. The first Jewish exiles and some of the temple vessels were taken during this year.[1]

Babylon's languages and literature included classical Akkadian (a syllabic cuneiform language) and the trade language of Aramaic (an alphabetic language using Hebrew letters). Half of Daniel is written in Aramaic. Nebuchadnezzar acquired the library of Assyria's Ashurbanipal (seventh century BC), which contained administrative, historical, and cultic texts. He also preserved the Akkadian religion, including a hierarchy of gods. Bel ("Lord") Marduk was the chief deity. Young palace servants, like Daniel and his friends, were indoctrinated into this culture.[2]

Contemporary accounts of Jerusalem's fall are scarce. The Babylonian Chronicle references Nebuchadnezzar's invasion of "Hatti land" (Syria) in his seventh year (597 BC), which became his base of operations to conquer Judah and appoint Zedekiah as king. The taking of Daniel and friends along with some of the temple vessels in Jehoiakim's third year (605 BC) is not mentioned, and the portion that might have covered Jerusalem's final destruction in 586 BC is not extant.[3]

Interpretive Insights

1:1 *In the third year of the reign of Jehoiakim.* Jehoiakim (609–598 BC) was one of Judah's worst kings, falling tragically short of the godly lifestyle of his father, Josiah (2 Kings 23:36–24:6; 2 Chron. 36:4–8). Jehoiakim became

Nebuchadnezzar's first military campaign into Judah after defeating the Assyrian and Egyptian armies at Carchemish is short lived because he needs to return quickly to Babylon and secure the throne after his father's death. On that trip he takes with him vessels from the temple and a select group of young Judean men.

a puppet king to Egypt's Pharaoh Necho, then a vassal to Nebuchadnezzar, and died in Jerusalem around the time of Babylon's second siege (Jer. 22:18–19; 26:23). In contrast to Daniel, Jeremiah connects Nebuchadnezzar's first year with Jehoiakim's fourth (Jer. 25:1; 46:2). Two issues are important: counting, or not counting, the king's months of rule before his official crowning, and when the New Year begins. The differing dates yield no firm consensus.

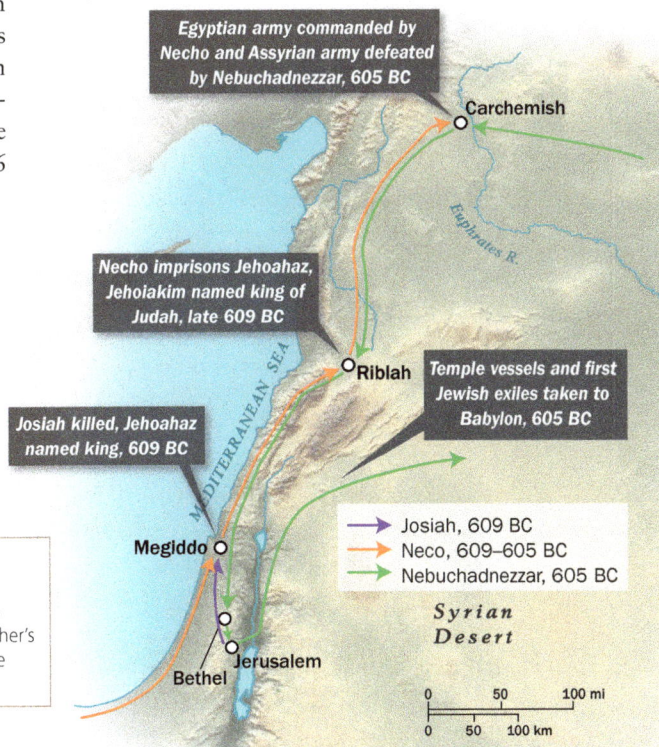

Egyptian army commanded by Necho and Assyrian army defeated by Nebuchadnezzar, 605 BC

Carchemish

Euphrates R.

Necho imprisons Jehoahaz, Jehoiakim named king of Judah, late 609 BC

Riblah

Temple vessels and first Jewish exiles taken to Babylon, 605 BC

Josiah killed, Jehoahaz named king, 609 BC

MEDITERRANEAN SEA

→ Josiah, 609 BC
→ Neco, 609–605 BC
→ Nebuchadnezzar, 605 BC

Syrian Desert

Megiddo

Bethel
Jerusalem

0   50   100 mi
0   50   100 km

Daniel 1:1–7

Perhaps Daniel uses the Babylonian calendar, while Jeremiah uses the Egyptian/Judean—making Jeremiah's date one year higher.[4] Both writers are clearly referring to autumn of 605 BC through spring of 604 BC.

Jerusalem . . . besieged. This event is not mentioned outside Daniel, suggesting it was not important to other historians. Yet it is significant here in that it marks the start of the approximately "seventy years" of Judah's exile (605–538 BC), the book's historical-literary framework.

1:2 *the Lord delivered Jehoiakim.* "Lord" (*'adonay*) speaks of God's sovereignty over kings and kingdoms, while the repetition of the verb "to give" (*natan*; NIV: "delivered") in 1:2, 9, and 17 connects the chapter's three sections. This text does not state that Jehoiakim and a large number of Judeans were deported at this time; rather, it reports his subjugation and the removal of some temple articles, including gold and silver goblets that reappear at Belshazzar's feast about seventy years later (5:1–3). The writer of Chronicles confirms these events (2 Chron. 36:6–7). Taking sacred objects often implies the victory of one god over another; yet here, Judah's Lord sovereignly gives his temple vessels into foreign hands in judgment on his people (cf. 2 Kings 24:1–4; 2 Chron. 36:15–21).[5]

the temple of his god in Babylonia. Marduk was Babylon's chief god, although Nebuchadnezzar's throne name invokes the protection of Marduk's mythical son Nabu. The NIV's "Babylonia" is literally "Shinar," recalling another failure and judgment, at the tower of Babel (Gen. 11:2). Elsewhere, Yahweh threatens a return to this place if postexilic Judea fails to heed the former prophets' warnings (Zech. 1:1–6; 5:11).

1:3 *chief of his court officials.* Ashpenaz's title suggests the training of Daniel and his friends for palace service. Although the Hebrew *saris* ("court official"; KJV: "eunuch") may suggest castration (perhaps to safeguard the king's harem), their description as being "without blemish" (1:4 ESV) makes this unlikely. Mentioning their status as "Israelites from the royal family" reflects the policy of pressing Judah's future leaders into Babylonian service, which impoverished the Israelites and enriched the Babylonians. The use of "Israelites" rather than "Judeans" recalls their Davidic ancestry from the once-united Davidic-Solomonic Empire around 1000 BC—the summit of Israel's kingdom in the Old Testament.

1:4 *young men . . . showing aptitude for every kind of learning.* The appearance and potential of these youths for gaining knowledge, yet with discernment (NIV: "well informed, quick to understand"), prequalifies them for training but also points to God's gifts to them, recognized later by Nebuchadnezzar (1:19). The "language and literature" of the Chaldeans includes learning both Akkadian and Aramaic, although Akkadian is likely emphasized because of their training in court documents. The "literature" involves a range of ancient Mesopotamian texts, including cultic texts for interpreting visions and dreams (cf. 1:17).[6]

1:5 *a daily amount of food and wine from the king's table.* Receiving rations from the king's storehouses does not mean they eat with the king (the NIV's addition of "table" is misleading). Nor does the Hebrew *pat-bag* specify "meat" (contra KJV). Though the word occurs only here in the Hebrew Bible, it is found elsewhere in Persian literature, describing baked sweet bread made with barley, wheat, and wine.[7] The Babylonians likely followed the Persian practice of training exiles in their mid- to late teens "for three years," to assimilate them into a pagan culture, where their Judean heritage would become unimportant.

1:7 *The chief official gave them new names.* The youths' Hebrew names honor the one true God, Yahweh. The name Daniel translates, "Elohim is my judge"; Hananiah, "Yahweh is gracious"; Mishael, "Who is like Elohim?"; and Azariah, "Yahweh helps." Read together, these reveal the incomparably sovereign Lord Yahweh, who exacts national and personal justice, while rendering compassionate help to faithful servants.[8] Though the author does not explain these names, Hebrew readers can easily discern their meaning. The exact meanings of the Babylonian names are debated, although certainly they were intended to honor Babylonian gods in similar ways—perhaps referencing Bel (Belteshazzar), Nabu (Abed-Nego), and Aku (Meshach and Shadrach). However, it is likely the writer deliberately corrupts their spellings in protest.[9]

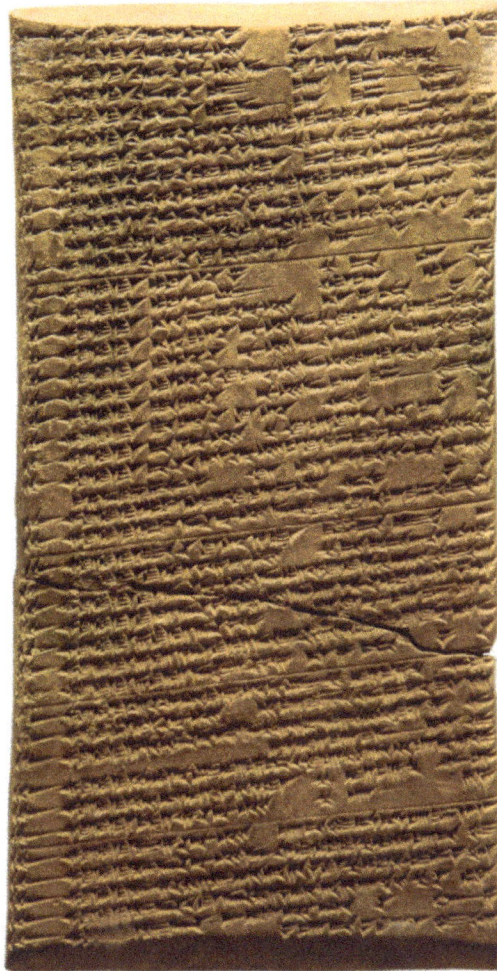

Theological Insights

Daniel 1:1–7 reveals the person and work of God in three ways. First, the Lord is sovereign over earthly kings and kingdoms, taking them down and setting them up as he pleases. Second, God sometimes allows the innocent to suffer with the guilty when his people are judged as a community. Third, Yahweh, the covenant-keeping God of Israel, is just, gracious, incomparable, and an ever-present help in times of need.

Teaching the Text

1. *The Lord is in control of this world.* Divine sovereignty is often relegated to theological and philosophical debates. This text, in contrast, demonstrates the practical relevance of God's control over nations, rulers, and individuals. The contemporary world poses even greater threats to human existence than those of the ancient Near East. We sometimes wonder whether God still rules over creation or whether powerful human leaders and uncontrollable forces of "nature" have taken over. Assure your listeners that God remains sovereign over our world and our personal lives. Encourage them to live their lives not in fear but rather with confidence and trust, even in a hostile environment. Remind them of our citizenship in God's kingdom, which will be established in the end.

2. *God's people are responsible to one another.* The judgment of a nation such as Judah, because of its corporate sin, often sweeps away young and innocent persons with the guilty majority. Daniel and his friends are examples of this reality. Remind your audience that believers today also have corporate responsibility. What individuals do affects the whole community of believers, and what the community does affects each individual. Remind them that God expects fidelity from his people no matter how difficult or unfair our circumstances. He holds us accountable for our beliefs and actions and allows challenges to our faith so that we may be refined and purified witnesses to our world.

3. *God is sometimes visible in the details.* Sometimes while reading a familiar Bible story from an ancient era, we can miss significant details that a reader from that time would have caught. Help your congregation or class learn the practice of looking for God in the details of a text. In this passage, the Hebrew names of the four Judean youths capture aspects of God's person and work essential to the larger narrative of Daniel 1–6. God is just (Daniel) and incomparable (Mishael); indeed, Yahweh is gracious (Hananiah) and rescues in times of need (Azariah). Cultural pressures we face today—secular or pagan—can cause us to forget who God is and how he works in our lives. The book is not about the greatness of Daniel and his friends. Rather, it is intended to reveal God to us.

What not to teach. First, avoid teaching this text in isolation from its historical, cultural, and literary contexts. Second, focus on the clearest message of the text rather than obscure details (e.g., Jehoiakim's third/fourth year, whether the Judeans are made eunuchs, the meaning of their pagan names). Third, do not rush over the prologue to come more quickly to stories of fire and lions or visions of the future. Instead, allow the text to move your teaching at its own pace and on its own terms.

Illustrating the Text

God is on his throne and in control of this world.

Hymn: "O Father, You Are Sovereign," by Edith Margaret Clarkson. Hymn writing was Clarkson's first love, from her publication of *Let's Listen to Music* in 1947 until her passing in 2008. It sprang from a lifetime of serious Bible study, challenging personal experiences, and a disciplined lyrical expression. At its 1992 national convention, the Hymn Society in the United States and Canada formally honored her contribution to hymnody by making her a fellow. Consider these words from "O Father, You Are Sovereign," which won the *Christianity Today* hymn-writing contest in 1982:

> O Father, You are sovereign
> In all affairs of man;
> No powers of death or darkness
> Can thwart Your perfect plan.
> All chance and change transcending,
> Supreme in time and space,
> You hold your trusting children
> Secure in Your embrace.
>
> O Father, You are sovereign
> The Lord of human pain,
> Transmuting earthly sorrows
> To gold of heavenly gain,
> All evil overruling,
> As none but Conqueror could,
> Your love pursues its purpose—
> Our souls' eternal good.[10]

Sin hurts everyone in the family of God's people.

Literature: *The Three Musketeers*, by Alexandre Dumas. In his writing of this nineteenth-century historical novel, Dumas makes popular a motto of brotherhood that unites the famous trio Athos, Porthos, and Aramis, though it is actually suggested by their friend D'Artagnan: "All for one, and one for all." This expression of loyalty and interdependence bonds them together through their many perilous adventures. But it also shows us why we must address sin in the community of God's people. The sin of one affects all, and sin by many affects each one. Because of this, we must learn to think of ourselves less individually and more interdependently. We must repent of individual sins for the sake of all and repent of communal sins for the sake of each one.

Look for God in the details of Scripture and in life.

Children's Book: In the 1990s a series of children's books appeared, written by Jean Marzollo and Walter Wick, titled *I Spy*. These include amazingly detailed photos and drawings that invite their readers to ponder complex images to discover tiny, hidden details. For example, a tableau of a medieval castle siege might contain hidden characters or accoutrements that must be spotted. The idea of the series has continued to live on in puzzles, board games, educational tools, and online games.[11] One can see the little details in the complexity of the entire scene only by looking for them with more than a casual glance. In the same way, God is constantly moving behind the scenes, acting on our behalf in ways we easily fail to notice. However, if we look for his fingerprints amid the small details, we are sure to find abundant evidence of his activity.

Daniel's Resolve Incurs God's Favor

Big Idea *God honors and sustains those who trust him and demonstrate their trust through faithful obedience, even though God's work is often not public.*

Understanding the Text

The Text in Context

See the unit on 1:1–7 for a discussion of the larger context, structure, and comparisons of this chapter. This is the second and central of three pericopes within the chapter that are marked by the idea of someone or something God "gives" (*natan*; 1:2, 9, 17). This aspect of the narrative is pivotal to the chapter's plot, yet at the same time it moves the story forward from tragedy to blessing and honor in exile. God's presence with his faithful servants who are in difficulty is the chapter's theological core. This interplay of resolve and reward foreshadows the trials the four Judean youths encounter in the parallel narratives of Daniel 3 and 6, as well as those of God's people under persecution in the second half of the book. Within this framework, 1:8–16 divides into three parts: Daniel's resolve to religious purity (1:8–10), his request for testing the four (1:11–14), and results of the testing (1:15–16).

Historical and Cultural Background

Selected individuals received provisions of food and wine from King Nebuchadnezzar's

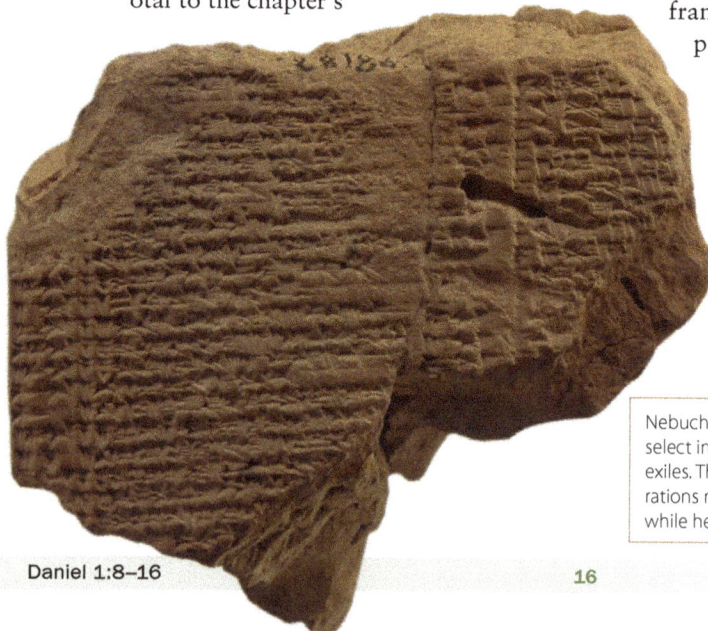

Nebuchadnezzar supplies food and wine to select individuals including political refugees and exiles. This cuneiform administrative tablet lists rations received by Jehoiachin, king of Judah, while he was a Babylonian captive (580 BC).

storehouses. Such persons were members of royal families, administrators, those in visible and influential professions (such as court officials in training), political refugees and exiles, and even soldiers on duty outside the palace.[1]

The nature, quality, and preparation of these provisions varied according to the intended group. The king and his dinner guests were among those who received the richest of dishes, such as meats like pork and horseflesh. Akkadian texts that speak of the care and feeding of the gods mention this food as first being offered to Marduk or Nabu with the hope of divine blessing. But this practice was restricted to those privileged to eat with the king, along with priests who sometimes circulated such foods.[2]

Court officials and those in training, such as Daniel and his friends, fell into a different category. They might receive prepared dishes of meat and produce or perhaps unprepared supplies of produce without meat. Such foods still qualified as coming from royal provisions, although it is unlikely these were offered to the gods. In general, the richer dishes were thought to be more nourishing for the recipient.[3]

Interpretive Insights

1:8 *But Daniel resolved not to defile himself with the royal food and wine.* The leader of the Jewish youths "set his heart" (NIV: "resolved") to avoid defilement, which may indicate a direct response to Ashpenaz's assigning (literally, "setting") their new names (1:7).[4] Though the Semitic *leb* is traditionally rendered "heart," it also carries connotations of "emotion, thought, or will."[5] Given the context, the NIV's

Key Themes of Daniel 1:8–16

- Daniel sets his heart to remain pure, and God shows him favor and compassion.
- God works behind the scenes on behalf of Daniel, Hananiah, Mishael, and Azariah through their pagan captors.
- God sustains the Judean youths through good health because they remain faithful.

Interpretive Challenges of Narrative in the Old Testament

Teaching "Bible stories" connects people with the Old Testament, because relating to other human beings is easier than extracting principles from Mosaic law, genealogies, portions of the wisdom literature, or the sometimes-esoteric prophetic oracles. However, we can easily misuse narrative when the essential message—that is, revealing the person and work of God—is missed or forgotten. Two key principles help keep the primary purpose in focus. First, relate to people in the narrative, but do not idealize them. Though Hebrews 11 commends many Old Testament characters for their faith, Ephesians 2:8 reminds us that even our faith is God's gift. Further, reading biblical narratives often reveals shortcomings on the part of the people being described. Here, Daniel resolves not to defile himself, and God gives favor and compassion. Our response should be not to model Daniel but to put our faith in the same God he serves. Second, look intentionally for God in the text. Sometimes he is easily seen, such as in his explicit and direct actions in Daniel 1:2, 9, and 17. At other times he is mysterious and hidden, such as in the lengthy discourse on the Greek kings in Daniel 11. In both cases we must ask: "What does this teach me about God?" In the latter case, we must remember that he is at work in the darkness as much as in the light.

paraphrase "resolved" is appropriate. Daniel may be observing Mosaic dietary laws, although "wine" is not among the "unclean" foods (cf. Lev. 11). He may have in mind food offered to Babylonian idols, but food from a "produce" diet is also offered to idols. Or he may wish to limit his indebtedness to the king, yet his training as a courtier further obligates him to the king. Instead of choosing only one option,

Daniel 1:8–16

Daniel seems to be moved by a combination of these concerns (and perhaps others) to resist full assimilation in order to retain his Jewish heritage.[6]

1:9 *Now God had caused the official to show favor and compassion.* As in 1:2 and 17, the verb "to give" (*natan*; NIV: "caused to show") links the three pericopes of this chapter and focuses the reader's attention on God as the primary character. Here the gift of God's "favor" (*hesed*) speaks of covenant loyalty toward a faithful servant, and it connotes the corresponding faithfulness of obedient believers (cf. 9:4). Here the provision comes through a pagan official over whom the Lord exercises sovereign control. Just as he uses Nebuchadnezzar to bring Judah's judgment, so he uses Ashpenaz and the unnamed guardian he appoints.

1:10 *I am afraid of my lord the king, who has assigned your* *food and drink.* This narrative contrasts Daniel's courage with the fear of the chief courtier, who refuses his request. Ashpenaz's concern is understandable, as examples of Nebuchadnezzar's wrath demonstrate (2:12; 3:13, 19–22). Yet Daniel and his friends share an equal risk. Though they might doubt Yahweh's intentions (since he has brought them into exile), they choose to trust him instead. This prepares the reader for chapters 2–6, where the resolve and courage of the youths is contrasted with the humbling of Babylonian kings.

1:12 *Please test your servants for ten days.* Daniel persistently, yet diplomatically, restates his request to the guardian, only now with a proposal to test him and his friends privately. "Testing" here connotes vindicating a person through faithful obedience under hardship, such as God's tests of Abraham (Gen. 22:1) and Hezekiah (2 Chron. 32:31). However, the focus quickly shifts from the youths to the God who is able to help. The number "ten" is symbolic elsewhere in Daniel: "ten times better" meaning clearly superior (1:20), "ten horns . . . ten kings" spanning Hellenistic Greek history (7:7, 20, 24), and "ten thousand times ten thousand" representing a myriad of angels (7:10). Perhaps it functions similarly here. Approximately ten days is sufficient time for the effects of their diet to be noticeable to the guardian,

Daniel asks for vegetables and water rather than the food and wine the king has provided. Perhaps he used terra-cotta plates and cups like the ones shown here, which were characteristic of the Neo-Babylonian period.

Daniel 1:8–16

but short enough to avoid attracting undue attention from Ashpenaz.

Give us nothing but vegetables to eat and water to drink. Again, the contrast is not explicitly vegetables versus meat, although meat may be involved. Rather, it is likely an unprepared ration of water and any foods grown from "seeds" as opposed to richly prepared foods. Such simple rations do not break Mosaic laws, are not offered to the gods, and do not unduly obligate the youths to the king.

1:14 *So he agreed to this and tested them for ten days*. As Daniel assumes leadership among his peers, the guardian moves from being appointed "over" Daniel (1:11) to a more passive, even subservient, yielding to Daniel's request—with God remaining in control of all.

1:15 *At the end . . . they looked healthier and better nourished*. Literally, they look "good and fat of flesh," appearing well nourished compared to those eating richer food. The result is not what Ashpenaz expects. Though it does not have the sensationalism of fire and lions (chaps. 3 and 6, respectively), the hand of God is revealed in the lives of the faithful. As a general principle, Israel's instructional wisdom suggests that obedience to torah leads to a long and prosperous life (Prov. 3:1–10), whereas its reflective wisdom allows for important exceptions. As Job asserts, both "good" *and* "trouble" come from God (Job 2:10). So Daniel and his friends experience both the judgment of Judah's exile and God's blessing of their commitment to purity.[7]

1:16 *So the guard took away their choice food . . . and gave them vegetables instead*. The narrative does not specify how long the youths remain on these rations. It appears that Daniel does not observe this practice all his life, as he seems to interrupt his consumption of "choice food," "meat," and "wine" for three weeks during his early eighties (10:1–3). Perhaps this practice is important only while he and his friends are in their formative years in Babylon.

Theological Insights

Three theological truths meet the reader in 1:8–16, the narrative center of the book's prologue. First, God honors a believer's resolve for religious purity. Second, sometimes God works behind the scenes—even through unbelievers—to accomplish his will. Third, God sustains faithful servants who trust in him.

Teaching the Text

1. *God cares for those who trust him*. The intended lesson from this narrative is that it is in God's character to honor the heart-felt resolve of faithful believers. When teaching this text, keep Daniel's faithfulness in perspective by highlighting God as the active agent in the story. Daniel is merely a recipient of God's giving. It is our responsibility as believers "not to defile" ourselves spiritually because we serve a holy God—not because we should try to be like Daniel. Never allow the faithfulness of any believer to eclipse the message of the person and work of God in a text. You might wish to cite Jesus's words to his disciples to drive the point home: "So you also, when you have done everything you were told to do, should say, 'We are unworthy servants; we have only done our duty'" (Luke 17:10).

2. *God works behind the scenes*. Apparently, only the chief official and his guard know about the unusual food being provided for the Judeans. Perhaps fear of the king concerns everyone involved. But God is willing to work quietly, even in relative secret, to grow the spirituality of young believers for years of service later. Challenge your listeners to look for the many ways God works daily through others in our lives—even unbelievers. Sometimes such persons unwittingly reflect God's favor and compassion, while others help young believers mature by bringing adversity. The overarching principle of God's sovereign control extends to the work of such individuals.

3. *God sustains faithful servants*. Great care must be taken here to teach only what the text teaches. Maintaining this special routine to avoid defilement makes the youths look "good and fat of flesh" and therefore more pleasing to those overseeing them (see the comments on 1:15, above). God is able to do this for faithful servants. However, the text does not claim that God physically rewards every faithful believer at every time and in every place. Without diminishing God's provision for the Judeans—and for many believers today—be sure to inform your audience that looking good and healthy may be a gift withheld until after this life is over. Again, God is sovereign and retains the prerogative to choose, but he will give just and gracious rewards in the end.

What not to teach. First, this text does not teach that "Daniel diets" or "Daniel fasts" (cf. 10:2–3) yield healthier bodies and more spiritual lives. Although healthy eating is important and fasting is sometimes appropriate (cf. Matt. 6:16; 9:14–15), Daniel's temporary practices are not presented as a model for either. Second, Daniel's request to be "tested" is about obedient living and knowing God's favor (cf. Mal. 3:10). It should not lead to capricious tests to prove something about God (cf. Matt. 4:7).

Illustrating the Text

God genuinely cares for his people.

Bible: Psalm 34. In his beautiful acrostic poem in Psalm 34, young David praises God for his deliverance from a time of deep personal despair while under the persecutions of Saul (cf. 1 Sam. 21:10–15). In summary, David extols, glorifies, and exalts the name of God (Ps. 34:1–3) and then recounts how the Lord is lovingly responsive to, and protective of, those who seek him in times of fear (34:4–7). David invites his audience to learn of God's goodness from his experience, to turn from their sins and pursue goodness (34:8–14). He assures them that God is attentive to the cries of the righteous, hears them when hearts are broken, and is able to protect and rescue his faithful servants (34:15–22). God lovingly demonstrates his care for faithful servants.

God's work behind the scenes is ever present.

Quote: *Theology of the Old Testament,* **by Walther Eichrodt.** Eichrodt, one of the most famous Old Testament theologians of the twentieth century, has keenly observed:

> The man [or woman] who knows God hears his step in the tramp of daily events, discerns him near at hand to help, and hears his answer to the appeal of prayer in a hundred happenings outwardly

small and insignificant, where another . . . can talk only of remarkable coincidence, amazing accident, or a peculiar turn of events. That is why periods when the life of faith is strong . . . have always been times rich in miracles, even though there have been no world-shaking occurrences to record, whereas those epochs in which the strength of the religious life has diminished . . . are insatiable in their desire to experience miracles, and yet remain unsatisfied even when the most wonderful things are going on all around them.[8]

Intentionally becoming more aware of God's work in our lives can help us to know him better and make us more thankful for his gracious interventions on our behalf.

The blessing of God's sustaining power may come inwardly or outwardly.

Testimony: Consider asking two select people to share personal testimonies about times when God strengthened and sustained them as they resolved in their hearts to do the right thing through difficult circumstances. Find one person who experienced more outward evidence of God's immediate blessings and another who was only sustained inwardly and had to endure continuing hardships during this time. Be sure to coach them both to focus on extolling God's actions and strength, not their own. The point is to demonstrate God's ability to deliver and bless, though he may choose to do so in widely varied ways and at very different times.

Ashpenaz is Nebuchadnezzar's chief official assigned to Daniel, Hananiah, Mishael, and Azariah. Court officials are depicted as part of the royal entourage in this Assyrian relief from Khorsabad that shows the king's son, Sennacherib, on the far left, with a row of courtiers following behind him (721–705 BC).

Daniel 1:8–16

God Gifts Daniel and His Friends

Big Idea *In the bigger picture of the Lord's sovereignty over human kingdoms, God gifts and honors those who are faithful to him, especially in challenging times.*

Understanding the Text

The Text in Context

See the unit on 1:1–7 for a discussion of the larger context, structure, and comparisons of this chapter. Daniel 1:17–21 is the last of three pericopes within the chapter that are marked by someone or something God "gives" (*natan*; 1:2, 9, 17). It brings the story of the Judeans' exile and concern regarding assimilation to a resolution. What is public in the first pericope and private in the second is now made public as the king tests and approves Daniel and his friends. Once again, God appears as the active agent who gifts and honors his faithful servants.

Within this framework, 1:17–21 divides into three parts: God's gifts to the Jewish youths (1:17), the king's assessment of their giftedness (1:18–20), and a postscript regarding Daniel's long time in exile (1:21). The author structures this chapter's conclusion to prepare the reader for a display of Daniel's God-given skills for interpreting Nebuchadnezzar's dreams (chaps. 2 and 4) and for explaining Belshazzar's wall writing (chap. 5). Yet Daniel's special gifting also leads to a surprising contrast when he cannot comprehend his own visions in the latter half of the book (7:15, 28; 8:27; 10:8, 15; 12:8). Finally, the mention of Cyrus (1:21) anticipates the historical markers in the following Aramaic (6:28) and Hebrew (10:1) sections, alluding to the exile's end.

Historical and Cultural Background

In contrast to instructional wisdom acquired through learning and experience (Proverbs), Egyptian and Mesopotamian texts (mostly the latter) speak of mantic or prophetic wisdom, which is given to Daniel alone in this narrative.[1] The exercise of this kind of wisdom was the work of diviners in decoding dream or vision symbols like those images that Nebuchadnezzar (chaps. 2, 4) and Belshazzar (chap. 5) experience.[2]

Babylonian counselors in the royal court included "magicians" (cultic diviners or astrologers) and "enchanters" (dream interpreters or conjurers). Egyptian magicians were among Babylonian court advisors, complemented by Mesopotamian enchanters. Together, their task was to defend the king against apparently hostile omens, as Daniel does in chapter 2. They normally did this through training in Akkadian dream and omen manuals that identified images, providing the sages with necessary information to devise strategies to neutralize the threat through cultic incantations and rituals.[3]

Interpretive Insights

1:17 *To these four young men God gave.* The resumptive opening (more precisely, "And as for these four") provides a grammatical pause in the narrative flow that recalls the first pericope before providing the reader with the narrative's conclusion. The Hebrew words used to describe their gifts are "knowledge" (*madda*), "insight" (*sakal*; NIV: "understanding"), "wisdom" (*hokmah*; NIV: "learning"), and "discernment" (*bin*; NIV: "understand"). These not only mirror the same four terms used to describe the youths' potential in the first pericope (cf. 1:4) but also imply the training in Israelite proverbial wisdom that they most likely received in Judah (cf. Prov. 1:1–7). In this rich theological tradition, wisdom is learned through decades of purposeful, daily living in the light of torah. But here "God gives" this to Daniel and his friends in a short time and at a young age. The NIV's phrase "literature and learning" connotes "insight in all the literature," including pagan literature, coupled with the wisdom of moral discernment in reverence for Yahweh (cf. Prov. 1:7).

Court advisors who served as "magicians" and "enchanters" were well acquainted with dream and omen literature like the dream omens recorded in this Old Babylonian cuneiform tablet from Sippar (1900–1600 BC).

Daniel could understand visions and dreams. Daniel alone receives prophetic ("mantic") wisdom for understanding dreams and visions. In Mesopotamian tradition this was acquired through a lifelong study of cultic texts, yet God preempts the pagan process with spiritual endowment, anticipating the demonstrations of God's grace toward Daniel in future challenges (2:19–23, 30; 4:18; 5:11–16). It also introduces him as a prophet (cf. Num. 12:6, where God gives visions and dreams to prophets), which is evident in his predictive

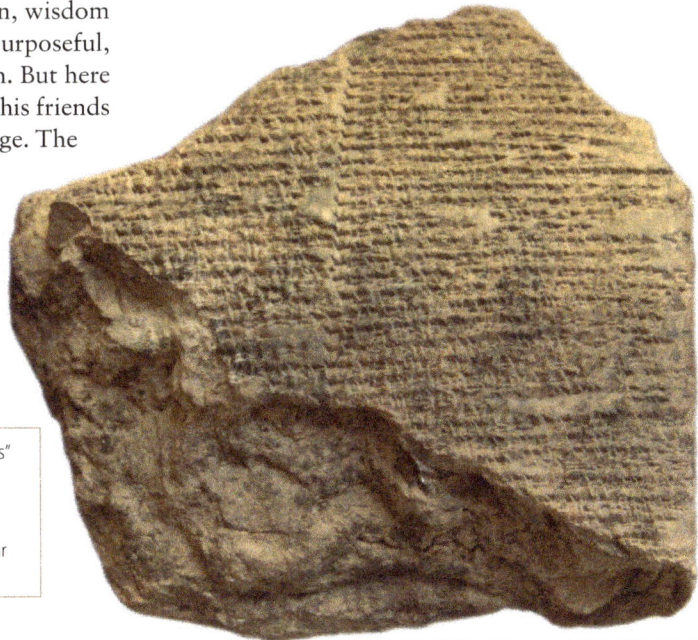

Wise Men in the Book of Daniel

Nebuchadnezzar employs at least five classes of sages, designated "wise men" (Aramaic *hakkim*) in Daniel 2 and 4–5. Exact distinctions within this group are difficult to discern because of their overlapping functions. Egyptian "magicians" (*hartom*; also "scribe") also appear in the Joseph and Exodus narratives (e.g., Gen. 41:8; Exod. 7:11), and in Daniel 1–2 and 4–5 (revealing international resources in Babylon). Egyptian "sorcerers" (*kashap*; "spell caster") occur elsewhere in the Pentateuch (e.g., Exod. 7:11; Deut. 18:10), the prophets (e.g., Jer. 27:9), and once in Daniel (2:2). Akkadian "enchanters" (*'ashap*; also "astrologer, soothsayer, conjurer") are found only in Daniel 1–2 and 4–5. Babylonian "diviners" (Aramaic *gazar*; also "astrologer, soothsayer, fate-determiner, exorcist") occur only in Daniel 2, 4–5. Finally, the Hebrew term *kasdim* (Aramaic *kasda'in*) denotes ethnicity ("Chaldeans") or religious profession ("astrologers, a priestly guild of diviners"). It is used in Daniel 2 and 4–5 with other wise men, implying their profession, whereas in Daniel 1, 3, and 9 it contrasts with the Judeans, reflecting their ethnicity: "Babylonians" (NIV translates "astrologers" in chap. 3).

confrontations with Nebuchadnezzar and Belshazzar (chaps. 4 and 5, respectively).[4]

1:18 *At the end of the time set by the king to bring them into his service.* The reference to "three years" of training in 1:5 partially clarifies this intentionally imprecise phrase (literally, "end of days")—although the former is likely a rounded number (cf. the similar language in Nebuchadnezzar's judgment for "seven times" in 4:16, 23, 25, 32). Literally, the text reads only "bring them" (NIV adds "into his service"), implying that Nebuchadnezzar summons them only to be examined. Then, if they pass, they will enter palace service.

1:19 *so they entered the king's service.* Literally, "they stood before the king," as anticipated by the same phrase in verse 3. Coupled with the timing of the events, this suggests the appointment of the Judeans during Nebuchadnezzar's second year (cf. 2:48–49). If this is accurate, verse 19 provides more details regarding the longer process of being prepared to officially stand before the king.[5]

1:20 *wisdom and understanding . . . ten times better than all the magicians and enchanters.* The Hebrew construct *hokmat binah* is better read as "wisdom of understanding." This is important for counterbalancing the "three-year" indoctrination system and a lifetime of a more inductive form of assimilation. The comparative number "ten times better" is both symbolic and hyperbolic, meaning "much" or "many" (cf. "seven times hotter" in 3:19).[6] The result of the examination foreshadows future encounters where Nebuchadnezzar and Belshazzar learn of Daniel's gifts pragmatically (e.g., Nebuchadnezzar's dreams in chaps. 2 and 4, and Belshazzar's wall writing in chap. 5). The two castes of royal counselors mentioned here have distinctive roots in Egyptian and Mesopotamian cultures, respectively.[7] They are part of five designations for Babylonian "wise men" in Daniel (see the sidebar). The four Judean youths are compared generally to the "magicians and enchanters," even though abilities in the area of prophetic wisdom apply only to Daniel. This speaks to his unique giftedness but does not imply the use of pagan practices by him or the others, which is prohibited by Mosaic law (Deut. 18:10–12).[8]

1:21 *Daniel remained there until the first year of King Cyrus.* This statement does not signal a change in Daniel's location or activities later in his life (i.e., "*only* until . . . "). The Judean sage last appears in the palace during Cyrus's first year (5:31) and receives his last vision in the king's third year (10:1–4)—probably while Daniel is in his mideighties. Cyrus's first year (539 BC) marks the release of the Jews and the return of the temple vessels (cf. Dan. 1:1–2; 2 Chron. 36:17–23; Ezra 1:1–4). Surprisingly, the historic event of the return of the Jews to their homeland is not mentioned anywhere in Daniel. Instead, this verse symbolizes the shifting of power from Babylon to Persia.[9] Cyrus's first year is also chosen because it marks the end of the approximately "seventy years" of exile for Judah (605–538 BC; Jer. 25:11; 29:10). This coincides with the historical markers in Daniel 5:30–31 and 6:28 and parallels the opening date of this chapter (605 BC; 1:1). The reference also foreshadows the tumultuous events that occur in Daniel's life: the rise and fall of four more kings, the near-death experiences of the four Jews (chaps. 3 and 6), Daniel's prophetic encounters with kings (chaps. 4–5), and the final collapse of Babylon (5:30–31).

God blesses Daniel, Hananiah, Mishael, and Azariah with knowledge and understanding, and when they enter the king's service they are described as being "ten times better than all the magicians and enchanters in his whole kingdom" (1:20). In the ancient Near East, royal prisoners of war and exiles were not usually depicted with this type of recognition. In this Assyrian relief from the palace at Nineveh (645–635 BC), captive Elamite kings, still wearing their crowns, are mocked as they perform the tasks usually reserved for lowly servants.

Theological Insights

Three characteristics of God can be discovered in 1:17–21. First, he is the giver of essential, proverbial wisdom, as well as special giftedness, to faithful servants in difficult situations. Second, God faithfully honors dedicated believers, sometimes in very public forums and sometimes over a lifetime of service. Third, Yahweh is the sovereign Lord who orchestrates the rise and fall of kings and kingdoms.

Teaching the Text

1. *God is able to give wisdom to the faithful.* In the modern world, God remains the source of essential wisdom and special giftedness. When teaching this text, distinguish between God's gifts of knowledge, insight, wisdom, and understanding (in a general sense to live a righteous life) and those needed for specific kinds of ministry (in a special sense, for Daniel, interpreting

visions). Draw specific examples from the book of Proverbs that demonstrate the spiritual dimension of a righteous life of wisdom in "the fear of the LORD" (e.g., Prov. 1:1–7). Discuss the challenges that arise when believers today face hostile workplace environments and educational systems. Teach them to look to God for special wisdom to understand the perspectives and viewpoints of others, yet to exercise great caution and care to avoid merely assimilating these attitudes undiscerningly.

2. *God is able to publicly honor dedicated believers.* Like the good health the youths receive in private in the previous pericope (1:8–16), the public honors that God gives them here are a demonstration of his ability to provide for them, as well as to prepare them for the future. On the one hand, those who are given such honors today are morally obligated to return to God the full credit for their successes. Daniel, in fact, does this by crafting his prologue around the idea of the one true God who gives (cf. 1:2, 9, 17). On the other hand, those who also serve faithfully today yet are not given such public recognition can rejoice that God uses persons behind the scenes as well and that all honors given to mortals ultimately reflect the honor that God alone deserves.

3. *The sovereign Lord governs human kingdoms.* The cryptic ending to this pericope and the chapter as a whole may at first appear almost irrelevant to the narrative. On the contrary, it completes the larger picture of Daniel's ministry and Judah's exile ("seventy years") in Babylon. Today, much like in the days of Daniel and his friends, political, economic, and ideological world powers are rising and falling around us, sometimes taking an awful toll on the

otherwise confident witness of dedicated believers. The assurance that God is in control of world events has never been more relevant or needed. Help your listeners to see the practical, as well as the theological, ramifications of God's sovereignty.

What not to teach. Be careful not to imply that natural potential, human achievements, or even faithfulness to God guarantee a believer's success today, any more than these virtues did for Daniel's contemporary Jeremiah (cf. Jer. 20:18). In fact, Jesus's disciples are told to anticipate rejection and suffering because of their faith and faithfulness (John 15:18–20). Emphasize that God is able to give such success, although, in his wisdom, he may choose not to do so.

Illustrating the Text

God is the giver of wisdom to the faithful.

Film: *The Wizard of Oz.* The beautiful Hebrew poem of Proverbs 1:1–7 defines the book's purpose and reveals the important principle of serving God by employing the wisdom that is readily available. In the classic film *The Wizard of Oz* (1939), Dorothy is accidentally transported from her home in Kansas to the magical Land of Oz, where she encounters many fantastical characters, like the Cowardly Lion, the Wizard, and Glinda the Good Witch. While a little girl from Kansas may seem young and weak compared to characters like Glinda who can use powerful magic, Dorothy's persistence and use of basic wisdom guide her on her journey and allow her to defeat the Wicked Witch of the West and return home. How much more can the gift of God's wisdom, in whatever capacity, enable our lives for faithful service, regardless of our abilities or status!

Whatever platform God gives us for the work of his kingdom, we should use it wisely.

Sports: *Relevant Magazine* labeled 2012 "The Year of the Outspoken Christian Athlete."[10] At the top of the list were Denver Broncos quarterback Tim Tebow, the Masters golf champion Bubba Watson, and the first American gymnast to win Olympic gold medals in both the individual all-around and team competitions, Gabby Douglas. Each used his or her position on the world stage to give glory to God by acknowledging publicly their relationship with Christ. They thanked God for his grace in making them successful. We need to be wise in how we use the admiration and respect of others as a point of entrée to share the gospel. The world may begin by celebrating us, but we want it to ultimately celebrate the person and work of God. Equally important is the behind-the-scenes platform of the vast majority of Christians. Reflect on personal experiences with other believers that have influenced your walk with God. We may not have a platform as prominent as these Christian athletes, but we too play a vital role in being an encouragement and witness to everyone around us.

We are called to minister as earthly kingdoms rise and fall.

History: At its height in the beginning of the nineteenth century, the British Empire was the largest world power in history. By 1922 it governed over 450 million people (one-fifth of the earth's population at that time) and covered more than 13 million square miles. It was known as "the empire on which the sun never sets."[11] Viewed against the larger backdrop of human experience, however, its greatness was relatively short lived. By July 2013 it had been reduced to only one out of twenty-eight countries that constitute the much smaller and less powerful European Union. Other powerful countries of the world today can learn from this example. The ultimate kingdom of the sovereign God—in which we are privileged to play a small part—is the only one that endures forever.

Daniel remains in Babylon until it is conquered by King Cyrus. That conquest and the king's subsequent reforms are recorded in the Cyrus Cylinder (539–530 BC), shown here. The reforms of Cyrus included the return of captive peoples to their homeland and the restoration of their temples.

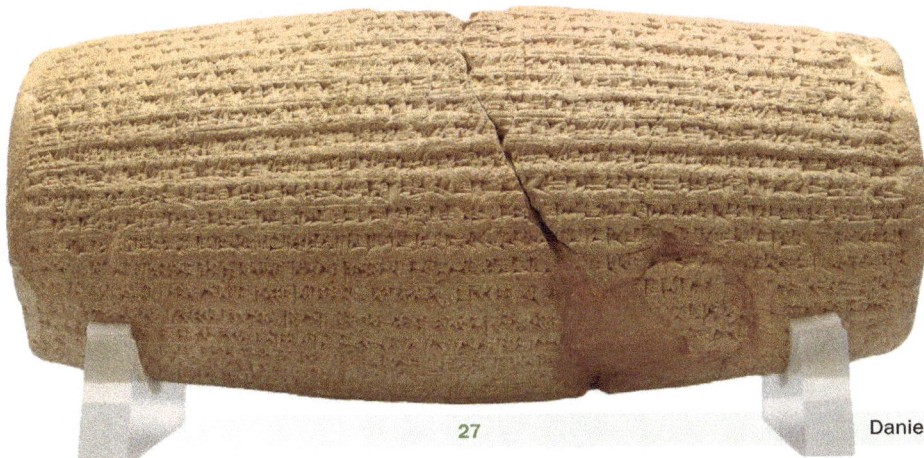

Daniel 1:17–21

Nebuchadnezzar Is Troubled by a Dream

Big Idea *God sometimes allows mere mortals, however powerful, to discover the bankruptcy of their belief systems before revealing himself through his messenger.*

Understanding the Text

The Text in Context

Daniel 2:1–49 is woven into the book's overall literary structure in two ways. First, it advances the narrative of chapters 1–6, in which the first four focus on Nebuchadnezzar (chaps. 1–2 with historical markers and 3–4 without) and the last two show the transition from Belshazzar of Babylon to Darius the Mede (chaps. 5–6). Second, it begins the first of three parallel pairs of chapters (2 and 7) in the book's concentric Aramaic center section. Comparatively, Daniel 2 and 7 contain "visions" (Aramaic *hezu* in 2:19, 28; 7:1; cf. Hebrew *hazon* in 8:1) that address the replacement of the same four representative earthly kingdoms by God's kingdom. However, chapter 2 utilizes a narrative style in which Daniel interprets Nebuchadnezzar's dream, whereas chapter 7 employs apocalyptic language in which Daniel's dream must be interpreted by a mediating angel.

Against this backdrop, Daniel 2 divides into three parts: the first (2:1–16) and last (2:31–49) set the king's dream opposite its interpretation, framing the theological center (2:17–30), which brilliantly reveals the character of the one true God of heaven. Within this framework, 2:1–16 divides into three parts: the announcement of Nebuchadnezzar's dream (2:1–4), the contentious arguments between the king and his sages (2:5–11), and a death sentence for all the wise men (2:12–16).

Historical and Cultural Background

This dream takes place in Nebuchadnezzar's second year, while he was gaining control over his new kingdom in the face of challenges from the west. He made a failed attempt to invade Egypt in his fourth year, and a rebellion arose from Judah in his seventh year.

Mesopotamian "sorcerers" (those who cast spells) and "astrologers" (a priestly guild of diviners) were added to the king's array of wise men. Similar groups served Median king Astyages and Persian kings Cyrus and Xerxes, whose kingdoms arose after Nebuchadnezzar's death (562 BC).[1]

The dream's content comes from the gods, but its interpretation requires the Akkadian omen manuals. Normally, the king would tell his dream to his advisors, who would interpret it and apply selected cultic rituals for his benefit and protection. Those suspected of misleading the king could face execution.[2]

The duties of the "commander of the king's guard" were sometimes unenviable. When a king conquered a city, the commander systematically dismantled and destroyed it, disposing of the victims by means of brutal execution or humiliating deportation.

Interpretive Insights

2:1 *In the second year of his reign, Nebuchadnezzar had dreams.* This historical marker suggests that the Jewish youths are in training for only two years (cf. "three" in 1:1–5). However, if they have begun in Nebuchadnezzar's accession year (fall of 605 BC), this could be the start of their third year (late in his second regnal year: 603/602 BC).[3] Otherwise, their aptitude and giftedness could allow them to progress quickly, or God could choose a sage-in-training to shame Babylon's wise men. The plural "dreams" may connote a recurring dream (also called a "vision" in 2:28) that literally "strikes" Nebuchadnezzar's "spirit" (NIV: "his mind

Key Themes of Daniel 2:1–16

- Nebuchadnezzar's great wealth and power are worthless for determining the meaning of his disturbing dream.
- Babylon's wise men cannot answer the king, because their false, pagan gods are not accessible to help.
- A very young Daniel is given the opportunity to bring light and hope into a dark and desperate situation.

was troubled"). His insomnia exacerbates the problem, making it difficult to revisit the dream. This is especially alarming in the formative years of his kingdom.

2:2 *So the king summoned . . . sorcerers and astrologers.* Two groups are added to Nebuchadnezzar's growing array of international wise men (see the sidebar "Wise Men in the Book of Daniel" in the unit on 1:17–21). "Sorcerers" appear only here in Daniel but are referenced elsewhere in the Old Testament (e.g., Exod. 7:11). The

Nebuchadnezzar summons his magicians, enchanters, sorcerers, and astrologers to interpret his dream. One method used to understand the messages of the gods was known as extispicy, reading the internal organs, usually the liver, of sacrificed animals. In this Assyrian relief from the palace at Nimrud (865–860 BC), a priest, wearing the flat hat, stands over a slaughtered animal. Its entrails would be studied and the omen literature consulted to receive answers to yes-or-no questions.

Some biblical versions include the apocryphal story of Susanna. In this oil painting by Valentin de Boulogne (1594–1632), titled *The Judgment of Daniel* or *The Innocence of Susanna*, Daniel speaks out on her behalf, and because of his wisdom she is saved from execution.

Hebrew *kasdim* is best understood in this context to mean a priestly class of "astrologers" (NIV), although it can also be rendered in an ethnic sense as "Chaldeans" (i.e., "Neo-Babylonians").

2:3 *I have had a dream . . . and I want to know what it means.* The Masoretic Text literally reads: "to know the dream" (NIV adds "what it means"). This cryptic phrase raises speculations among commentators as to whether Nebuchadnezzar forgets his dream[4] or does not understand it. The sages' customary request (cf. 2:7) that he recount it to them suggests the latter.

2:4 *astrologers answered the king.* Either the "astrologers" take the lead throughout the narrative, or the term here connotes all the "Chaldean" wise men. The phrase "answered the king" is followed in the Masoretic Text by the Hebrew proper noun *'aramit* ("Aramaic"). Although the NIV omits this term, it should be retained (cf. ESV, NASB, NKJV, NRSV) because it highlights the linguistic shift from Hebrew (1:1–2:4a) to Aramaic (2:4b–7:28).[5] The

salutation "May the king live forever!" was standard protocol for addressing royalty in the ancient Near East.

2:5 *This is what I have firmly decided.* Scholars more recently have come to understand the Aramaic *'azda'* as a Persian loanword meaning "firm, certain" (not "gone from me" as in the earlier KJV). Kings would usually reveal dreams to sages to remove any evil influence, so the sages could protect the king.[6] However, Nebuchadnezzar is unwilling to do so, creating a desperate situation. His threat regarding dismemberment and destruction of homes is real, as evidenced by his treatment of Jewish kings and rebels (2 Kings 25:6–7; Jer. 29:21–22) and his enraged attempt to burn Daniel's friends alive (Dan. 3). Benefits for compliance are equally significant, for the builder of Babylon the Great can bestow enormous material and political rewards.

2:8–9 *you are trying to gain time . . . misleading and wicked things.* Nebuchadnezzar's accusation that his wise men are stalling to plot against him suggests he fears a conspiracy and is pressing them to confess their treason. In this context, the phrase "misleading and wicked things" should be read as implying "lies invented with evil motives."

2:10–11 *No one can reveal it to the king except the gods, and they do not live among humans.* The tone of the sages deteriorates from respect to despair as they realize Nebuchadnezzar's resolve. They do not appeal to their gods for help but rather assume it is not forthcoming. Babylonian gods "do not live among humans" but remain distant, disinterested, and unwilling to help (cf. Isa. 47:12–15). This sad picture contrasts with "the God of heaven" (2:18), who is near to listen when the Judeans pray, is interested in their dilemma, and is willing to help (2:19–30).[7]

2:12–13 *the king . . . ordered the execution of all the wise men of Babylon.* Nebuchadnezzar's frustration and outrage lead to his irrational behavior (cf. his rage in 3:13, 19). The participle "beginning to execute" (NIV: "to put . . . to death") implies the imminence of his decree, raising tension in the narrative and perhaps implying that some of the sages were already being killed. The "wise men of Babylon" most likely includes all those within the city of Babylon (cf. 4:29–30), not the broader "province" or kingdom (cf. 2:49). The status of the Judeans in the training program at this time is uncertain, as they are associated with the sages but not advanced enough to be called with them. Regardless, they are now under imminent threat of death.

2:14 *Daniel spoke to him with wisdom and tact.* The Aramaic phrase literally means, "he answered with good taste" (NIV adds "wisdom"), a diplomatic response that flows from Daniel's God-given and wisdom-driven gift of discernment.[8] These words recall the previous narrative where God gives Daniel "favor and compassion" in his interaction with the official and the

Susanna

The story of Susanna is a Greek addition appended to the canonical book of Daniel as chapter 13 in the Septuagint (Old Greek and Theodotion) and in Catholic and Orthodox Bibles (see NRSV), but it is not in the Masoretic Text followed by Jews and Protestants.[a] It is discussed here because it depicts Daniel as a young man in Babylon who, with his wisdom, helps fellow Judeans in a time of crisis. The story (63 verses) tells of a wealthy Jewish couple living in Babylon: Susanna and Joakim. Although Susanna is a God-fearing woman, two corrupt Jewish elders try to rape her, and then they falsely accuse her of sexual misconduct with another man. Because of their testimony she is nearly condemned to death, until Daniel, then a young boy, rescues her through his superior wisdom. Consequently, he is greatly esteemed among the Jews. The folktale extends Daniel's activities and influence beyond the palace and highlights other godly Jews in Babylon—notably, a woman.

[a] See C. A. Moore, *Daniel, Esther, and Jeremiah*, 23–38, 77–116; Collins, *Daniel*, 420–39.

guard (1:8–14). Also, the special gifting to Daniel there (1:17) provides hope at the outset of the crisis here.

2:16 *Daniel went in to the king and asked for time.* By leaving unanswered questions about Daniel's first appeal to Nebuchadnezzar, the writer not only preserves a sense of mystery but also condenses the narrative in order to move quickly to the central hymn of praise (2:19–23).

Theological Insights

Three truths about God are embedded in 2:1–16, which are easily discernible from the context. First, without reliable knowledge of the one true God, the most powerful and wealthy king cannot coerce or buy an understanding of God's work in his life. Second, without reliable knowledge of God, the wisest sages are left in a darkness that comes from their distant, secretive, and disinterested false gods. Third, such desperate situations form perfect opportunities for a messenger of the God of heaven to speak true wisdom to needy people.

Teaching the Text

1. *The limits of worldly power.* The most powerful rulers today regularly use their considerable wealth and influence to ensure successful lives. Yet they often are helpless to resolve personal crises, especially of a spiritual nature. Nebuchadnezzar believed that his gods were trying to tell him something, but he was unable to understand the message. Moreover, the advisors he employed were equally worthless. Help your listeners to understand that wealth and power today cannot address the spiritual challenges of knowing God and understanding his plans for our lives and that spiritual advisors are only as helpful as the reliability of their source of wisdom.

2. *The bankruptcy of false religions (and secular philosophies).* The failure of the sages in Nebuchadnezzar's day was related to their distant, secretive, and disinterested pagan gods. False religions are still common in today's world, although in many places they are replaced with secular philosophies. In either case, persons seeking wisdom from these sources continue to meet dead-end streets, absent a reliable word from the one true God. Remind your congregation or study group that Yahweh still helps his people (Exod. 2:23–25; 1 Sam. 7:12), lives among us (Exod. 25:8), and remains accessible to us through Scripture (Jer. 29:13). Encourage believers to look to the one true God for guidance in daily

If the astrologers cannot both recount and interpret Nebuchadnezzar's dream, he threatens to have them cut into pieces. This section of a band from the Balawat Gates depicts the dismemberment of an enemy soldier (Palace of Shalmaneser III, 858–824 BC).

living, as well as for expectations regarding the future of their world.

3. *Opportunities for believers in a dark world without knowledge of God.* The limitations of human power and wisdom must be faced head-on in today's preaching and teaching. But go beyond this by helping your audience to see the dark world around them as an opportunity to be messengers of God's word. The mention of Daniel at the end of this pericope recalls God's "favor and compassion" (1:8–14) and special gifting (1:17). Call your people to remember in the darkness what God teaches us in the light. Help them look for opportunities in the dark and desperate world around them, which is too often without knowledge of the one true God, who knows the future, as well as our personal challenges, and cares to get involved in helping us.

What not to teach. Do not get distracted by speculations on dates, classifications of wise men, whether the king "forgot" his dream, what kind of conspiracy might have existed, or why Daniel was not called sooner. Moreover, this passage does not teach that God speaks through dreams today. However, even if he chooses to do so, only the Bible—carefully interpreted under the guidance of God's Spirit—can confirm God's will for our lives.

Illustrating the Text

Worldly power cannot solve spiritual problems.

Biography: Chuck Colson. Colson was a well-known figure who personally experienced the bankruptcy of life without Christ and found the limits of political power in solving spiritual problems. Although he had extensive influence as special counsel to the president in the Richard Nixon administration (1969–73), Colson discovered that it was faith in Christ rather than political authority that transformed him into a great leader. Even though he had once been an incredibly powerful public figure (the White House "hatchet man"), no amount of money or fame was able to save him from imprisonment as a result of his involvement in the Watergate scandal. The only solution to his spiritual need was his conversion, accompanied by the realization that what mattered most was not what he did but what a sovereign God chose to do through his subsequent ministry in Prison Fellowship.

False religions and secular philosophies must be carefully avoided.

Culture: Cautions against false religions can be more easily delineated, and therefore, temptations in this area seem less threatening. However, the appeal of secular philosophies is often more subtle and can even infiltrate Christian circles. False religions include the teachings of Mormons and Jehovah's Witnesses regarding the person and work of Christ, which depart from historically orthodox Christianity by denying a trinitarian theology. Secular philosophies appear in both modernist and postmodernist thinking. Whereas modernists (late nineteenth to early twentieth century) boast a certainty of knowledge based on experimentation and scientific thinking, postmodernists (late twentieth century) are skeptical of such certainty, tending toward a moral and intellectual relativism based on "what works" for each individual. Understanding and embracing the importance of the inspired and authoritative Christian Scripture as the only reliable source of true knowledge can provide divine guidance as believers navigate the treacherous waters of life.

We are the light of the world.

Film: *Schindler's List.* It is often the presence of darkness that causes people to long all the more strongly for light. Consider compelling classic films set in historical times of great turmoil and despair, such as *Schindler's List.* Overwhelmed by the enormity of the task, at the end of the war Oskar Schindler laments, "I could have got more out. . . . If I'd made more money . . . Why did I keep the car?" Even though he has been responsible for rescuing eleven hundred Jewish people, despair remains. Ask selected congregants to share briefly their despair and sadness regarding modern national crises, such as the tragic and brutal 9/11 attack on New York City's World Trade Center (2001) or the devastation of Hurricane Katrina in New Orleans (2005). Did they ever have the opportunity to be the light of God's wisdom during such times of darkness and to share that light with others? As Christians we have the unique opportunity to be the light of Christ in a world of darkness longing for light (cf. Matt. 5:14).

Daniel's Praise for God's Wisdom

Big Idea *God knows all, reveals what he chooses, and rules over history, whether for humbling kings and sages or for answering the prayers of his faithful servants.*

Understanding the Text

The Text in Context

See the unit on 2:1–16 for a discussion of the larger context, structure, and comparisons of this chapter. Against this backdrop,

Daniel refers to YHWH as "the God of heaven," a title that was used for Ahura Mazda, depicted on this Persepolis relief. Ahura Mazda was the chief deity of Zoroastrianism during the Persian period, sixth century BC.

2:17–30 forms the center of the larger narrative, containing a praise poem focused on the God who "gives" (Aramaic *yᵉhab*; 2:21, 23) wisdom and knowledge. This pericope links the theological core of this chapter with the structural outline of the previous one (cf. Hebrew *natan* "to give" in 1:2, 9, 17). Within this framework, 2:17–30 divides into three parts: Daniel's request for prayer (2:17–18), a poem of praise to God (2:19–23), and Daniel's audience with the king (2:24–30).

Historical and Cultural Background

Though poetry is common in Hebrew literature, it is relatively scarce in extrabiblical Aramaic texts. Because of this, the six theocentric poems embedded in the Aramaic prose narratives of Daniel are remarkable from a literary perspective (2:20–23; 4:1–3, 34–35; 6:26–27; 7:9–10, 13–14).[1]

The phrase "God of heaven" appears frequently as a title for deity in sixth-century Persian documents, referring to Ahura Mazda, the chief deity of Zoroastrianism, and in the fifth-century Egyptian Elephantine Papyri, which contain the longer phrase, "God of heaven and earth."[2]

Interpretive Insights

2:17 *his friends Hananiah, Mishael and Azariah.* This is the last reference to Daniel's friends by their Hebrew names, which poignantly speak of the incomparable God, Yahweh, who gives compassionate help to his faithful servants. Curiously, in 2:49 and throughout the next chapter only their pagan names are used. After that, these three Judeans disappear from the text of Daniel.

2:18 *He urged them to plead for mercy.* The Aramaic term *rahamin* ("mercy") is from the same Semitic root as the Hebrew word translated as "compassion" in 1:8–9. These two passages represent the turning points of their respective narratives through similar interplays between Daniel and God. The title "God of heaven" is frequently used for Yahweh in other postexilic biblical literature (Ezra 1:2; 6:10; 7:12, 21; Neh. 1:4–5; 2:4).[3]

2:19a *During the night the mystery was revealed to Daniel in a vision.* The

Theocentric Structure of Daniel's Prayer

Concentric structures occur often in Daniel, either across multiple chapters (2–7), within a single chapter (3 and 6), or within a short section, like the praise poem in 2:19–23.

A Daniel blesses the God of heaven, who has revealed the mystery to Daniel (2:19b).
  B Daniel blesses the name of God, who possesses wisdom and power (2:20).
    C God changes times, seasons, and kings (2:21a).
      D God gives wisdom and knowledge (2:21b).
    C′ God reveals that which lies in darkness, and light dwells in him (2:22).
  B′ Daniel praises his ancestors' God, who gives wisdom and power (2:23a).
A′ God has made known that which Daniel had asked: the king's dream (2:23b).

In the outer parallel sections (A, B, B′, A′), the one true God is identified by the reference to his "name" (Yahweh) and the "ancestors" (Abraham, Isaac, and Jacob). Also, his wisdom and power are set in the context of his ability to reveal mysteries, the specific concern of Daniel's prayer. In the next section (C, C′), the work of God involves changing kings and kingdoms, as well as periods of darkness and light—eventually leading to God's kingdom (2:44–45). The single center section (D) focuses on God's gifts to Daniel, which are essential to his role in this chapter.[a]

[a] Steinmann, *Daniel*, 124–26; Prinsloo, "Two Poems," 100–101.

apocalyptic terms "night," "mystery," "revealed," and "vision" reflect Nebuchadnezzar's dream and vision (2:1, 28) as well as preview Daniel's four apocalyptic visions (chaps. 7; 8; 9; 10–12). Although this initial "vision" (revealed in 2:31–45) is not usually counted with the other four, the use of the Aramaic term *hezu* ("vision") here and in 7:1, along with its Hebrew equivalent *hazon* in 8:1, links these three symbolic visions.[4]

2:19b, 23b *Daniel praised the God of heaven . . . I thank and praise you.* The NIV's "praised" in verse 19 could also be rendered "blessed" God (*bᵉrak*; also in 2:20), meaning to kneel in gratitude, honor, and recognition of God.[5] In the parallel phrase, "I thank and praise you" (2:23), Daniel switches to a more personal tone by using first- and second-person pronouns. The two Aramaic terms used for "thank" and "praise" are practically synonymous, amplifying the young Judean's praise. By adding the plural "us" in 2:23d, Daniel includes his friends as recipients of divine mercy.

2:20, 23a *Praise be to the name of God . . . God of my ancestors.* The divine name Yahweh (NIV: "LORD") occurs only in chapter 9. However, the phrase "name of God" functions in verse 20 as a reverent substitute for the sacred covenant name. Its parallel, "God of my ancestors" (2:23), reminds the reader of God's covenant with Abraham, Isaac, and Jacob (Exod. 3:13–17). Throughout most of the Old Testament, the name Yahweh was commonly spoken and written among the Hebrews. The twofold mention of God's "wisdom and power" speaks to that which God possesses and that which he may give to those on whom he chooses to have mercy.

2:21a, 22 *He changes times and seasons . . . He reveals deep and hidden things.* God's power to change the course of nature is applied to his removal of one king and appointment of another in his place. The revelation of what is "hidden" in "darkness" reflects the prophetic wisdom Daniel receives in 1:17. Yet it also anticipates dark, apocalyptic events in the distant future announced in 2:29–45 and in the visions of chapters 7–12.

2:21b *He gives wisdom to the wise and knowledge to the discerning.* The language of "wise" and "discerning" is reminiscent of the introduction to Proverbs (1:1–7), although here it connotes both proverbial and prophetic wisdom. The emphasis on God as the "giver" recalls the structure of the book's prologue (1:2, 9, 17).[6]

2:24–25 *Do not execute the wise men of Babylon.* Daniel's direct and assertive language to Arioch at this time parallels his earlier initiative to put himself before Nebuchadnezzar (2:14–16). In contrast to his apparently unannounced appearance before the king then, Daniel now follows protocol with Arioch to see Nebuchadnezzar. This action slows the pace of the previous narrative, allowing us to pause before the formal introduction to follow. The mention of Daniel's exilic status accents both his aloneness and his religious heritage, recalling the events that begin the book (1:1–7). It also subtly reminds Nebuchadnezzar of the God he thinks he has won a round against by subjugating Jehoiakim.

2:26 *Belteshazzar . . . "Are you able to tell me what I saw . . . ?"* Daniel is never referenced in the book by his Babylonian name without a nearby mention of his Hebrew name (1:7; 2:26; 4:8–9, 18–19; 5:12; 10:1). This presents an interesting contrast with the sole use of the pagan names of his three friends throughout chapter 3. The repetition of the king's twofold demand (cf. 2:5) sets this text in parallel with the king's exchange with the failed sages (2:8–11). What they cannot do, Daniel's God is able to accomplish (cf. the similar exchange in 3:15, 17, 29).

2:27–28 *No wise man . . . can explain to the king the mystery . . . but there is a God in heaven*. The text adds a fifth group of wise men here, "diviners" (NIV) or "fate determiners," yet still no technical distinction is made between categories that appear as general and inclusive. Daniel's initial "No . . ." is strikingly similar to that of the wise men earlier (2:10–11), raising the tension in the narrative. Knowing the short temper of Nebuchadnezzar (2:12, 15), one can imagine a pause in Daniel's speech, for effect, as the dream is about to be revealed. God's speaking to and through Daniel forms an antithesis to the distant gods and failed sages of Babylon (2:10–11).[7] The phrase "days to come" connotes general time units, which designate a long-term future, yet one that begins with the end of Nebuchadnezzar's rule.

2:29–30 *not because I have greater wisdom than anyone else alive*. This is a clarifying moment in the narrative as God's ability (2:28) is set against Daniel's inability. Although the young Judeans are "ten times better" than anyone in the kingdom (1:17–20), their gifts pale in significance before God's ability.[8] Any tendency to heroize Daniel is challenged by his explicit rejection of such honor. Instead, he remembers God's mercy (2:18) and wisely turns the spotlight on the true giver of wisdom (2:28).

With the deflection of the king's (and the reader's) attention from Daniel to God, the contest becomes one between Yahweh and the false deities of Babylon (cf. 2:10–11)—a competition in which Yahweh is clearly the victor. The wise men's conviction that divine knowledge is inaccessible is countered by Yahweh's gracious willingness to share wisdom with his servant.

Theological Insights

Daniel 2:17–30 explicitly announces several important truths about God. Since the poem is central to both the pericope and the chapter, make it central to your message. First, the covenant-keeping God is deserving of worship because he embodies

> Daniel gives God the praise as the revealer of mysteries. No wise man, enchanter, magician, or diviner using all the literature, manuals, and tools, such as this liver model (1900–1600 BC), can explain Nebuchadnezzar's dream. In the ancient Near East, clay models of livers were created to help diviners interpret what the gods were communicating when a liver was inspected.

The gods of Babylon are powerless to reveal wisdom or rescue those dependent on them. This plaque (800–550 BC) may have been created as a protective amulet because it depicts a "mushhushshu" dragon, the sacred animal of Marduk, the principal Babylonian god.

wisdom and power. Second, the one true God is able and willing to give knowledge and revelation, rescuing his faithful servants. Third, the sovereign God of history changes times, seasons, and human rulers—all as he pleases.

Teaching the Text

1. *God is worthy of praise*. Daniel's response to the dilemma of the wise men is to acknowledge that the one true God possesses wisdom and power. Only God has the wisdom to foresee the future and the power to oversee it. Draw on Israel's rich, redemptive history by citing a couple of key biblical examples where someone seeks God in prayer and worship, and in turn, Yahweh is proven worthy (e.g., David in 1 Sam. 21 and his corresponding acrostic prayer in Ps. 34; see "Illustrating the Text" in the unit on 1:8–16). Encourage your listeners to include a regular time of thanksgiving in their prayers, acknowledging God's person and work throughout Scripture as well as in their personal lives.

2. *God reveals and rescues*. Daniel's affirmation of God's ability sharply contrasts with the bankruptcy of Babylon's gods. They can neither reveal wisdom nor rescue those who look to them. On the contrary, Daniel's God is able and willing to hear and answer. Invite your listeners to come to God for understanding in times of confusion and for deliverance in times of need. Assure them that God is willing and able to respond on our behalf, even if he chooses to do so at a different time or in a different way from what we anticipate or request. Remind them that if his answer draws attention to them, the credit should be returned to the God who is worthy. Call them to testify that "there is a God in heaven" who communicates to mortals through those who seek him.

3. *God changes times, seasons, and kings*. God's sovereignty is focused on revealing the king's dream but is expressed in terms of the created order and human rulers. As the primary mover in history, God can change even the fixed order of the universe and the most powerful monarchs to accomplish his purposes. The changing world we face today is not outside God's control. Instead, he directs its movement, changing the balance of world powers as he desires. Encourage your listeners to trust the God who controls history, rather than to fear the changes that take place around them.

What not to teach. First, do not linger over the unanswered questions of Daniel's two appearances before the king—it is not important to the text's message. Second, this prayer is not intended as a model prayer in structure or content. Focus on the truths about God's person and work. Third, do not read the text's drama and poetry in a monotone voice. Develop your skills as a good storyteller and reader of poetry.

Illustrating the Text

God deserves all our praise because of who he is.

Church History: The Westminster Shorter Catechism (1646–47) teaches that the primary goal of all human beings should be "to glorify God, and to enjoy him forever."[9] How often do you take time in everyday life to glorify God through intentional praise? God's worthiness is independent of our emotions or attitudes, even in times of fear for our lives, which are of secondary importance to glorifying God. He is praiseworthy, independent of our circumstances, and always deserves active, intentional worship.

True wisdom is revealed to us by God's will consistent with his Word.

Culture: For over forty years Walter Martin's *Kingdom of the Cults* has exposed the error of seeking supernatural insight through cultic organizations, like New Age cults, or major religions, like Islam and Hinduism—all of which deviate from biblical Christianity. Also, the "self-help" movement, named after Samuel Smiles's *Self-Help* (1859), gained popularity through such works as Dale Carnegie's *How to Win Friends and Influence People* (1936) and Norman Vincent Peale's *Power of Positive Thinking* (1952) and then became a postmodern cultural phenomenon by the end of the twentieth century. Consider friends or family who have pursued these avenues and found them wanting. Such sources are unreliable and often harmful in contrast with God's revealed wisdom in Scripture.

God remains in sovereign control, even amid times of chaos.

History: In December 2010 the Arab Spring erupted in the Middle East as a revolutionary wave of demonstrations, leading to civil wars and extending from northern Africa to east of the Arabian Peninsula. Many countries, including Egypt, Syria, and Iraq, had been swept into the fray by 2014. Imagine yourself as a believer in Jesus living in one of these countries. Or imagine yourself as a Messianic Jew in Israel or a Christian Arab in the predominantly Muslim Palestinian Territories. You are threatened on every side, even by your own people. It was in the midst of this kind of conflict that a small yet important evangelical witness for God's sovereign control over human affairs emerged as the Bethlehem Bible College in 1979. Prophetic voices here call believers on multiple sides of the conflict to affirm their joint citizenship in God's kingdom and embrace their sisters and brothers in Christ across ethnic, political, and theological divides. Our own spheres of despair may seem insignificant compared to the Middle East crisis yet can threaten to consume our lives and overwhelm us with uncertainty and fear. As Paul reminds Timothy, "God gave us a spirit not of fear but of power and love and self-control" (2 Tim. 1:7 ESV).

Daniel Interprets Nebuchadnezzar's Dream

Big Idea *The wise and powerful God of heaven reveals the essential course of redemptive history, which replaces transient human kingdoms with his everlasting kingdom.*

Understanding the Text

The Text in Context

See the unit on 2:1–16 for a discussion of the larger context, structure, and comparisons of this chapter. Within this framework, 2:31–49 divides into three parts: Daniel's retelling of the dream (2:31–35), his interpretation of the dream (2:36–45), and Nebuchadnezzar's response (2:46–49).

Historical and Cultural Background

Statues built in Babylon and Persia were sometimes cast in a combination of different metals, such as bronze and iron, and then joined and covered with gold and silver. None matches this text exactly. Dreams involving statues in Egyptian (thirteenth century) and Mesopotamian (seventh century) literature usually relate to kings going to war.[1] This military connotation would have been important in the formative years of Nebuchadnezzar's reign.[2]

Hesiod writes of five ages of gold, silver, bronze, "heroic" (no metal), and iron (*Works and Days*, eighth century BC), and Ovid, of four ages of gold, silver, bronze, and iron (*Metamorphosis*, first century BC–first century AD). Further, the sequence of Assyria, Media, and Persia appears in Herodotus (*Hist.* 1.95, fifth century BC) and Ctesias (in Diodorus Siculus, *Bib. hist.* 2.1–34, fourth century BC), whereas the *Sibylline Oracles* 4 (third–first century BC) speaks of Assyria, Media,

In the ancient world, metal statues were often cast in bronze or iron and then plated with gold or silver. This figurine of the god Baal (fourteenth to twelfth century BC) found near Ugarit was made of bronze and plated in gold. Only the head remains gold covered.

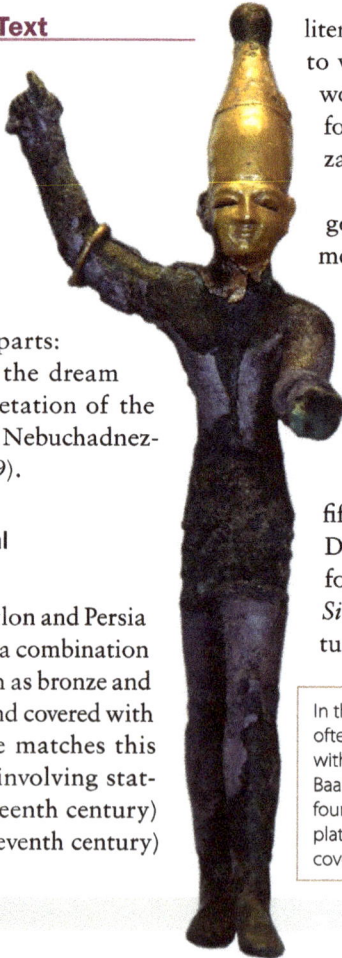

Persia, and Greece—with a later addition appending Rome as a fifth kingdom.[3] None matches Daniel's vision exactly.

Interpretive Insights

2:31–33 *a large statue . . . awesome in appearance.* Literally, the description begins with "one large statue," emphasizing its unity. The NIV's "awesome" (Aramaic *deḥal*, "fear, dread"; *HALOT*, 1850) might better be translated as "dreadful." The golden head is a single unit, while the other three parts include pairs (arms, legs, feet). The top-to-bottom sequence of the metals (and clay) reflects two comparisons: the decrease in density and value and the increase in strength. However, neither is pointed out in the text (2:36–45).

2:34–35 *a rock was cut out, but not by human hands.* This description implies supernatural intervention (cf. 8:25). The extreme contrasts of replacement speak to the strength of God's kingdom over the frailty of earthly kingdoms. Although some understand the rock and the mountain as references to Jesus,[4] the contexts here and in chapter 7 suggest a more inclusive reference to God's kingdom, which destroys all earthly kingdoms as a composite whole.

2:36 *we will interpret it.* The plural verb raises the question of the presence of Daniel's friends, who are also recipients of the vision's meaning (cf. 2:23). More likely, it is used here as an "editorial" or "deferential" plural.[5]

2:37–38 *Your Majesty . . . The God of heaven has given you.* Daniel's interpretation begins specifically with Nebuchadnezzar's kingship, using the second-person singular "you" or "yours" eleven times in verses 31–39a. He is the greatest monarch

Key Themes of Daniel 2:31–49

- God reveals his ability to know future events of human history.
- God reveals his power to orchestrate human history so as to establish his everlasting kingdom.
- Nebuchadnezzar's rule, Daniel's insights, and the Judeans' promotions are all gifts from the God who alone is worthy.

of his time and, therefore, the fitting golden head of the statue. His forty-three-year rule (605–562 BC) is followed by Babylon's decline under five weaker kings until its fall in 539 BC. The idea of God "giving" connects this pericope with Daniel's prayer (2:19–23) and the previous chapter (1:2, 9, 17), setting the interpretation into its larger theological context.

2:39 *After you, another kingdom . . . Next, a third kingdom.* The language switches from "king/kingship" to a second "kingdom" that arises after Nebuchadnezzar's death yet remains "inferior" to his unparalleled reign over Babylon. The Median Empire was growing strong at this time (562–550 BC) yet could not conquer Babylon by itself. In contrast, the third kingdom would rule far more of the then-known world than either of the previous, clarifying the inferiority of the second kingdom. Whereas Media and Babylon were about the same size, Persia assimilated both of them (in 550 and 539 BC, respectively) on its way to becoming the largest empire known until this time, stretching from India to Ethiopia (539–331 BC; cf. Esther 1:1).

2:40–43 *there will be a fourth kingdom . . . a divided kingdom.* Media and Persia play only a transitional role here, as in chapters 7, 8, and 10–11. They are passed over quickly to keep the focus on the first and

God's Covenants and Kingdom

God's kingdom promises in Daniel 2 and 7 are rooted in his covenantal promises, alluded to in Daniel 9. Four major covenants outline Old Testament history. The Abrahamic, Mosaic, and Davidic covenants together form the old covenant, in contrast with the new covenant announced by Jeremiah and inaugurated by Jesus. Each recognizes God's sovereignty and humanity's responsibility. God calls Abraham to faithful living and promises to bless him (Gen. 12:1–3; 17:1–2). Moses says Israel will be God's nation if it obeys his law (Exod. 19:5–6). God promises David a dynasty, and Israel the land, if they remain faithful (2 Sam. 7:11b–16; 2 Chron. 7:17–22). Similarly, new covenant believers receive the gift of faith yet must live it out in obedience (Eph. 2:8–10; James 2:14–24).[a]

There is continuity within the old covenant as the Abrahamic leads to the Mosaic, providing context for the Davidic, and also as Abraham's offspring is fulfilled in Jesus (Gal. 3:16). There is also discontinuity, as the superior and more inward new covenant replaces the inferior and more outward old covenant (Heb. 7:22; 8:6–7, 13). In part, the promise to Abraham concerns the land from the "Wadi of Egypt to the great river, the Euphrates," which the Davidic-Solomonic Empire comes to occupy (Gen. 15:18; cf. 1 Kings 8:65; 2 Kings 24:7). Conversely, the kingdom of the new covenant (mentioned over one hundred times in the Gospels) is essentially spiritual (cf. Luke 17:20; 19:11–13; John 18:36).[b] Although theologians debate what forms Jesus's kingdom takes, the complex mix of divine sovereignty and human responsibility, as well as the spiritual essence of the kingdom, remains.

a Pierce, "Covenant Conditionality."
b On Daniel as a central backdrop to the NT "kingdom of God," see Wenham, "Kingdom of God and Daniel"; Evans, "Daniel in the New Testament," 2:490–519.

fourth kingdoms. The brief description of the fourth kingdom here is more fully developed in chapters 8 and 11, where similar language describes Greece as the last kingdom named in Daniel. Its twofold division into Ptolemaic and Seleucid states—which were strong and brittle, and a mixture of peoples—becomes the historical trajectory of Daniel 7–12.[6]

2:44 *In the time of those kings, the God of heaven will set up a kingdom.* The plural "kings" may refer to those within the fourth kingdom or to God's longer-term work across the four kingdoms. The reference to the simultaneous destruction of the statue's four parts suggests the latter. Christian commentators differ widely on the time and manner of the establishment of God's kingdom (see "Additional Insights" following this unit).

2:45 *will take place in the future. The dream is true and its interpretation is trustworthy.* Regarding "the rock" that crushes the statue, see the comments on verses 34–35 above. In chiastic style, Daniel reverses the order of the metals as he completes his interpretation of the king's dream and vision, nullifying any supposed significance earlier. The phrase "in the future," (literally, "after this") points beyond Nebuchadnezzar without specifying how far. The affirmations "true" and "trustworthy" take the reader back to the drama's origin, contrasting the unreliability of Babylon's gods and sages (2:1–16) with the certainty of Yahweh's revelation (2:17–30).

2:46 *Nebuchadnezzar fell prostrate before Daniel and paid him honor.* The verbs used here connote worship when used with God or gods (see the comments on 3:5, where the same verbs are used regarding the image). This meaning is reinforced by the language of "offering and incense." If this is Nebuchadnezzar's intention toward Daniel, there is no suggestion that he accepts such worship (cf. 2:30).[7]

2:47 *your God is the God of gods and the Lord of kings.* Nebuchadnezzar turns his praise to Daniel's God, who is above all gods and kings, and the "revealer of mysteries."[8] This summarizes the description of Yahweh's character in 2:19–23 and 27–30 but does not mean that Nebuchadnezzar has converted to monotheism or will honor Yahweh long term—the following narrative in Daniel 3 suggests the opposite.

2:48 *the king placed Daniel in a high position*. Daniel's rewards and promotion include being made "ruler" (a high administrative office) over the "province" of Babylon and its sages—the latter phrase defining the extent of his promotion. "Province" implies one of Babylon's districts around the city, consistent with Daniel's restriction to the "royal court" (2:49). His supervisory role over the "wise men" does not suggest that he takes part in their cult or that he retains this position throughout his life (4:9 is the last mention of this status).

2:49 *the king appointed Shadrach, Meshach and Abednego*. Daniel asks that his friends be appointed over the "work" or "service" (NIV: "administrators") of the province (a secondary role to Daniel's), placing them among the people while Daniel remains in the palace. The distinction may explain Daniel's absence in chapter 3.

Theological Insights

Not surprisingly, 2:31–49 applies truths from the chapter's central prayer in 2:19–23. First, the God of wisdom graciously gives to faithful servants the special wisdom necessary to address difficult challenges for his glory. Second, God's sovereign power

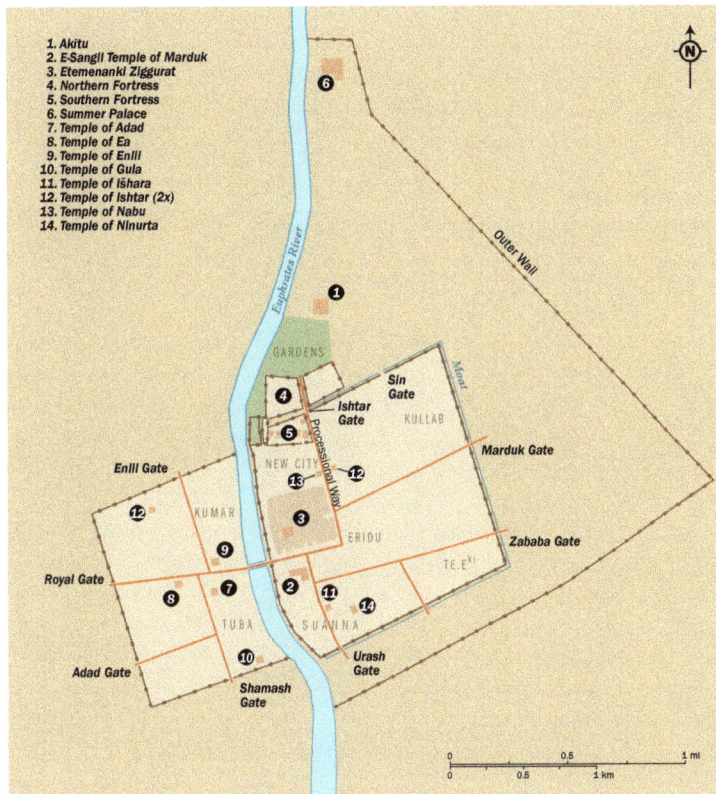

1. Akitu
2. E-Sangil Temple of Marduk
3. Etemenanki Ziggurat
4. Northern Fortress
5. Southern Fortress
6. Summer Palace
7. Temple of Adad
8. Temple of Ea
9. Temple of Enlil
10. Temple of Gula
11. Temple of Ishara
12. Temple of Ishtar (2x)
13. Temple of Nabu
14. Temple of Ninurta

Nebuchadnezzar elevates Daniel to a high administrative position over the "entire province of Babylon" (2:48). This map shows the layout of Babylon during the time of Nebuchadnezzar.

to change kings and kingdoms is realized in the replacement of earthly kingdoms with God's eternal kingdom. Third, God alone is worthy of the honor and praise that come through human accomplishments and rewards.

Teaching the Text

1. *God's work in human history*. There will always be a keen interest in knowing the future, whether distant or near. Moreover, God can and will reveal such details in time—although perhaps not in our lifetime. This

passage contains a partial and more general revelation of some of those details. Admonish your listeners to look carefully for the essential message in a mysterious passage like this one. Use broad strokes to paint a picture of God's active role in exchanging kings and kingdoms for his purposes. Help them to see that God remains in control of human history even when powerful and oppressive kingdoms dominate the world in which we live. State your opinion on the identity of the kingdoms—with clearly evident respect for other views—but do not allow this issue to become the theme of your message.

2. *God's establishment of his kingdom.* The most important thing about knowing God's future plans for humanity is that, in the end, God's everlasting kingdom will be established. Focus your presentation of this wonderful truth on the language of the text. Emphasize the assurance believers can have regarding the certainty of God's kingdom. Inform them that when it is fully established, it will no longer be in competition with opposing kingdoms but will fill the earth. Help them find true peace in knowing that this

Daniel receives another honor from Nebuchadnezzar. He is placed in charge of all the wise men of Babylon. One of the categories of sages in ancient Mesopotamia was the *apkallu*. Portrayed in fish cloaks (as here), they were modeled after the great sages of old who instructed humanity in the arts of civilization (eighth to sixth century BC).

righteous kingdom will endure forever, in contrast to the transient, unreliable, and sinful kingdoms of this world. Keep your focus on the truth and trustworthiness of these important facts, which the text highlights and on which all evangelicals agree.

3. *Human achievements and honors.* Two human achievements appear in this context that must be kept in perspective. First, Nebuchadnezzar's status as "king of kings" and "head of gold" (2:37–38) is subordinated to "the God of gods and the Lord of kings" (2:47). Second, the accolades (which approximate worship), as well as the public honors for Daniel and his friends, recall Daniel's early affirmation that such gifts are from the God who alone is worthy. Warn your congregation or class against the danger of taking personal achievements and honors too seriously.

What not to teach. First, this text is not about Daniel's skill as a young trainee but about the God who blesses him. Second, its purpose is neither to identify the four kingdoms nor to explain how these kingdoms relate to a larger systematic theology of the end times. Acknowledge the considerable diversity of opinions on how God's kingdom fits into the picture (see "Additional Insights" following this unit), yet hold your speculations on these matters lightly while staying focused on that which is clear in the essential message of the text.

Illustrating the Text

God is at work throughout history to accomplish his will.

Bible: The narratives of Joseph (Gen. 37–50) and Daniel (Dan. 1–6) are strikingly similar; therefore, many scenes from the former can serve well as illustrations for the latter. In the story of Joseph's slavery and rise to prominence in the Egyptian government—more than a millennium before Daniel's time in Babylon—God explicitly weaves together the fabric of human history to accomplish his purposes. Not only is Joseph's life as an individual marked by God's hand and work (for example, receiving from God the interpretation of Pharaoh's dream), but also the larger events in history occurring in the narrative (such as the widespread famine) are all orchestrated by God and presented as working together to accomplish his will. In the end, Joseph affirms this truth to his brothers: "You intended to harm me, but God intended it for good to accomplish what is now being done, the saving of many lives" (Gen. 50:20).

One's country of origin does not matter— eternal citizenship does.

Human Experience: Imagine crossing a national border and being questioned about your citizenship. Consider the discomfort or uneasiness of knowing that you may be forbidden to enter or imprisoned if you are attempting to enter a place where you do not have citizenship. By contrast, upon entering into God's kingdom, our human country of origin will neither advantage nor disadvantage us, for our right to enter is established by our inclusion as God's children in Christ, which makes us citizens of heaven—the only kingdom that truly matters. It is in God's kingdom that we will ultimately spend all eternity, and he can surely be trusted to be faithful to his word and bring all passing human kingdoms to an end in favor of the establishment of his eternal rule of righteousness.

Earthly honors must be held lightly.

Sports: American professional road-racing cyclist and cancer survivor Lance Armstrong won the brutal Tour de France a record seven consecutive years (1999–2005). Tragically, because of his use of illegal, performance-enhancing drugs, he was stripped of his honors in 2012 and disqualified from the sport for life. Consider the pomp and circumstance of human accolades of such accomplishments, and reflect on how it might feel to win these honors, give acceptance speeches, and frame the fabled "yellow jerseys" to hang in your office or home. As enchanting as this thought may be, all temporal human rewards must never claim the right to define us or become so desirable that one's life be shipwrecked in pursuit of such a fleeting goal. Excellence and recognition are not inherently sinful, yet they must always be pursued for the sake of obedience to God's call and for his ultimate glory, never for our own desires for human achievement and honor.

The Kingdoms in Daniel 2 and 7

Although there is no clear New Testament "interpretation" of Daniel's kingdoms, this excursus summarizes the evangelical arguments for Rome or Greece as the fourth kingdom—with a brief explanation of why the Greek view is preferable.[1]

Roman View

The **Neo-Babylonian Empire** (605–539 BC) is the first kingdom, represented by Nebuchadnezzar, its first and greatest king (2:37–38; 7:4).

Medo-Persia (539–331 BC) is the second kingdom, conquering Babylon (5:28) and retaining a dual heritage (6:8). A bear raised up on one side (7:5) and a ram with two uneven horns (8:20) appropriately represent this kingdom, in which Persia is dominant. Its inferiority (2:39) may relate to its government, culture, or morality—since silver is less valuable than gold (2:32).

Greece (331–146 BC) is the third kingdom, ruling with authority (2:39; 7:6) from Egypt to India. Alexander's conquests were swift like a winged leopard, and his empire was divided among his four generals after his death (7:6; 11:3–4). The fact that Greece plays a major role in chapters 8 and 11, but only a minor role in chapters 2 and 7, is consistent with the intended audiences of the Aramaic (gentile) and Hebrew (Jewish) sections of Daniel.[2]

Rome (146 BC–AD 476) is the fourth kingdom. Though it is not explicitly named in Daniel, 11:30 alludes to it. Its description as a divided empire that oppresses God's "holy ones" (2:40–43; 7:19–20, 23–25) fits Rome's treatment of Jews and Christians.

There is no consensus on the identity of Rome's "ten horns" or "little horn" (7:8), or when the little horn and his kingdom were—or will be—conquered and replaced by God's kingdom. Images and metaphors

In his dream, Nebuchadnezzar sees an enormous statue with a head of gold, chest and arms of silver, belly and thighs of bronze, legs of iron, and feet of iron and clay. Here is an artist's depiction of the image in Nebuchadnezzar's dream.

from Daniel appear in the New Testament regarding Jesus, antichrist, and future events but may apply to either Jesus's first or second coming—or both.[3]

Greek View

Nebuchadnezzar's **Babylon** (605–562 BC) comes first. Daniel speaks strictly in personal pronouns and images regarding him and his "kingship" (2:37–38; 7:4) rather than using the terminology of "kingdom."

Media is the second kingdom. It rises to greater power (2:39a; 7:5) after Nebuchadnezzar's death yet remains "inferior" (2:39a) to Babylon (562–539 BC). This inferiority is contrasted and clarified by the "authority to rule" given to the third kingdom (2:39b; 7:6). Darius the "Mede" is mentioned frequently in Daniel (5:31–6:1; 6:6, 9, 15, 25, 28; 11:1), and the "Medes" are connected often in Scripture with Babylon's fall (Isa. 13:17; Jer. 51:11, 28; Dan. 5:31). Further, a shared culture is not the same as a dual empire: Greco-Roman culture exists; a combined Greco-Roman Empire never has. Finally, the kings and people of "Media and Persia" are always mentioned in the plural—there is no "king" of "Medo-Persia" in Daniel.

Persia (539–331 BC) is the third kingdom, ruling with authority over the then-known world (2:39; 7:6) from Egypt to India and most often playing an independent role in Scripture (2 Chron. 36:20–23; fourteen times in Ezra; four times in Esther; Ezek. 38:5; Dan. 10:1, 13, 20; 11:2). It is never called "Medo-Persia" in any extant texts. Cyrus's conquests were swift like a winged leopard, and "four" kings represent Persia in 11:2. Moreover, Daniel's historical markers in its mirror-image chapters (7:1; 8:1) allude to the transition from Media to Persia following the book's pivotal center in Daniel 7.

Greece (331–146 BC) is the fourth kingdom. Its description as a twofold divided empire (Ptolemies and Seleucids) that oppresses God's "holy ones" (2:40–43; 7:19–20, 23–25) fits its treatment of the Jewish people, especially under the Seleucid king Antiochus IV (175–164 BC). All commentators agree that Greece is named as the clear focus of chapters 8 and 11 (8:21; 11:2) and that Antiochus IV is the little horn (cf. 8:9), "master of intrigue" (8:23–25), and "contemptible person" (11:21–35). Moreover, the "ten horns" fit the number of Hellenistic rulers before Antiochus (see table 2, "Greek Kings in Daniel 11:5–35," in the unit on 11:2–20). Antiochus's desecration of the temple sparked the Jewish revolts (164–104 BC) that led to a reestablished Judean kingdom (104–64 BC). The strong linking of chapters 7 and 8 (historical markers, literary style, and descriptions of the last, oppressive kingdom) make Daniel 8 the earliest commentary on the four kingdoms of chapters 2 and 7. Also, the writer's truncated interpretations of the second and third kingdoms (Babylon in 2:39; Media in 7:17) are consistent with a focus on Greece as the last kingdom in chapters 2, 7, 8, and 10–12.

As with the Roman view, there is no consensus on how Greece is replaced by God's kingdom. The use of Daniel in the New Testament is best understood as an application of Daniel's rhetoric and theology to believers' experiences under Rome (symbolically called "Babylon"; e.g., 1 Pet. 5:13; Rev. 14:8). This applies to the spiritual inauguration of God's kingdom at Jesus's first coming and still foreshadows its full establishment at his return.[4]

Nebuchadnezzar Builds the Statue

Big Idea *God sometimes allows believers to face dark times of crisis in which their faith and faithfulness are challenged, even with the penalty of death.*

Understanding the Text

The Text in Context

Daniel 3:1–30 is woven into the book's overall literary structure in two ways. First, it advances the narrative of chapters 1–6, in which the first four focus on Nebuchadnezzar (chaps. 1–2 with historical markers and 3–4 without) and the last two show the transition from Belshazzar of Babylon to Darius the Mede (chaps. 5–6). Second, it begins the second of three parallel pairs of chapters (3 and 6) in the book's concentric Aramaic center section. Comparatively, Daniel 3 and 6 reveal nearly identical patterns: royal decrees combine with malicious accusations against the Jews, which lead to crises and deliverances, which lead to royal counterdecrees. At the center of each chapter the question of God's ability to deliver is asked and answered in the affirmative. When read together, these narratives keep Judah's "seventy-year" exile in view by setting Babylon's first king opposite its last, recalling the parameters of the prologue (1:1, 21). Taken alone, Daniel 3 reflects a concentric structure with three pairs and a center section.[1]

A   Nebuchadnezzar's first decree to worship the image (3:1–7)

  B   The Jews are accused (3:8–12).

    C   The Jews are threatened (3:13–15).

      D   The Jews commit to honor the one true God (3:16–18).

    C′ The Jews are punished (3:19–23).

  B′ The Jews are vindicated (3:24–27).

A′ Nebuchadnezzar's second decree to worship God (3:28–30)

Against this backdrop, 3:1–12 connects with the previous chapter by the "statue"/"image" terminology (the same Aramaic term *tselem* appears in 2:31 and 3:1) and the earlier switch to the Judeans' Babylonian names (compare 2:17 with 2:49). In addition, the mention of the Judeans' appointment over the province of Babylon (2:49; 3:1, 12)—while Daniel remains in the palace (2:49)—anticipates the language of the accusations against them and Daniel's absence in this narrative. Whereas Daniel distinguishes himself above his peers in chapters 1–2, Shadrach,

Meshach, and Abednego now move to the foreground. This creates a feeling of chronological movement, even though this text lacks a historical marker. Within this framework, 3:1–12 divides in three parts: building the statue (3:1–2), the royal decree and compliance of the people (3:3–7), and the accusation against the Jews (3:8–12).

Historical and Cultural Background

Herodotus describes two large golden images in Babylon: one of Marduk (Bel) on his throne beside a table (probably for food offerings), the other of a man standing in the god's presence—possibly the king (*Hist.* 1.183). Shalmaneser III (ninth century BC) is depicted on the Balawat temple gates, where sacrifices could be made. Such settings allowed kings to associate with the gods, yet without identifying themselves as one of them. Sacrificial ceremonies at the city gates were often used when provincial officials swore loyalty to kings, such as Nebuchadnezzar early in his rule. Assyria's Ashurbanipal brought administrators to Babylon to swear allegiance to him in the seventh century BC.[2]

Proportions of an "image" are difficult to discern, as the height may include the image alone, or its height atop a pedestal, or carvings on a high cliff. This could explain the statue's dimensions in this text (3:1). Also, the "plain of Dura in the province of Babylon" cannot be located with certainty, as many sites from

this era use the Aramaic *dur* as a prefix to connote a "walled place." It is likely situated outside the city, yet within the province where Daniel's friends are administrators.[3]

Interpretive Insights

3:1 *King Nebuchadnezzar made an image*. These events may involve Nebuchadnezzar establishing his rule around 605 BC or relate to a revolt against him during his tenth year (594–593 BC; Jer. 27:1–22; 51:59–64). The Septuagint adds the "eighteenth year of Nebuchadnezzar" (587/586 BC) to this verse, when a large deportation of Judeans took place (cf. Jer. 52:29)—although this would hardly call for a ceremony of this magnitude. Regardless of which hypothesis is correct, the narrative suggests a time between chapters 2 and 4. Therefore, the three Jewish "youths" could have been

King Nebuchadnezzar makes an image of gold ninety by nine feet. Obelisks of this height were constructed in Egypt, and one of the largest still remaining can now be seen near the Basilica of St. John Lateran in Rome. Originally erected by Thutmose III in Karnak during the fifteenth century BC, it is 105 feet high, and its square base is 9 feet wide at the bottom.

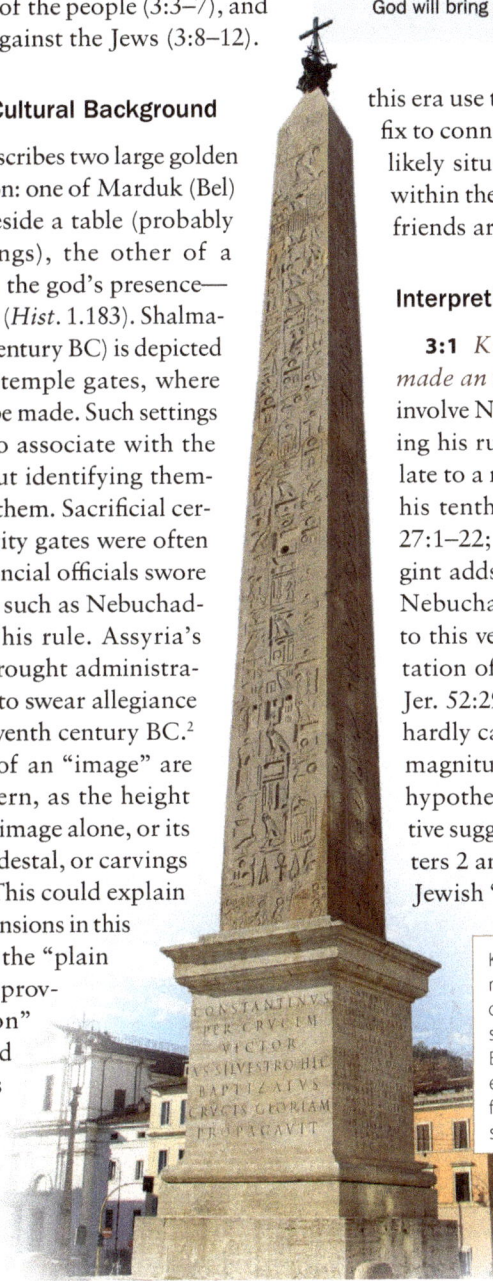

An orchestra that includes horns, flutes, zithers, lyres, and harps is assembled to signal the time to worship the erected image of gold. This eighth-century BC orthostat from Karatepe, Turkey, shows musicians playing their instruments: a drum, harps or lyres, and a flute.

somewhere between their late teens and midthirties. The use of the Aramaic *ts^elem* in 2:31 and 3:1 to describe the "statue/image," along with the reference to gold (plating) on the image (cf. the gold head in chap. 2), links the two narratives. Its sixty-by-six-cubit dimensions (ninety by nine feet) reflect the Babylonian sexagesimal counting system and probably include the combined height of the statue and its pedestal.[4] The image more likely represents a deity—Marduk or Nabu—as Babylonian kings were not divinized.[5]

3:2–4 *He then summoned . . . all the . . . provincial officials.* The attendees appear in descending order and are described with two Semitic terms ("satraps" and "prefects") and five Old Persian loanwords (from before the third century BC). These reflect the establishment of Persia by Cyrus (539 BC), shortly before Daniel's death, a possible occasion for the writing of the book. The addition of "other provincial officials" links the narrative to the administrative province of the three Judeans (2:49). The herald's "nations and peoples of every language" is hyperbolic, meaning all those under Babylonian influence. The edict's scope and list of officials run parallel to 6:7.[6]

3:5 *As soon as you hear . . . all kinds of music.* The list of instruments includes three Semitic terms, "horn," "flute," and "harp" (highlighted in the Aramaic text with definite articles), and three Greek loanwords. The latter reflect Greek interaction with the ancient Near East at Daniel's time.[7] "All kinds of music" implies a large orchestra assembled for the occasion. The language of "worship" (Aramaic *s^egid*) in the mouth of the king and the Judeans (3:5, 7, 10–12, 14–15, 18, 28) connotes the idea of deity. The use of the same term for Nebuchadnezzar's actions toward Daniel in 2:46 ("paid him honor") involves both "honoring" him and "worshiping" his god.

3:6 *Whoever does not . . . worship will immediately be thrown into a blazing furnace.* Instances of capital punishment through fire are rare in the ancient literature. One is found in Herodotus (*Hist.* 1.86),[8] while another occurs in Jeremiah 29:22, where Nebuchadnezzar burns "Zedekiah and Ahab" (not the biblical kings). The situation in this text likely refers to furnaces for making bricks and smelting metals on the construction site of the image. These had openings on top and at ground level and could hold several persons. Nebuchadnezzar is using the furnace as a weapon of opportunity. Mention of immediate execution suggests it was in operation at the time of the decree.

3:7 *as soon as they heard the sound . . . fell down and worshiped the image.* The narrator's tedious repetition of the names of the instruments (also in 3:10, 15) creates an environment in which conformity feels normal, while resistance stands out.[9] The sea of people bowing before the image reinforces this feeling.

3:8–12 *some astrologers came forward and denounced the Jews.* The Aramaic *kasda'in*, like its Hebrew counterpart in 2:2, can denote profession, "astrologers" (2:2, 4–5, 10; 4:7; 5:7, 11), or ethnicity, "Chaldeans" (1:4; 9:1; NIV: "Babylonians").[10] In chapters 2, 4, and 5, it is used in a group context with the other castes of wise men and thus implies profession. Here it is used alone and in contrast to "Jews," which reflects ethnicity. This is court jealousy, as in the singling out of Daniel in chapter 6, not anti-Jewish persecution.

whom you have set over the affairs of the province of Babylon. Pointing out Nebuchadnezzar's responsibility for these disloyal subjects is an implicit attack on his abilities as king. The use of the Judeans' Babylonian names without reference to their Hebrew names (cf. Dan. 1–2) disconnects them from their Jewish heritage, causing them to appear more vulnerable. This creates tension as the narrative builds to its climactic center point. The threefold charge brought against them includes disrespect of the king personally, disrespect of his gods, and disobedience to his command. This recalls the first two commandments in Exodus 20:4–6, and also parallels

the reference to the "law" and the charges brought against Daniel in 6:5 and 13.

Theological Insights

As in the opening scene of the previous chapter (2:1–16), God makes no direct appearance in 3:1–12—the context is purely pagan. Yet through the religious language employed in the narrative, three important ideas emerge as the theological backdrop to the drama. First, the demand to worship a pagan image reminds the believing reader that God alone is worthy of worship. Second, God allows these Jews in the context of exile to experience overwhelming pressure to conform. Third, the contrast of the Jews' status with the threat of their demise recalls their missing Hebrew names, which might assure us of God's incomparable compassion and deliverance in a time of crisis.

Teaching the Text

1. *God alone is worthy of worship.* This text is clear that the three Jews pay no attention to Nebuchadnezzar, and they do so by refusing to serve his pagan gods. Compare the prohibitions in the first two of the Ten Commandments, which speak to the practice of worshiping other gods and their images (Deut. 5:7–8). In the pluralistic and relativistic society of the modern Western world, the temptation for believers to consider other religions (gods) as equal to their own view of God can be significant, or they may be tempted to embrace a secular view that God does not exist. Challenge your listeners to a singular dedication to the one true God, despite the many pressures around us to do otherwise. Encourage

them to build this conviction into the hearts and lives of their children, who may face an even more challenging world than ours (Deut. 6:4–9).

2. *God allows the faithful to be tested.* Situations can change quickly in life. The king honors these three, and then jealous colleagues drag them before the king, who is no longer impressed with them. God still allows unexpected challenges in the lives of believers today and still expects us to remain faithful, despite the consequences. The mention of the vast array of "officials" from across the empire, along with the repeated emphasis on the Babylonian symphony, intensifies the social pressure on the Jews. Encourage your listeners to stay strong in their faith when powerful colleagues and the noise of the world around them begin to shake their confidence. Help them to focus on the person and work of God, experienced through our relationship with him.

3. *Remember God in the darkness.* The use of the pagan names for the three Jews in chapter 3, without their Hebrew counterparts, darkens the atmosphere of this narrative. Regretfully, most readers today do not even know the Hebrew names of the three, let alone their meanings. Remind your audience of the rich theology contained in these names that could encourage Shadrach, Meshach, and Abednego in this time of crisis (see the comments on 1:7). Knowing that the God whom believers serve today is still the incomparable (Mishael) and compassionate God (Hananiah) and is the ultimate rescuer (Azariah) can be of great comfort in circumstances similar to those of the three Jews long ago.

What not to teach. First, this text does not present a precise historical backdrop to the narrative. Therefore, avoid the temptation

The penalty for not worshiping the image is to be thrown into a blazing furnace. Although not as large as the one described in Daniel 6, this is an example of a copper-smelting furnace from the twelfth century BC, Timna, Israel.

to assign a specific age to the Jews, as they could have been anywhere between their late teens to midthirties. Second, this narrative is not about deifying Nebuchadnezzar, since Babylonian kings did not claim to be deities. Third, do not bore your listeners with detailed explanations about the provincial officials and musical instruments.

Illustrating the Text

There's not enough room for multiple gods in your heart.

Popular Culture: Associated with numerous American Western films since the 1930s (and later borrowed for the rock single by American pop group Sparks in the 1970s), the cliché "This town ain't big enough for both of us" indicates that the egos of two persons are so inflated or so incompatible that both of them residing in the same town is impossible. Trying to embrace the one true God and false deities at the same time tears apart the hosting heart. God jealously refuses competition for worship. Resist the temptation to value other persons and things so highly that they get in the way of exclusive, wholehearted worship of God.

God uses tests to bring him glory and to refine his people.

Film: *The Lord of the Rings.* In J. R. R. Tolkien's *Lord of the Rings*, hobbits Sam and Frodo endure suffering on a lengthy quest to defeat the forces of evil. Near the end of the 2002 film *The Lord of the Rings: The Two Towers*, Sam reflects on the value of tests for accomplishing a greater purpose:

> It's like in the great stories, Mr. Frodo—the ones that really mattered. Full of darkness and danger, they were. And sometimes you didn't want to know the end, because how could the end be happy? How could the world go back to the way it was, when so much bad had happened? But in the end, it's only a passing thing, this shadow. Even darkness must pass. A new day will come. And when the sun shines, it will shine out the clearer. . . . Folk in those stories had lots of chances of turning back, only they didn't. They kept going because they were holding on to something. . . . There's some good in this world, Mr. Frodo. And it's worth fighting for.

Similarly, God sometimes puts trials before those who love him, for their own growth and for the ultimate good of his perfect will, which is well worth fighting for.

God's goodness is often most obvious in places of darkness.

Quote: Bono. Drawing from his own experiences caring for those in places of extreme desperation and poverty, Bono—the famed lead singer of U2, the Irish rock band from Dublin, and an active philanthropist—shared these reflections on the comfort that the presence of God brings even in the darkest places:

> God is in the slums, in the cardboard boxes where the poor play house. God is in the silence of a mother who has infected her child with a virus that will end both their lives. God is in the cries heard under the rubble of war. God is in the debris of wasted opportunity and lives, and God is with us if we are with them.[11]

Remember the profound truth that God is often most discernible, knowable, and touchable when we join him in working in the most difficult, impossible, and allegedly "God-forsaken" places and lives.

Three Judeans Remain Faithful

Big Idea *God is worthy of committed and steadfast obedience even when powerful rulers threaten believers, at the edge of their faith, with imminent death.*

Understanding the Text

The Text in Context

See the unit on 3:1–12 for a discussion of the larger context, structure, and comparisons of this literary unit. Against this backdrop, 3:13–23 is the core of the chiastic narrative, which intensifies the drama and provides a background for the coming deliverance. The only speech given by Shadrach, Meshach, and Abednego in Daniel is the central, theological emphasis of this pericope and chapter. Amid personal crisis, the Judeans declare that God is worthy of their fidelity whatever the cost, mirroring Daniel's resolution in chapter 6. Within this framework, 3:13–23 divides into three parts: the threat against the three Judeans (3:13–15), their commitment to honor the one true God (3:16–18), and Nebuchadnezzar's attempted execution of Daniel's three friends (3:19–23).

Historical and Cultural Background

Greek names of musical instruments are repeated throughout this chapter, including wind, animal horns, flutes, stringed lyres, and harps. One of these instruments cannot be identified precisely but translates into English as "symphony" (Aramaic *sumponyah*;

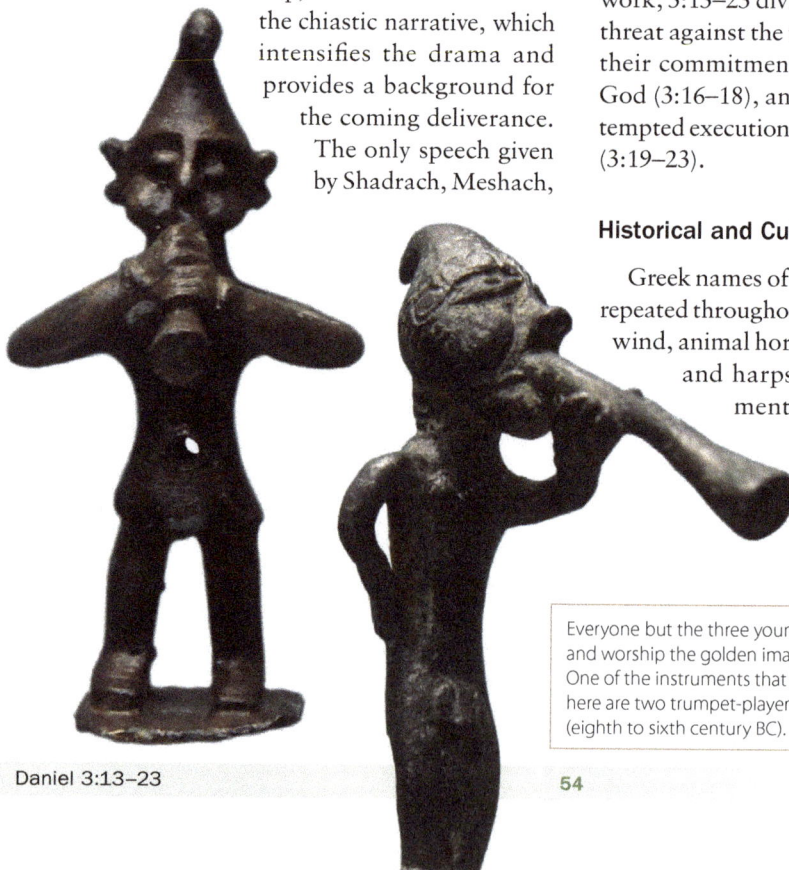

Everyone but the three young men from Judah fall down and worship the golden image when the music plays. One of the instruments that sounds is a horn. Shown here are two trumpet-player figurines from Turkey (eighth to sixth century BC).

3:5, 7, 10, 15; NIV: "pipe") and is known as early as the eighth century BC from Homer's writings. The presence of these words in Daniel is consistent with Babylonian interaction with Greece as early as the sixth century BC. In addition, Nebuchadnezzar's rations lists attest to the presence of Greeks in Babylon, including foreign musicians.[1]

In ancient Mesopotamia furnaces were primarily intended for making bricks, pottery, and metals. As such, they appeared near the places where their materials were used. Constructed of bricks or clay (often lined with stone), they had a side door for inserting and extracting materials and a domed-roof opening for ventilation. Death by burning appears in Hammurabi's Law Code (25; eighth–seventh century BC),[2] yet furnaces were probably not created for this purpose.[3] Depending on their use, temperatures ranged from 1,650 to 2,700 degrees Fahrenheit. Therefore, heating the furnace "seven times hotter than usual" is certainly hyperbolic.[4]

Interpretive Insights

3:13 *Furious with rage, Nebuchadnezzar summoned.* The high positions of Shadrach, Meshach, and Abednego most likely warrant the unusual royal summons in place of their being executed immediately by the king's subordinates. Nebuchadnezzar's uncontrolled temper recalls his behavior in 2:12—perhaps speaking to his sense of insecurity—and contrasts with Darius's concerns for Daniel in 6:14–19. The use of the Judeans' Babylonian names without their significant Hebrew counterparts (cf. 1:6–7, 11, 19; 2:17) creates an atmosphere of isolation from their heritage,

Key Themes of Daniel 3:13–23

- Nebuchadnezzar gives Shadrach, Meshach, and Abednego a second chance to compromise their faith or die.
- Nebuchadnezzar challenges the ability of any god to rescue someone from his power.
- The Judean youths choose to remain faithful even in the face of what looks like a certain and horrible execution.

making them appear more vulnerable in this crisis.[5]

3:14 *Is it true . . . that you do not serve my gods or worship the image . . . ?* The Hebrew term for "worship" (*sᵉgid*) is also used in 2:46, where Nebuchadnezzar "paid honor" to Daniel, thereby "worshiping" his God. A similar correlation appears here: bowing to the image implies serving pagan gods. In total, three charges are brought against the Jews: they pay no attention to the king, they do not serve his gods, and they do not worship the image. Here, Nebuchadnezzar repeats the last two, but he utilizes only the last one in his interrogation—as it can serve as proof of the previous two.

3:15 *if you are ready . . . what god will be able to rescue you . . . ?* The conditional clause parallels the statement of the Judeans in 3:17. Again, their high positions may warrant this second chance, although the repetition of "immediately" (3:6, 15) lessens Nebuchadnezzar's credibility. The NIV's addition of "very good" is implied but not stated in the Masoretic Text. Nebuchadnezzar's remark is rhetorical, yet emphatic, literally asking, "What god at all . . . ?" By it, he inadvertently sets up the confession of fidelity by the Judeans (3:17–18), followed by God's deliverance in 3:24–30. His question recalls the sages' assertion in 2:11 that only the gods are able to

The Prayer of Azariah and the Song of the Three Jews

A lengthy deuterocanonical insertion (68 verses) appears between Daniel 3:23 and 3:24 in the Septuagint (both the OG and Theodotion) and Roman Catholic and Eastern Orthodox Bibles (see NRSV), but not in translations of the Masoretic Text by Jews and Protestants.[a] It consists of the Prayer of Azariah (1–22), a brief prose section describing the angel's intervention (23–28), and the Song of the Three Judeans (29–68). Most scholars agree that this intrusive tale was not part of the original corpus of Daniel but was added around 100 BC.

The addition positively embellishes the cryptic and slightly ambiguous statement in the original text of Daniel 3:17 (ESV: "If this be so"), which may be why it was inserted. The Masoretic Text speaks solely of "God's" ability to deliver Shadrach, Meshach, and Abednego (3:17, 28). In contrast, the addition portrays God as "Lord" (perhaps a substitute for the divine name Yahweh) of history, attentive to Israel's corporate and personal needs, by using the Hebrew names of the Judeans: Hananiah, Mishael, and Azariah. As Lord of the universe, the Creator is exalted above creation. The liturgical, penitent prayer of the three resembles Daniel 9:4–19, suggesting that the author of the addition may have had knowledge of that text.

  [a] See C. A. Moore, *Daniel, Esther, and Jeremiah*, 23–76; Collins, *Daniel*, 195–207.

reveal mysteries, although here he puts his power above that of any god. His defiance counters the Judeans' persistence.

3:16 *replied to him, "King Nebuchadnezzar, we do not need to defend ourselves."* Verses 16–18 form the literary and theological center of the chapter. The NIV does not follow the Masoretic punctuation of this text, which reads, "[They] replied to the king, 'Nebuchadnezzar, we do not . . .'" Thus, they do not use his royal title when speaking to him. The bold, informal manner of address suggested by the Masoretic Text would have commanded Nebuchadnezzar's attention and, at the same time, fueled his rage. The fact that these three Judeans offer no defense is tantamount to a guilty plea to the three charges laid against

them. Its simplicity focuses the reader's attention on God's worthiness to be served exclusively, no matter the cost.

3:17 *If we are thrown into the blazing furnace, the God we serve is able to deliver us.* This cryptic statement is more difficult to translate than most modern translations reflect.[6] Literally, the first clause reads: "If it be *so*" (KJV, NASB; cf. ESV)—begging the question: "If *what* be so?" The NLT concurs with the NIV in rendering, "If we are thrown into the blazing furnace," while the NRSV translates, "If our God whom we serve is able to deliver us." This may be a reference only to the inevitability of their execution, yet the grammar allows for the possibility of their having an understandable moment of doubt. Both renderings find justification in legitimate antecedents in 3:15. The NIV's rendering of the clause appeals to the threat, "you will be thrown . . ." and is clearly the more palatable reading.[7] Yet the NRSV's interpretation appeals to the nearer antecedent, "what god will be able?" In context, this intriguing, yet slightly ambiguous, assertion allows readers to identify with the Judeans, setting them up for the second, and more important, conditional statement.

3:18 *But even if he does not, we want you to know.* In contrast to the preceding verse, the commitment of Shadrach, Meshach, and Abednego is clear: they choose to remain loyal to their God even if it means facing a horrifying death. The suspense with which their only recorded speech ends creates tension in the text. The proof that God is able to deliver is finally expressed clearly in the concluding section of the chapter (3:24–30).

3:19–22 *Nebuchadnezzar was furious . . . his attitude toward them changed.* The bold rhetoric and unrepentant attitude of the Judeans infuriates the king even further (cf. 3:13). Literally, the Aramaic reads, "and the image [*ts^{e}lem*] of his face changed," a subtle pun on the "image" he has set up for worship. Making the furnace as hot as possible from the bottom, while sending his strongest soldiers to the top (the furnace was probably adjacent to a hill), contrasts the irrational actions of Nebuchadnezzar with the steadfast demeanor of those facing execution. The description of them as being fully clothed accents the urgency of Nebuchadnezzar's command and, ironically, enhances the coming miracle.

3:23 *these three men, firmly tied, fell into the blazing furnace.* Restating the execution (cf. 3:20) provides a breathtaking image of the Judeans falling into the flames. The Masoretic Text places a paragraph divider after this statement, creating a dramatic pause before the response of the king (cf. the similar drama in 6:16–18). This may be the occasion for the deuterocanonical insertion at this point in the Septuagint (see the sidebar).

Theological Insights

Daniel 3:13–23, the chiastic center of the larger narrative, speaks to three theological realities. First, the one true God is incomparable to false gods; he can do what they cannot. Second, God is able to rescue those who faithfully serve him, despite their doubts, and even from the hands of the most powerful rulers. Third, God is worthy of the ultimate sacrifice regardless of whether he chooses to exercise his divine prerogative to deliver.

> Shadrach, Meshach, and Abednego are thrown into the fiery furnace when they refuse to worship the image Nebuchadnezzar has erected. This fragment from a fourth-century AD sarcophagus lid shows Daniel's three friends in the fiery furnace.

Teaching the Text

1. *The true God compared to false gods.* Nebuchadnezzar experiences the failure of his gods to rescue him from his dream dilemma (Dan. 2), yet now he forgets this truth and challenges the ability of any god—especially the Jewish God. Remind your listeners that it is easy to forget the times in the past when God has worked on our behalf and, therefore, to question his intent or ability at a later time. Encourage them to review often the times when God has proven himself faithful in their lives. The king inadvertently poses just the right question in this context, one that God answers explicitly in the conclusion to the narrative. Challenge your audience to be attentive to questions others pose—no matter how negative their intent—that provide an opportunity to speak on God's behalf or for God to work directly.

2. *Commit to the God who is able.* When teaching this text, acknowledge the ambiguity of the response of the three Judeans (see the comments on 3:17 above). A reasonable argument can be made that they have a moment of doubt about God when they are pushed to the edge of their faith. There is no need to make sure these persons always act perfectly. On the contrary, help your audience to identify with them, remembering a time when they may have experienced doubts about God. The point to make from this passage is that, in the end, the three Judeans choose what is right. Further, encourage believers today to help other believers in similar circumstance as part of a community rather than to judge their times of doubt.

3. *The God who is worthy of sacrifice.* It is fine to point out the courage and fidelity of the Judeans under these circumstances. However, courage and fidelity alone are not the point. In fact, that same behavior toward a false god would be a fool's errand. Rather, only the one true God deserves such behavior. He is inherently worthy of the greatest sacrifices, whether or not he chooses to deliver. Affirm the uncomfortable truth that God may choose not to deliver us from hardships in life, no matter how faithful we have been. Emphasize that eternal deliverance will come in the end (cf. Dan. 12:2–3). But do not promise that temporal deliverance is guaranteed if we just have enough faith or live a righteous life—no biblical text teaches this.

What not to teach. Avoid heroizing the three Judeans. The question Nebuchadnezzar raises is about God, as is their answer to him. Their commitment flows out of their belief about the person of their God. Keep this truth at the forefront of your preaching and teaching. The call to action should not be "Dare to be like Shadrach, Meshach, and Abednego" but rather "Dare to believe that our God is worthy of our fidelity in any challenges that may confront us, for his name's sake."

Illustrating the Text

Commemorate and remember God's greatness over false gods.

Bible: Unlike Nebuchadnezzar, we must be intentional in remembering the work of God and being encouraged by his incomparable greatness over any other gods. Throughout the Old Testament, God reminds his people that he redeemed them from Egypt (e.g., Exod. 20:2; Deut. 20:1; Judg. 6:8; 1 Sam. 12:6–8; 2 Kings 17:36; Ps.

Polycarp, bishop of Smyrna, was martyred in the second century AD, burned alive by the Romans. He is included as one of twenty-five martyrs represented in the *Procession of the Holy Martyrs* mosaic at the Basilica of Sant'Apollinare Nuovo in Ravenna, Italy, crafted around 560. In this reproduction of a portion of that mosaic, Demetrius, Polycarp, Vincent, Pancras, and Chrysogonus are depicted (from left to right).

81:10; Dan. 9:15). The exodus was an undeniable expression of his supremacy over the power of Pharaoh and the false gods of Egypt—a great victory that Israel is called to remember. To forget God's past deliverances is to bring destruction on oneself, just as Israel did (Deut. 8:10–20), and Nebuchadnezzar does as well. Commemorating the extraordinary cases of God's faithfulness in our lives, like the exodus, gives a believer courage and faith for the present.

Confidence in God is stronger than doubt.

Quote: Nelson Mandela. Mandela (1918–2013) is remembered as a nonviolent anti-apartheid freedom activist, politician, and philanthropist in South Africa who eventually served as the country's president from 1994 to 1999. From his teens he demonstrated remarkable courage in opposing the oppression of his people, even in the face of severe personal persecution. Yet consider one of his most frequent and often remembered assertions: "I learned that courage was not the absence of fear, but the triumph over it. The brave man is not he who does not feel afraid, but he who conquers that fear."[8] When we are faced with frightening circumstances and overwhelming human

powers, fear and doubt are sometimes unavoidable. How we handle these human responses—while trusting God in spite of them—is what enables us to learn from our experiences to rest in the knowledge that God is greater than our fears.

Serving God is worth even the ultimate sacrifice.

History: The cost of discipleship is something we all experience, though the physical price may not be the same for everyone. Sacrifice may mean smaller things, such as living in less than ideal conditions while serving God, or it may mean paying the ultimate price of laying down one's life for faith in Christ. Consider the faithfulness of the early Christian martyrs, such as Stephen, Peter, or Polycarp, even in the face of torture, mutilation, and death. According to Christian tradition, Polycarp was taken from his home by Roman authorities and bravely faced trial, threats, and eventually burning at the stake, remaining strong in his trust that God would give him the strength to endure the fire. Though God does not always grant deliverance in this lifetime, he always faithfully grants eternal deliverance to those who trust in him.

God Rescues the Faithful from the Furnace

Big Idea *Reflecting his kingdom purposes, God is able to demonstrate his sovereign power and gracious care to those who trust and obey him.*

Understanding the Text

The Text in Context

See the unit on 3:1–12 for a discussion of the larger context, structure, and comparisons of this literary unit. Against this backdrop, 3:24–30 is the last section of this narrative, which delights the reader with the deliverance of the Judeans and Nebuchadnezzar's praise to God—mirroring the ending of chapter 6. Within this framework, 3:24–30 divides into three parts: Nebuchadnezzar's response to God's deliverance of the Jews (3:24–27), his decree to praise their God (3:28), and his promotion of the Jews and punishment of their enemies (3:29–30).

Historical and Cultural Background

Angelic messengers also play significant roles in the Ugaritic Baal cycle, and the equivalent to the Semitic term *mal'ak* ("angel") is found in Phoenician literature.[1] Likewise, Homer uses the Greek term *angelos* ("angel") as early as the eighth century BC. This evidence is consistent with Nebuchadnezzar's apparent familiarity with angels in this text.[2]

The Semitic "son of the gods" is a common expression for representing a supernatural being. However, since this phrase comes from Nebuchadnezzar's lips, one

Nebuchadnezzar spots another figure in the flames of the furnace and says it "looks like a son of the gods" (3:25). He later declares that God's angel has been sent to rescue the three young Jewish men. The designer of this clay lamp (fourth to sixth century AD) chose to depict the fourth person with wings and a halo.

should not expect deep, messianic, theological insight. Rather, a polytheistic king like him would use it to describe a member of Babylon's pantheon of gods.[3]

Interpretive Insights

3:24 *King Nebuchadnezzar leaped to his feet in amazement.* The abrupt shift from the Judeans falling into the flames (3:13–23) to the king's reaction to their instantaneous deliverance emphasizes God's ability to save.[4] Just as Nebuchadnezzar's question in 3:15 sets the stage for the Judeans' confession of loyalty to God, so his question here does the same for his confession of God's ability. Further, just as Daniel confronts him with the truth, "there is a God in heaven who reveals mysteries" (2:28), so here Nebuchadnezzar discovers that God can deliver those who serve him. Whereas 3:13–23 is focused on the king and the Judeans, the first and last pericopes include others standing nearby—here, the "advisers" who confirm the number of men in the furnace. This begins a series of eyewitness examinations that prove the miracle.

3:25 *Look! I see four men walking around in the fire.* Another emphatic interjection begins this sentence, announcing more evidence that God is at work. Those bound and thrown into the flames (3:19–23) are now instantly and inexplicably loosed and unharmed. Moreover, a fourth person appears with them who looks like "a son of the gods" (literal translation of the Aramaic *bar 'elahin*; cf. ESV, NASB). In contrast, the KJV and the NKJV maintain a christological reading of this text by translating, "the Son of God."[5] However, several factors support the NIV's reading. First,

Nebuchadnezzar's perspective suggests that the Aramaic *'elahin* be understood as a genuine plural ("gods"), contrasting Daniel's use of the singular (*'elah*) when a single deity is intended (3:15, 29; 4:8). Second, the king describes the person as one who "looks like" a divine being, but he clarifies later that it is an "angel" (3:28). Third, the phrase "sons of God" appears elsewhere in

Chapter and Verse Divisions in the Hebrew Bible

In the Hebrew Bible, as well as in modern Jewish Bibles (e.g., NJPS), the introduction to Nebuchadnezzar's letter (Dan. 4:1–3 NIV) is numbered as 3:31–33. Hence, in the Masoretic Text, the two chapters are numbered 3:1–33 and 4:1–34. This created parallel, poetic praise endings for three narratives (3:1–33; 4:1–34; 6:1–28), which makes good sense structurally. However, there is a clear consensus among commentators today—both Christian[a] and Jewish[b]—that these three verses should be understood as the beginning of Daniel 4, making the numbering of that chapter 4:1–37 (NIV).

Originally, Old Testament manuscripts had no verse or chapter divisions. The oldest known copies with verse indicators—although without numbering—date to the sixth to ninth century AD. The practice of numbering chapters and verses evolved during the thirteenth to sixteenth century AD. Traditionally, Archbishop Stephen Langton numbered the Hebrew/Aramaic and Septuagint (Greek) texts according to the Latin Vulgate. At this time, what we know today as Daniel 4:1–3 was mistakenly associated with the narrative of Daniel 3.[c] In response, English (Wycliffe, fourteenth century; KJV, seventeenth century) and German (Luther, sixteenth century) versions corrected it to form the beginning of chapter 4. The strongest argument in favor of this choice seems to be the first-person language of Nebuchadnezzar throughout chapter 4 (except for vv. 28–33). Therefore, the opening poetic doxology in 4:3 forms a literary and theological parallel to the closing poetic doxology in 4:34–35.

[a] E.g., Longman, *Daniel*, 116.
[b] See the discussion of rabbinical debates in Goldwurm, *Daniel*, 132–33.
[c] See also Slotki, *Daniel*, 29–30.

the Old Testament, referring to angels or mortals—but never to deity (Gen. 6:2–4; Job 1:6; 2:1 [see NIV footnote]). Fourth, Hebrew and Aramaic have no "capital letters" (only one case); therefore, capitalizations in English texts are purely interpretive. Fifth, Hebrew and Aramaic can designate definite articles ("the"), but one does not occur here. Sixth, nowhere in the New Testament is this text recognized as referring to Jesus.

3:26 *Nebuchadnezzar then approached the opening of the blazing furnace.* This accurately represents ancient Mesopotamian furnaces, as the king can see the Judeans through the ground-level opening. Nebuchadnezzar's reference to their exclusive service to "the Most High God" both recalls their confession (3:17) and anticipates the king's praise (3:28). This designation of God throughout chapters 3–7 is attributed to gentiles (4:2, 17, 34) as well as Jews (4:24–32), and both ascribe to him universal sovereignty.[6]

3:27 *satraps, prefects, governors and royal advisers.* These four titles abbreviate the longer list in 3:2–3, which may include the "Chaldean" accusers from 3:8 (see NIV footnote). Their third-party examination recalls and confirms the initial observation of Nebuchadnezzar in verse 25. The evidentiary details of no harm or smell of smoke prove the miracle (cf. Heb. 11:34).

3:28–29 *Praise be to the God of Shadrach, Meshach and Abednego.* Nebuchadnezzar praises the only God who "can save in this way," answering the question he raises earlier: "What god will be able to rescue?" (3:15). Perhaps he wishes to appease their God, whom he has offended earlier (3:15). The language of the text suggests no more than that he makes the faith of the Jews legitimate along with other religions. His words fall short of a personal conversion. In fact, his confession would be strengthened by his use of the Judeans' Hebrew names (see the comments on 1:7). His choice of *mal'ak*, "angel," clarifies the rescuer's identity. Perhaps based on this statement, the Babylonian Talmud identifies the person in 3:25 as the angel Gabriel (*Pesahim* 118a, b).[7] The threatened punishment for the accusers is consistent with that used by other Mesopotamian kings.[8]

More important, mention of the Judeans setting aside the king's command redirects honor toward their God and away from Nebuchadnezzar's gods.

3:30 *the king promoted Shadrach, Meshach and Abednego*. This may be a "promotion" beyond what he gives in 2:49 (cf. 3:12). The Aramaic term *ts^{e}lah* can also denote causing someone to "prosper" or have "success" within an already existing position, perhaps with riches and public honor.[9] The reference to the "province of Babylon" parallels the chapter's beginning.

Theological Insights

In 3:24–30, the dramatic conclusion to a well-known story, the reader encounters the Most High God in three ways. First, God proves himself able to rescue those who choose to put their trust in him. Second, God is worthy of, and justly rewards, the trust and obedience of believers. Third, when angels appear and miracles occur, these are meant to point to the sovereign God, who acts to establish his kingdom.

Teaching the Text

1. *God is able*. Although God does not need to prove himself to mere mortals, he often does so through his grace and kindness to those who seek him. The Judeans'

promotions, their colleagues' accusations, and Nebuchadnezzar's blasphemous rage demonstrate the one true God's ability to rescue—in contrast to weak and worthless pagan gods. Help your listeners to find confidence in God's ability in contrast to their own, even if he sometimes chooses not to rescue us from any given crisis in this present life. Assure them that he ultimately acts on our behalf and for his glory. Moreover, his actions are not for believers alone but serve also as a witness to a world that regularly doubts God's ability or his intentions.

2. *God rewards those who trust him*. The text connects God's willingness to rescue with the description of the Judeans as God's servants who trust him and are willing to die rather than compromise their faith. Emphasize to your listeners that faith and faithfulness, taken together, make a difference in the way God works with his people. This is consistent with Old Testament wisdom that teaches blessing for the righteous and judgment for the wicked (cf. Prov. 1:1–7). Although proverbs are not absolute promises that God always keeps in this life, they reveal general principles

The satraps, prefects, governors, and royal advisors whom Nebuchadnezzar has summoned to this dedication/worship event observe the miraculous rescue of Shadrach, Meshach, and Abednego by the God of Israel. This eighth-century BC relief from the palace at Zincirli shows a procession of court officials.

Daniel 3:24–30

by which God governs his moral universe. Therefore, we as believers should live holistic lives of faith and obedience because God is worthy and delights in blessing the righteous.

3. *Miracles point to God's person and work*. Although the deliverance in this story is spectacular, the story is not about the miracle—rather, it is about the God who is able to rescue. To this end, Nebuchadnezzar praises the one true God, who is sovereign over the personal crisis of his faithful servants. Keep this bigger picture before your audience so that they do not miss the story's point. Remind them to stay focused on God's ability, rather than on the greatness of their faith. The three Judeans may experience a moment of doubt, yet God honors their commitment based on the amount of faith they possess and their choice to invest it in him.

What not to teach. First, do not become preoccupied with the identification of the fourth person in the furnace. His descriptions come in the form of narrative, and from the mouth of a pagan king.

This mysterious intermediary plays a brief and secondary role in comparison with the primary character: "the Most High God" of the Judeans. Second, Nebuchadnezzar's decree does not indicate a permanent conversion of him or his people. Third, do not spend time in a sermon on the question of the Masoretic Text's ending of this chapter. The outcome of that discussion does not affect the theology of either chapter 3 or 4.

Illustrating the Text

God is always able to rescue, yet he may only do so in the life to come.

Human Experience: When baking cookies or preparing a sauce, a cook will often take a small taste before it is finished. When the finished product is served and the enjoyment of the food is shared with others, everyone experiences the same excitement and happiness. Though the cook had a small taste already, these taste tests are not the substance of the meal: everyone eats the meal, while only a few taste ahead, and the meal is filling, while the taste tests never satisfy. In the same way, a feast of salvation is in store for all of God's own, and the finished product is just as sweet for all, whether they have already tasted or not. Some may get to taste ahead of time (miracles of deliverance, healings, and particular manifestations of the Spirit), but no one knows the full joy of the feast (unveiled fellowship with Jesus) until it has fully come.

Righteousness is responding to seemingly impossible situations by trusting God.

Film: *Mission: Impossible.* The classic television series *Mission: Impossible* (1966–73) and its subsequent movie franchise live up to this title in presenting the protagonist Ethan Hunt in situations of extreme danger from which success or rescue seems "impossible." However, viewers who witness these scenarios time and time again come to realize that no matter how terrible things become, there remains a sense of confidence that, just as in the past, the heroes will again make it out alive. Daniel's three Judean friends facing the "impossible" situation of their plight in the furnace would also know of many examples of God's rescue in Israel's past, such as when the emerging nation was trapped between the Red Sea and Pharaoh's army with no possible route of escape (Exod. 14:9–10). The knowledge of deliverance in the past can and should instill confidence that God is able to rescue even from seemingly "impossible" circumstances.

Miracles are windows that point to God's kingdom.

Bible: **John 9.** Rather than being a point of focus in itself, a miracle is better thought of as a window to reveal more clearly the power and majesty of God and his kingdom in our present lives. In John 9, the healing of the man born blind emphatically depicts miracles as pointing beyond themselves to our faith in God. The Pharisees conduct interrogations of the man and his parents, analyzing the circumstances of the miracle closely, yet they are shown to be shockingly ignorant of the identity and eternal importance of the one who performed the miracle. By contrast, consider the blind man, who looks through his experience of healing to the one who healed him and comes to believe in Christ (9:30–33, 38). The wonder of the miracle is never the goal; rather, the miracle serves as a window through which to see the person and purpose of the miracle-working God behind it.

Daniel 3:24–30

Nebuchadnezzar's Testimony and Tree Dream

Big Idea *In contrast to this world's belief systems, God communicates his sovereignty to powerful leaders through his Spirit in faithful servants.*

Understanding the Text

The Text in Context

Daniel 4:1–37 is woven into the book's overall literary structure in two ways. First, it advances the narrative of chapters 1–6, in which the first four focus on Nebuchadnezzar (chaps. 1–2 with historical markers and 3–4 without) and the last two show the transition from Belshazzar of Babylon to Darius the Mede (chaps. 5–6). Second, it begins the third of three parallel pairs of chapters (4 and 5) in the book's concentric Aramaic center section. Comparatively, Daniel 4 and 5 present contrasting Babylonian kings and varying structures, yet they share the same general content and theme: God's judgment of proud rulers. Read together, they keep Judah's "seventy-year" exile in view by setting Babylon's first king opposite its last, recalling the parameters of the prologue (1:1, 21).

This chapter is also arranged chiastically: the first pericope (4:1–18) sets Nebuchadnezzar's dream opposite its fulfillment in the last (4:28–37), while the center (4:19–27) focuses on Nebuchadnezzar's telling of his dream and Daniel's prophetic interpretation of it.[1] Within this framework, 4:1–18 divides into five parts: the king's doxological proclamation (4:1–3), the narrative's introduction (4:4–9), the tree vision's content (4:10–12), an angelic command to destroy the tree (4:13–16), and the purpose of the vision (4:17–18).

Historical and Cultural Background

Usually, a proclamation like Nebuchadnezzar's would be inscribed on a large stele in a place that was inaccessible to passersby, yet where all could read it. Smaller copies were sometimes made, as was done with the Behistun Inscription of Darius I Hystaspes (sixth–fifth century BC). Although the salutation of Nebuchadnezzar's decree in Daniel is similar to then-standard royal inscriptions, the personal testimony section is unusual. The salutation's form—a king's name, the letter's recipients, and wishes for peace—is common in Babylonian, Persian, and Greek letters. The omission of a verb and a formal greeting is also common in royal proclamations.[2]

The symbolism of a tree at the center of the world with roots accessing subterranean waters and branches touching the sky was well known in the ancient Near East. In the Myth of Erra and Ishum, the god Marduk describes a "meshu tree" whose roots descend through the oceans to the netherworld and whose top ascends to heaven. Assyrian literature speaks of sacred trees, such as the "tree of life" with a winged disk over it surrounded by animals, humans, and supernatural beings. This cosmic symbol of life and prosperity may personify a king, his kingdom, or a divine world order.[3]

Whereas a class of supernatural beings called "watchers" (Aramaic 'ir) is common in intertestamental literature (e.g., the "Book of Watchers" in 1 Enoch, as well as some of the Dead Sea Scrolls), no evidence exists prior to the third century BC of a specialized usage like that which appears in Daniel.[4]

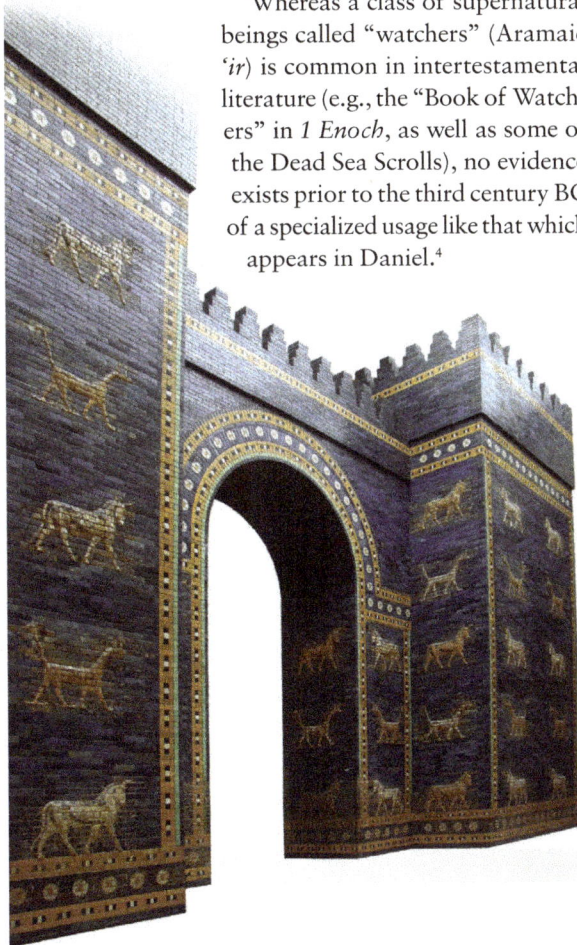

Interpretive Insights

4:1–3 *King Nebuchadnezzar, To . . . all the earth.* This rhetoric is royal hyperbole for the greatest imaginable reach of one's kingdom (Babylon covered only the Fertile Crescent). The combination of "signs and wonders" conveys the idea of a supernatural event, referring to the instantaneous affliction of Nebuchadnezzar and his equally sudden restoration. This proclamation continues the theme of God's everlasting kingdom from 2:44. Here, God's "signs and wonders" are evidence of his kingdom work among mere mortals like Nebuchadnezzar.

4:4 *I, Nebuchadnezzar, was . . . contented and prosperous.* The scene is set after Nebuchadnezzar secured his kingdom from his opponents (the last, Phoenicia, in 571 BC) and completed his massive building projects (see "Historical and Cultural Background" in the unit on 4:28–37) by the thirty-fourth year (571 BC) of his

At the time of his dream, Nebuchadnezzar describes himself as "contented and prosperous" (4:4). The Babylon he had built was a magnificent city. The beautiful Ishtar Gate, a portion reconstructed here, was one of the main entrances to the city and directed the processional way to the great temple of Marduk. The gate's elaborate decorations displayed the symbols of the Babylonian gods believed to empower the king.

forty-three-year reign (605–562 BC). The insertion of his "eighteenth year" (586 BC) into the Old Greek is less likely.[5] The emphatic first-person introduction is unique for a king. This style continues throughout the chapter, except for Daniel's comments in 4:28–33. Nebuchadnezzar's portions of the narrative tell the story through his eyes, with boastful language about his impressive rule (cf. 4:28–30).[6] The specific imagery of "prosperous" (literally, "growing") is used to describe healthy trees in Jeremiah 11:16 (NIV: "thriving") and 17:8 (NIV: "green"), while here it foreshadows the tree image in the king's dream.

4:5–7 *I had a dream that made me afraid.* In Nebuchadnezzar's first dream (2:1), his kingdom is one of several ultimately replaced by God's kingdom (2:36–45). Here, he personally is threatened with divine judgment for sinning against the God of heaven (4:26–27). Compared to the prolonged drama in 2:2–13, the sages in this narrative are told the dream but cannot, or will not, interpret it—perhaps due to its negative implications. Their failure sets the stage for Daniel's entrance. Although the Septuagint omits verses 6–7, making it appear that Daniel comes first, the Masoretic Text is preferred.

4:8–9 *Finally, Daniel came . . . the spirit of the holy gods.* Daniel may be summoned last because he is overseer of the sages (2:48), which highlights the importance of his arrival. The king refers to him by both his Hebrew and Babylonian names, noting that the latter references Nebuchadnezzar's god Bel.[7] His recognition of the "spirit of the holy gods" in Daniel recalls his supernatural gifting (1:17). Nebuchadnezzar understands Daniel's skills as the

influence of pagan gods, ignoring the "God of gods and the Lord of kings" (2:47) and "the Most High God" (3:26; 4:2). The text emphasizes God's Spirit at work in Daniel (cf. Joseph before Pharaoh; Gen. 41:38). The single reference to "magicians" is probably representative, as they are first in the list in 4:7. The affirmation "no mystery too difficult" alludes to God's revelation of "mysteries" through Daniel (2:28).

4:10–12 *the visions I saw while lying in bed.* The tree's size and place make it accessible to all seeking sustenance and protection. The metaphorical description of Assyria's demise in Ezekiel 31 (587 BC, eighteen years after Daniel's exile) forms a striking parallel to Nebuchadnezzar's dream. Although Daniel may have known of this text—because Ezekiel lived in Babylon at this time—this is not Daniel's dream. Rather, it is Nebuchadnezzar's first-person impressions of what he has seen.

4:13 *I looked, and there before me was a holy one, a messenger.* The repetition of the introductory phrase, "In the visions . . . ," creates a pause before the prosperous tree is reduced to a fettered stump. The interjection is abrupt, indicating a new phase in the dream—or even an awakening only to experience a second dream. The Aramaic term *'ir* describing the "messenger" denotes "one who is awake and watchful"[8] (NIV footnote: "watchman"; cf. 4:17, 23). Only here in the Hebrew Bible does it reference a heavenly being. The Old Greek translates, "angels," although Theodotion changes it to "watchers" (see the sidebar "Nondivine, Heavenly Beings in Daniel" in the unit on 3:24–30).

4:14–16 *Cut down the tree . . . let the stump . . . remain.* The plural imperatives

The tree that Nebuchadnezzar sees in his dream may have brought to mind the sacred trees depicted on Assyrian reliefs. Here two figures of King Ashurnasirpal, flanked by protective spirits, stand in front of a sacred tree. This relief was displayed behind Ashurnasirpal's royal throne in his palace at Nimrud (864–860 BC). A god in a winged disk is depicted above the tree. The winged creatures flanking Ashurnasirpal also coincide at many points with the watchers connected to Nebuchadnezzar's dream tree.

in 4:14a carry the same force as the passives in 4:14b–15a, implying a comprehensive judgment. Leaving the "stump and its roots" marks the transition from "tree" to "man" to "animal." The "iron and bronze" binding is a mixed symbol of imprisoned preservation.[9] The command to "let his mind be changed" reflects the Aramaic *lᵉbab* ("heart"; cf. Hebrew *leb*), which carries connotations of "emotion, thought, or will." The divinely induced mental disease of zoanthropy ("animal-man") is clarified in 4:33 more specifically as boanthropy ("ox-man"; see "Historical and Cultural Background" in the unit on 4:28–37).[10] The judgment is for "seven [appointed] times" (Aramaic *'iddan*), denoting a fixed and definite period, yet of unstated duration (cf. 2:8; 7:12). Although the NIV's footnote follows the popular interpretation "years" (suggested by the OG), the ESV captures the text's ambiguity with "periods of time."[11]

4:17 *The decision is announced by messengers.* Although Nebuchadnezzar may understand the verdict as originating with the watchers (the Aramaic construct suggests this; cf. NRSV, ESV), they are mere messengers of the decree of the Most High. The decree's purpose, "that all . . . may know" (NRSV) both recalls and foreshadows the public confessions of Nebuchadnezzar (4:1–3, 37), as well as his influence symbolized in "the tree." The decree's content is the theological climax: "the Most High is sovereign" (cf. 4:25, 32). This affirmation builds on God's "giving" Jehoiakim into Nebuchadnezzar's hands (1:2) and anticipates Nebuchadnezzar's repentance in 4:28–37.

4:18 *This is the dream that I, King Nebuchadnezzar, had.* The resumptive rhetoric of the king marks both the beginning and the ending of this pericope. The dream's interpretation should have been easy for Nebuchadnezzar's trained interpreters. Perhaps the dark judgment scene (4:13–17) had prevented them all from facing this reality, or the sages had feared the king's rage (cf. 2:12–13; 4:19). Yet their failure lays the foundation for God's prophetic work through Daniel in 4:19–27.

Theological Insights

Three aspects of God's person and purposes are embedded in 4:1–18, the introduction to Nebuchadnezzar's judgment. First, without knowledge of the one true God, worldly power and wisdom cannot adequately explain the experiences of mere mortals. Second, God works by his Spirit through his faithful servants in ways the world cannot duplicate or understand. Third, the Most High God is sovereign over all earthly kingdoms and rules them as he pleases.

Teaching the Text

1. *The emptiness of human wisdom and accomplishments.* It is no coincidence that the failure of pagan kings and sages is repeated in chapters 2, 4, and 5. Human beings too often look to worldly power and wisdom to answer spiritual questions or to seek deliverance from a crisis. Nebuchadnezzar should have remembered this lesson from his early years. Retell this aspect of the story, as the text of Daniel does, so that your listeners may remember that wealth and power cannot resolve the more important conundrums of life and that false religions or secular philosophies cannot answer life's deeper questions. In contrast, the one true God, as revealed in the Bible, is the only reliable source of power and wisdom.

2. *God works through his Spirit in believers.* Encourage your listeners to hear this story afresh from Nebuchadnezzar's perspective, imagining his great wealth and influence but, at the same time, realizing that even seemingly content unbelievers sometimes are forced to look to believers for help when they sense God's Spirit in us. This should encourage us to be prepared to explain our faith in appropriate, winsome, and productive ways. It also can make us aware that God's Holy Spirit is working in and through us today, as it was with Daniel. Challenge your audience to develop a deeper relationship with God through the work of his Spirit in their lives, so that their inner spiritual quality shows outwardly to others around them like a light to a dark world.

3. *God is sovereign over human kingdoms and rulers.* Employ good examples of how God displays his power and care today—perhaps through "signs and wonders"—emphasizing his kingship over our world by providing for our every need. Point out the effect such experiences can have on us to help us see God's goodness and greatness as we participate in his kingdom work. Show your listeners how the kingdom and dominion of God can have personal and practical application. For instance, knowing that the sovereign Lord of history is still in control of that history can help to alleviate the fear that many of us face as we encounter global threats in the daily news.

What not to teach. First, this text neither confirms nor denies "signs and wonders" today—this is not its focus. Second, do not get distracted by the question of "spirit of the holy gods" versus "Spirit of the holy God." The former is Nebuchadnezzar's perspective; the latter is Daniel's. Third, although

God may use loss of privileged status or personal illness as judgments for sin, we should never assume this is the case. Fourth, not all dreams are messages from God, and the work of modern-day "prophets" is different from those in the Bible.

Illustrating the Text

No amount of human wisdom can address spiritual needs.

Quote: Francis Schaeffer. Consider the hopelessness of those who do not know God and consequently live in a world they cannot understand or explain by relying on human wisdom. We were crafted for relationship with God, and the pressure of alienation from God and the failure of human philosophies and wisdom to adequately address a person's spiritual needs bring us to what theologian and philosopher Francis Schaeffer calls the "point of tension" and the resulting "roof" constructed in an effort to blind us to our innate, spiritual need:

> At the point of tension . . . the roof is built as a protection against the blows of the real world, both internal and external . . . but we must allow the person to undergo this experience so that he may realize his system has no answer to the crucial questions of life. He must come to know that his roof is a false protection.[12]

No human wisdom can explain our experiences or rescue us from the spiritual need that only God can satisfy.

Outward power is nothing compared to the inward working of the Spirit.

Popular Culture: Unlike many superheroes who have an inherently superhuman ability or others who use external weapons and technology, Marvel Comics' Iron Man has an electromagnetic power source implanted in his chest as part of a medical procedure to save his life. The device has so much power to spare that it allows him to deploy a suit of armor that protects him and affords him additional superhuman abilities. Iron Man is unique in that he is a regular human being transformed and saved from death by a foreign power source placed within him that not only saves his life but also enables him to save others. In many ways the indwelling of the Holy Spirit affords us this same opportunity as the Spirit works in us first to save our lives from the death of sin and also works through us for the furtherance of God's kingdom and the service of others.

God demonstrates his care through his sovereignty over rulers.

Biography: Corrie ten Boom. God continues throughout history to show his sovereignty, even over the most powerful and evil human rulers. Corrie ten Boom, a Dutch Christian whose family helped Jews escape the persecution of the Holocaust, experienced God's sovereign care during her imprisonment at the hands of the Nazis, enduring suffering through the comfort she found in him. Though the power of Nazi Germany may have been overwhelming by human standards, God was greater still and protected Corrie through her release after the war. Her account of the struggles she encountered and her faith in the sovereign God who cared for her is recorded in her book *The Hiding Place* (1974), which serves as a lasting example of God's greatness over human authorities.

Daniel Interprets the Dream and Confronts Nebuchadnezzar

Big Idea *The Most High God blesses and judges even the most powerful rulers of this world regarding their belief in him and their treatment of those they govern.*

Understanding the Text

The Text in Context

See the unit on 4:1–18 for a discussion of the larger context, structure, and comparisons of this literary unit. Against this backdrop, 4:19–27 forms the center of this narrative, shifting the story line from the telling of the dream to its interpretation and at the same time changing from first person to third when speaking of Nebuchadnezzar (continuing through 4:33).[1] It also presents Daniel the sage in his new role as prophet. Moreover, he functions in the classical sense of earlier Hebrew prophets in the Old Testament who confront persons on behalf of God and sometimes predict divine consequences if repentance is not forthcoming. This role links the present text to the narrative in its parallel chapter (5:15–31), although Daniel shows more tact with Nebuchadnezzar here than with Belshazzar there.

Daniel declares that Nebuchadnezzar is the tree in his dream. An anthropomorphic representation of a sacred tree may be depicted on this plaque, where a god holds tree branches from which goats nibble (first half of second millennium BC, ancient Ashur, Iraq).

Within this framework, the pericope divides into two parts: Daniel's concern for the king followed by his retelling of the dream (4:19–22) and Daniel's interpretation of the dream followed by his confrontation of the king (4:23–27).

Historical and Cultural Background

Whereas trees in ancient Mesopotamia were sometimes gilded with decorative metal bands, there is no reference in that literature to a stump being bound with metal to preserve its life.[2] The mention of the "dew of heaven" in this context, however, finds a parallel in Babylonian literature, where dew descends from the stars to bring the judgment of sickness or the blessing of healing, depending on an individual's circumstances.

The Akkadian equivalent to the Aramaic *'iddan* ("appointed time") simply means a "specified period" of some length (days, weeks, seasons, or years). Such a designation was common in the Babylonian sages' interpretation of omens, where they often cited phases of the moon, as well as favorable days or years. In addition, the number "seven" may carry a figurative meaning, like heating the furnace "seven times hotter than usual" (3:19).[3]

Interpretive Insights

4:19 *Daniel . . . was greatly perplexed for a time, and his thoughts terrified him.* Daniel's reaction to Nebuchadnezzar's report of his dream is open to at least three interpretations. First, Daniel may be showing concern for his earthly sovereign of thirty years. Second, he may fear Nebuchadnezzar will become enraged, because of past

experiences (cf. 2:12; 3:19–22). Third, he may be exercising diplomatic sensitivity (cf. 1:8, 12; 2:14). The last seems most likely in this text.[4] Similarly, Nebuchadnezzar's counterresponse may show care for Daniel, or he may be acting pragmatically to make sure Daniel tells him the dream. Either way, this smooth flow of events contrasts with that of the failed sages (4:6–7). Further, the narrator's shift to a third-person perspective paves the way for a demented Nebuchadnezzar's inability to speak due to his boanthropy ("ox-man") disease. Wishing that a king's judgment would go to his "enemies" appears elsewhere in the Old Testament where it is used to distance the messenger from an unwelcomed message and at the same time to sound an ominous note about what the message portends (1 Sam. 25:26; 2 Sam. 18:32).

4:20–21 *The tree you saw, which grew large and strong.* Daniel's retelling of the "tree" portion of the vision (4:20–21) contains only minor differences from Nebuchadnezzar's version (cf. 4:10–12). However, the "messenger" portion (4:25–26) omits significant details of the tree's destruction, the iron and bronze fetters, the changing of the king's mind, and his description as "the lowliest of people" (cf. 4:13–17). Daniel divides these two parts of the pericope with the statement, "Your Majesty, you are that tree!" (4:22). Once the Judean prophet has declared the king guilty, he moves quickly to Nebuchadnezzar's sentencing.

4:22 *Your Majesty, you are that tree!* Daniel's confrontational words are diplomatic; nevertheless, he functions like an Old Testament prophet here and in 5:22–28 (cf. Nathan's "You are the man!" in 2 Sam. 12:7).[5] This narrative completes three encounters between Nebuchadnezzar and the Judeans: Daniel confirms the king as "the head of gold" in his second year (2:37–38); his friends defy Nebuchadnezzar's orders and threats some years later (3:16–18); and Daniel confronts him most harshly in this text after thirty years of service. Later, he

describes Belshazzar's blasphemous actions with the temple vessels as arrogant and prideful (5:20).

4:24–25 *the decree the Most High has issued against my lord the king.* Daniel clarifies Nebuchadnezzar's words about the "decision" and "verdict" of the holy messengers (see the comments on 4:17) by omitting these intermediaries here to focus the reader's attention more directly on the sovereign will of God. However, there is no clarification here of the "seven times" that will end when Nebuchadnezzar recognizes God as King of all kingdoms—especially Babylon. This language continues a pattern of intentional ambiguity regarding numbers in Daniel.[6] Yet the message of God's sovereignty over kings and kingdoms—the book's central theme—appears clearly in every literary unit in the book.

4:26 *leave the stump . . . your kingdom will be restored to you when you acknowledge that Heaven rules.* By omitting the phrase "bound with iron and bronze," Daniel focuses exclusively on the idea of preservation for restoration.[7] The use of the Aramaic term for "heaven" recalls the tree "reaching the heavens" (4:11, 20; NIV: "touching the sky"), the holy messengers from heaven (4:13), and the "dew of heaven" (4:15)—and also anticipates the "powers of heaven" (4:35) and the "King of heaven" (4:37). "Heaven" occurs in either Hebrew or Aramaic twenty-four times in Daniel and is the language of the Most High in thirteen of these references (chaps. 3, 4, 5, 7). It functions as a circumlocution for God only here in the Old Testament, even though this usage is common in Jewish intertestamental texts (e.g., 1 Macc. 3:18–19, 50; 2 Macc. 7:11; 8:20). Daniel's

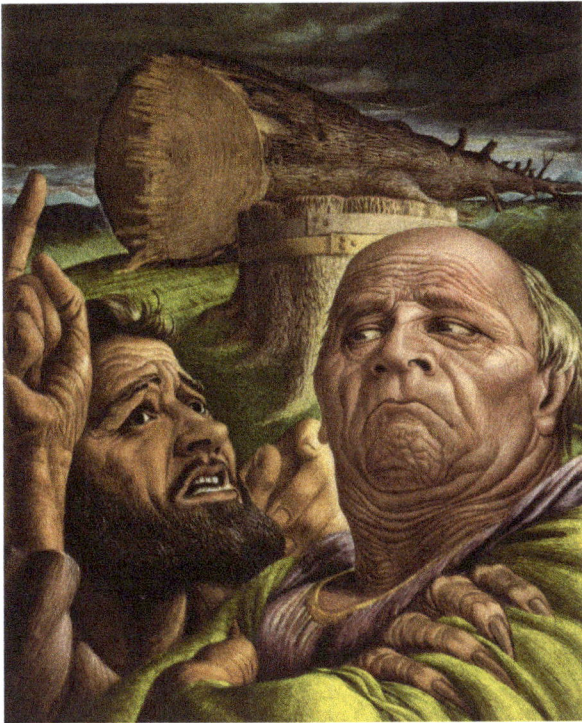

Daniel confronts Nebuchadnezzar with the message of God's judgment given in his dream. This painting by Guy Rowe captures Daniel's attempt to strongly advise a skeptical Nebuchadnezzar to "renounce your sins by doing what is right, and your wickedness by being kind to the oppressed" (4:27).

[NIV: "throw"]; Exod. 32:2 [NIV: "take off"]). These actions are stated generally as "doing what is right" and specifically as "being kind to the oppressed" (literally, the "poor and miserable"). Though "being kind" is not stated in the imperative form, it carries the same force as its imperative parallel, "break off."[9] This twofold description of a righteous king also characterizes the ideals of Solomon and Josiah (Ps. 72:2; Jer. 22:15–16), as well as the messianic descendant of David (Isa. 11:4). The clause "it may be that then" might be translated more literally, "if there is to be," thus clarifying the conditional nature of the hope offered (cf. Amos 5:15; Joel 2:12–14). There is no promise of restoration, no opportunity to bargain with God—only a divinely given prophetic mandate for a moral conversion that is demonstrated in one's life.[10]

Theological Insights

Daniel's prophetic confrontation of Nebuchadnezzar in 4:19–27 teaches the reader three things about God's relationship with humanity. First, the Most High God is the source of all human greatness. Second, God can reverse the accomplishment of mere mortals as he wills. Third, God provides opportunities for prophets to speak words of truth and sinners to break away from their sins by doing what is right.

Teaching the Text

1. *God is the source of human greatness.* Although Nebuchadnezzar is a pagan king, God remains the divine giver of all his greatness and, by extension, the spheres of influence of all human rulers. The symbol of

most direct statements of God's "sovereignty" or "rule" are concentrated in this narrative and in his retelling of this story to Belshazzar in 5:21.

4:27 *Renounce your sins . . . and your wickedness.* Once again Daniel speaks with wisdom and tact ("your Majesty") before calling Nebuchadnezzar to repent of his prideful and arrogant behavior, which he describes as "sins" and "iniquity" (NIV: "wickedness"; the two terms are used synonymously). The NIV's "renounce" is better rendered "remove, wipe away" (Aramaic p^eraq),[8] that is, demonstrating a mental renunciation by outward behavior (cf. the use of its Hebrew equivalent in Gen. 27:40

a tree makes this point well. It is planted by someone else and obtains its splendor through someone else's gifts. Comparing a powerful king and his extensive building enterprise to a tree diminishes the accomplishments of the ruler by emphasizing what he has received from the God of heaven. Encourage your congregation or study group to think of their successes in terms of God's gifting and blessing rather than their own achievements, and more in terms of what they receive than what they do. This includes notions of our own greatness, as well as what we are able to do for others

2. *God can reverse human accomplishments*. Well-established rulers or leaders whose influence spans several decades (like Nebuchadnezzar's) can easily begin to think of themselves as secure in their prosperity, even invincible. Remind your listeners that in comparison with God's sovereignty we are quite fragile and vulnerable. God can remove his gifting in our lives as quickly as he gives it. Apply this not only to leaders but to anyone whom God gifts in a way that allows him or her fame and a sphere of influence over others. Help them to learn to say, "It's not about me but about the God who gives." Encourage them to hold lightly the privileged position God gives, knowing these are sacred stewardships only for a time.

3. *God allows prophets to call sinners to repentance*. The Bible calls God's people to be prophetic. That is, we should speak the truth of Scripture to the world around us, which includes calling sinners to repentance. Sin and wickedness need to be acknowledged and renounced. Exhort your listeners to be honest, acknowledging the sin in their own lives, as well as exposing it in the world around them. Doing what is right includes (in part) kindness to the poor and miserable. God's people today need to develop sensitive hearts to those hurting both inside and outside the church, and to reach out to them in God's name. We need to be messengers of grace, extending the hope of restoration with

Nebuchadnezzar may have felt secure in his prosperity especially since he had done many things to win the favor of the Babylonian gods. This cuneiform tablet excavated from Babylon is known as the East India House Inscription. Here Nebuchadnezzar calls himself "the exalted prince, the favorite of the god Marduk, the beloved of the god Nabu." The inscription describes many of the temples Nebuchadnezzar erected and gives details about the building of the temple to Marduk. Nebuchadnezzar concludes by saying, "For thy glory, O exalted Merodach a house have I made. May its greatness advance! May its fullness increase!" But he had failed to acknowledge the sovereignty of the most High God.

God and his people for any person who genuinely repents.

What not to teach. Even as a prophet, Daniel does not guarantee the king's prosperity, which is held as a divine prerogative. Warn your listeners—especially as nonprophets—against the temptation of predicting what God will do. Yet, in balance, assure them that our actions have consequences with God—whether good or bad. Help them to appreciate the interpersonal dynamic that comes with a living and interactive relationship with the one true God.

Illustrating the Text

Greatness comes from God, whether used for good or for ill.

Film: Star Wars. God is the source of all human greatness, whether we use it for good or evil. In George Lucas's Star Wars films (1977–2005), two of his characters most gifted in "the Force" are Jedi knights Obi-Wan Kenobi and Anakin Skywalker. Both are respected and admired for their power, which comes from the same source, and are in many ways comparable in their abilities, having once been master and pupil. Yet Obi-Wan uses his power for good through the aid and guidance he provides to others, while Anakin uses his power to corrupt and control those around him, eventually becoming the dreadful Darth Vader. We are responsible for how we use God's gifts in whatever form he gives them.

God determines not only human greatness but also its duration.

Bible: Judges 13–16. Samson is an example of human greatness granted and removed in God's timing. He is raised as a Nazirite (cf. Num. 6:1–21), dedicated to the Lord, and instructed to abstain from drinking wine, touching dead bodies, and cutting his hair. Samson frequently uses abilities beyond the natural, as God's Spirit empowers him to kill a lion barehanded (Judg. 14:5–6) and fight victoriously when greatly outnumbered (14:19; 15:14–17). Though his strength is great, it is taken from him as a consequence of folly and disobedience (16:4–22) and restored only briefly to bring about God's judgment on the Philistines (16:23–31). Power and greatness are permitted at the discretion of God's will and must always be used for his specific purposes. No matter how remarkable the ability, God determines the bestowal and removal of human greatness.

God uses prophetic voices to speak truth and call for repentance.

Biography: Martin Luther King Jr. All believers are called to be prophets, in the sense that we proclaim God's truth to others, whether within the community of faith or without. Champion of the American civil rights movement, beloved pastor, and social activist Martin Luther King Jr. has been cherished for decades for sharing his "dream" as a man committed to speaking the truth in love. Bravely protesting the injustice of racial inequality surrounding him, King exemplified the vital importance of calling others to repentance, whether believers or unbelievers, and holding fast to the principle that he avowed: "A time comes when silence is betrayal."[11] It is God's call and desire that believers not stand on the sidelines but rather engage the sin in our world—whether personal or communal—as prophetic voices of truth to those around us.

Nebuchadnezzar's Judgment and Repentance

Big Idea *The sovereignty of God over heaven and earth is demonstrated in the judgment of sin and the restoration of those who genuinely repent.*

Understanding the Text

The Text in Context

See the unit on 4:1–18 for a discussion of the larger context, structure, and comparisons of this literary unit. Against this backdrop, 4:28–37 concludes this narrative, and brief statements of time ("twelve months" [4:29] and "at the end of that time" [4:34]) identify its two parts: God's punishment of Nebuchadnezzar (4:28–33; with subdividing markers at vv. 28, 31, 33) and God's restoration of him (4:34–37; with subdividing markers at vv. 34, 36). The latter resumes the king's first-person narrative, framing his confession with the resumptive "I, Nebuchadnezzar" (cf. 4:4, 18). It also reaffirms God's sovereign dominion (4:34) over Nebuchadnezzar's rule, granted by God and temporarily lost.

Historical and Cultural Background

Herodotus testifies to Babylon's greatness within a century of Nebuchadnezzar's reign (*Hist.* 1.178–81, 190–91; 3.151). The city contained two of Antipater of Sidon's "Seven Wonders of the Ancient World" (*Greek Anthology* 9.58): forty-foot-high, double-encased walls on which chariots could pass (each four miles long with defense towers), and the lush Hanging ("terraced") Gardens, built for Nebuchadnezzar's Median wife Amytis to remind her of her homeland (Josephus, *Ant.* 10.11.1; *Ag. Ap.* 1.19). Its eight gates included a double gate dedicated to the fertility goddess Ishtar, leading to Marduk's temple and a three-hundred-foot ziggurat. The thousand-yard Procession Way was lined on both sides with enameled brick walls showing 120 lions (symbols of Ishtar), as well as 575 dragons (Marduk) and bulls (Bel) arranged in alternate rows. The Euphrates was diverted into multiple canals to provide water for inhabitants, and a four-hundred-foot bridge connected the new city with the ancient capital.[1]

Nebuchadnezzar's description as a grotesque beast suggests a mental disease known as zoanthropy ("animal-man")—more specifically in this text boanthropy ("ox-man"). It is reminiscent of the ancient

Sumerian Enkidu in the Gilgamesh Epic and the Aramaic story of Ahiqar in exile,[2] who experience symptoms similar to Nebuchadnezzar's, causing them to be alienated from their worlds. Though a cuneiform text alludes to a personal problem of Nebuchadnezzar's that resulted in his son Awel-Marduk temporarily ruling in his place, it is too fragmentary for us to draw firm conclusions.[3]

Interpretive Insights

4:28–29 *All this happened . . . Twelve months later.* The dialogue between Nebuchadnezzar and Daniel (4:9–27) now becomes the prophet's commentary (4:28–33) on events that transpire a year after the initial confrontation. That which appears as a delay in fulfillment may be due to an initial (although temporary) compliance by the king, an expression of God's grace (cf. 2 Pet. 3:8–9), or simply God's prerogative to act as he pleases (Dan. 4:35).[4] In context, the duration of time recalls the vague historical marker in 4:4 and prepares us for the statements of immediacy to follow (4:31, 33).

The view from the palace roof gives the king an overview

of the city and may be the site of the famous Hanging Gardens (see "Historical and Cultural Background" above), although their location has not been identified.

4:30 *Is not this the great Babylon I have built . . . ?* Nebuchadnezzar's prideful outburst includes his understanding of the source and purpose of his accomplishments: his "power" and his "glory." These rhetorical questions serve as a catalyst for the dream's fulfillment and his impending punishment. They also contrast sharply with Daniel's calling him to do what is right in acts of kindness to the oppressed (4:27) and later rightly ascribing Nebuchadnezzar's accomplishments to God (5:18–19).[5]

The impressive beauty of "the great Babylon" built by Nebuchadnezzar can be seen in the glazed brickwork lions, shown here, that lined the Processional Way outside the Ishtar Gate (sixth century BC).

Daniel 4:28–37

The Prayer of Nabonidus

The Prayer of Nabonidus, a first-century BC Aramaic text from Qumran, tells a story similar to Daniel 4:4–37, yet about Nabonidus, a later king of Babylon, who is afflicted with an illness for seven years while in Teima (outside Babylon). In it, he prays to the Most High God and is pardoned, healed, and restored in an encounter with an unnamed Jewish magician. This story may have some literary dependence on Daniel,[a] although scholars who date the authorship of Daniel to the second century BC argue that the unknown writer of Daniel adapted the biblical account from a proposed earlier version of *The Prayer of Nabonidus*.[b] The fragmentary nature of the text makes exact correlations with the biblical account difficult. The major differences include the king's name, kind of illness, location, specific mention of "years," and anonymity of the Jewish exile.[c]

[a] See Steinmann, "The Chicken and the Egg"; also Hasel, "The Book of Daniel: Evidences Relating to Persons and Chronology."
[b] E.g., Collins, *Daniel*, 233–34.
[c] *ZIBBCOT*, 540–41.

4:31–32 *Even as the words were on his lips, a voice came from heaven*. That which seemed slow in coming is unexpectedly sudden. The phrases "a voice came from heaven" and "what is decreed" recall the messengers from heaven who first announce the decree (4:13, 17, 23). Likewise, the mention of removing Nebuchadnezzar's "royal authority" and acknowledging God's sovereignty build on similar statements in 4:17 and 25. Together, these expand on the cryptic introductory phrases "all this happened" and "twelve months later" (4:28–29).[6]

4:33 *Immediately what had been said about Nebuchadnezzar was fulfilled*. Again there is a sense of urgency (cf. 3:6, 15; 5:5), and a third reminder that God's word through his messengers ultimately is fulfilled. The summary of the dream's conclusion completes the three stages of this narrative: telling (4:9–18), confronting (4:19–27), and judging (4:28–33). The duration of the "seven times" (4:16, 25, 32)

is clarified somewhat by the reference to "feathers" and "claws." It takes weeks or months—but not necessarily years—for hair to grow excessively long and become coarse and matted, and for nails to curl. No extrabiblical record of Nebuchadnezzar's last thirty years mentions an experience like this (although the texts are sparse).[7] He or a descendant may have destroyed these documents for the pride of Babylon and its kings.

4:34 *At the end of that time*. This parallels the "seven times" that God appoints for Nebuchadnezzar's punishment. After being driven from the great civilization he has created, he lifts his eyes toward heaven in repentance, seeking divine help. The NIV rightly does not capitalize "heaven" here as it has done with "Heaven rules" in 4:26. In this context "toward heaven" reflects the decree that comes "from heaven" (4:31). The result is his "sanity" (or "knowledge," *manda*) is restored—just as he was "given the mind of an animal" (4:16). Nebuchadnezzar's threefold act of worship ("praised," "honored," "glorified"), as powerful as it sounds, falls short of confirming a genuine and permanent conversion.[8] He acknowledges God on some occasions (2:47; 3:28–29; 4:34–37) and opposes him on others (3:15; 4:25), casting doubt on his long-term commitment. Polytheistic kings like Nebuchadnezzar often valued one god above others (cf. his reference to Bel as "my god" in 4:8). More important, there is no denial of false gods in any of these passages. Since this instance is this king's last personal appearance in Daniel (except for the retelling of parts of this story in 5:18–21), there is no way to be certain of his beliefs in the end.

4:35 *All the peoples of the earth are regarded as nothing*. Nebuchadnezzar

When Nebuchadnezzar announces that Babylon has been built for his own power and to glorify his own majesty, what has been revealed to him in his dream comes to pass. "He was driven away from people and ate grass like the ox" (4:33). William Blake's artistic rendering of Nebuchadnezzar depicts him in his "animal state" (1795).

implicitly puts himself in this contrast of mere mortals with the sovereign God (cf. Isa. 40:15, 17). God's lordship also extends to the "powers of heaven" (Aramaic *hayil*, "powers," connotes "might, strength," and by extension, "armies"),[9] which are like humans in their subordination to the Most High. These are most likely spiritual beings (angels), synonymous with the "host of the heavens" in Daniel 8:10.

4:36–37 *At the same time . . . My advisers and nobles sought me out.* This resumptive phrase carries the same force as the appointed time determined in verse 34, followed by the second mention of Nebuchadnezzar's renewed mental health. The details of his restoration suggest palace sages and other administrative officials knew of his condition, at least within the city. Reinstating him to his throne reaffirms their loyalty toward the end of his reign.[10] The fact that he "became even greater than before" suggests a strong finish to his kingship, in contrast to the weaker successor kings (e.g., Belshazzar in chap. 5—this chapter's parallel). The phrase "King of heaven" occurs only here in the Hebrew Bible (although also in 1 Esd. 4:46) and is equivalent to "Lord of heaven" in this chapter's parallel narrative (5:23). It contrasts two sovereignties: the king of Babylon, who should do what is right and just (4:27), and the King of heaven, who always does this—and, in addition, humbles the proud (cf. Prov. 16:18–19).

Theological Insights

Daniel 4:28–37, the concluding pericope of this narrative, is especially rich with God's self-revelation. First, the righteous and just God keeps his prophetic word for punishment of sin. Second, God also shows his compassion by graciously restoring those who repent of their sins. Third, God is worthy of honor and praise because he reigns in his kingdom as sovereign over all human and spiritual powers.

Teaching the Text

1. *God punishes those who walk in pride.* Rather than merely telling your listeners to be humble, paint for them a picture of the sovereign God of kings and kingdoms, whom we can know and serve. Encourage them to listen for their own inappropriate, first-person pronouns of pride: "the great Babylon *I* have built . . . by *my* mighty

power and for the glory of *my* majesty" (4:30). Our speech often betrays worldly pride in our perceived accomplishments. Warn your people that, after an extended period of grace, a humiliating punishment for sin may come suddenly and without warning. Help them to acknowledge that the sovereign God is justified in all that he does.

2. *God restores those who repent of sin.* When exercising a prophetic voice today, we must remember that the Old Testament prophets not only announce judgment but also promise blessing, if repentance is forthcoming. Similarly, Daniel juxtaposes God's righteous judgment of Judah with a passionate plea for restoration (9:4–19). God's work with Nebuchadnezzar affirms that God is gracious and compassionate to restore the repentant sinner. Exhort your listeners to practice restoration of those who raise their eyes toward heaven, of those who are moving toward God rather than away from him. Warn them sternly to watch out for their own pride, especially a spiritual pride, when seeking to assist others.

3. *God is sovereign over heaven and earth.* When we look earnestly at the person of God, we are compelled to honor and glorify him. This is why it is so important to keep the focus of our preaching and teaching on who God is and how he works with humanity. The former drives the latter, and we are recipients of both—even though we often come to know God through the way he works with mere mortals in Scripture. Emphasize the one true God as the Most High ruler of an everlasting kingdom with both heavenly and earthly dimensions. God welcomes the questions and struggles of believers, but this expression of his character is a gift and privilege, not our entitlement. None of us has the right to question his wisdom.

What not to teach. First, God's sovereign prerogative does not mean that he capriciously inflicts suffering without cause, although we may not be able to see God's purposes during this life. Second, God does not always cause trials and illnesses, yet he can sometimes use these as wake-up calls to expose something that needs changing in our lives. Third, God does not always judge sin in what humans may consider a timely manner, or even in this life. But, in the end, he holds us all accountable for our actions. Fourth, Nebuchadnezzar's decree does not prove a permanent conversion of him or his people.

Illustrating the Text

Human pride can prompt the direct intervention of God.

Quote: *Mere Christianity,* by C. S. Lewis. The book of Proverbs includes many pithy, wise sayings about human pride and its consequences—for example: "To fear the LORD is to hate evil; I hate pride and arrogance, evil behavior and perverse speech" (8:13); "When pride comes, then comes disgrace" (11:2); "A fool's mouth lashes out with pride" (14:3); "Pride goes before destruction, a haughty spirit before a fall" (16:18); and "Pride brings a person low, but the lowly in spirit gain honor" (29:23). C. S. Lewis observes in his enduring classic, *Mere Christianity,*

In God you come up against something which is in every respect immeasurably superior to yourself. Unless you know God as that—and, therefore, know yourself as nothing in comparison—you do not know God at all. . . . A proud man is always looking down on things and people: and, of course, as long as you are looking down, you cannot see something that is above you.[11]

Repentance is the only path to restoration.

Quote: **Charles Spurgeon.** In his sermon "Two Essential Things," preacher and evangelist Charles Spurgeon once said:

> Evangelical repentance is repentance of sin as sin: not of this sin nor of that, but of the whole mass. We repent of the sin of our nature as well as of the sin of our practice. We bemoan sin within us and without us. We repent of sin itself as being an insult to God. Anything short of this is a mere surface repentance, and not a repentance which reaches to the bottom of the mischief.[12]

This exhortation reminds us that true repentance is not to be taken lightly but to be evidenced by a sincere practice of justice and righteousness (cf. Amos 5:21–24). God is full of grace and able to restore those who are genuinely repentant and turn toward God in their sin.

God's sovereignty is seen equally in punishment and forgiveness.

Bible: God's interaction with humanity, and specifically with his covenant people Israel, shows that he is praiseworthy in the exercise of his sovereign will in judgment and in restoration. This is evident from Israel's deliverance out of Egypt through the national exiles they face as divided kingdoms until Judah's restoration. As a result of its repeated idolatries, Israel incurs God's appointed consequences (Deut. 28:15–68) for breaking covenant with him. Their exile from the land at the hands of Assyria (eighth century) and later Babylon (sixth century) is orchestrated by God to fulfill the curses of disobedience; yet the restoration promised at the giving of the covenant (30:1–10) is also fulfilled when God returns his people to their land after his determined period of captivity—all in his own timing. God's interaction with his people displays on a grand scale that both punishment and restoration are equally important and praiseworthy examples of God's sovereignty.

When Nebuchadnezzar acknowledges the sovereignty of the Most High God, his honor and splendor are restored, and he returns to his throne, becoming "even greater than before" (4:36). Here is an artist's depiction of the ancient city of Babylon.

The Handwriting on the Wall

Big Idea *Sacrilege against God can lead to a divine confrontation that worldly wealth, power, and wisdom cannot adequately address.*

Understanding the Text

The Text in Context

Daniel 5:1–31 is woven into the book's overall literary structure in two ways. First, it advances the narrative of chapters 1–6, in which the first four focus on Nebuchadnezzar (chaps. 1–2 with historical markers and 3–4 without) and the last two show the transition from Belshazzar of Babylon to Darius the Mede (chaps. 5–6). Second, it completes the third of three parallel pairs of chapters (4 and 5) in the book's concentric Aramaic center section. Comparatively, Daniel 4 and 5 reflect different situations and structures, yet they share the same theme: God's punishment of proud rulers. This recalls Jehoiakim's subjugation (1:2), while keeping Judah's nearly "seventy-year" exile in view by contrasting Babylon's first and last king. Within Daniel 5, Belshazzar's blasphemy (5:1–9) is placed opposite his rebuke and judgment (5:18–31). The center section recounts Daniel's life experience with two summaries of his consistent message of God's sovereignty. The death of Belshazzar in 5:30 provides this chapter's historical marker.[1]

Against this backdrop, 5:1–9 is the first of three sections in the chapter connecting Belshazzar's blasphemy with Nebuchadnezzar's desecration of the temple—an event made more personal when Nebuchadnezzar is called Belshazzar's "father." It divides into three parts: Belshazzar hosts a banquet (5:1–4), the "hand" and wall writing appear (5:5–6), and the king summons the inadequate Babylonian sages (5:7–9).

Historical and Cultural Background

Nabonidus, Babylon's last official king, took the throne in 556 BC and within three years formed a coregency with his son Belshazzar. The latter was unknown outside the Bible from the third century BC until just over a century ago when several cuneiform texts with his name were discovered. Belshazzar managed Babylon for ten years while Nabonidus was in Teima for religious reasons. Belshazzar's status is clarified in the *Nabonidus Chronicle*.[2]

The banquet in this text occurs October 12, 539 BC (Herodotus, *Hist*. 1.191; Xenophon, *Cyr*. 7.5.15–25), two days after the Persians conquered Opis (modern Baghdad, about fifty miles north of Babylon) and nearby Sippar. Nabonidus fled at first, then later surrendered to Cyrus in

Nabonidus was Babylon's last official king. He is depicted on this sixth-century BC stele with upraised hand before three divine symbols: the crescent, the winged disk, and the star. These represent Sin, the moon god; Shamash, the sun god; and Ishtar or Venus. They are just a few of the ancient Near Eastern deities that would have been called on for protection.

Babylon. Praising Babylonian gods with Judean temple vessels may have brought to Belshazzar's mind victories of Nebuchadnezzar, invoking the pagan gods' protection during this military threat. In addition to Marduk, Nabu, and Sin (the moon god honored by Nabonidus), images of other deities from surrounding cities were moved inside Babylon's walls for safekeeping. Modern excavations have uncovered the palace complex, including what may well be the room referenced in this narrative—with the remains of a plastered wall with a niche for the king's throne (cf. Dan. 5:5).[3] Relevant to the general region and era is Herodotus's account that wives and concubines attended Persian feasts (*Hist.* 5.18).[4]

Key Themes of Daniel 5:1–9

- Belshazzar intentionally treats God's sacred temple vessels like common drinking cups at his banquet.
- God confronts the king's sacrilege by sending a mysterious hand to write on the wall.
- Babylon's wealth, power, and wisdom fail to resolve the crisis that results from sin and judgment.

Interpretive Insights

5:1 *King Belshazzar gave a great banquet.* The transition from Daniel 4 is abrupt, with no mention of Nebuchadnezzar's passing or the four kings before Belshazzar. In their original forms, Belteshazzar (Daniel's pagan name) and Belshazzar were likely identical (see the comments on 1:7).[5] The rounded number of nobles ("a thousand") symbolically represents all surviving high officials in Babylon after the military defeats nearby. The occasion could be to boost morale, to proclaim Belshazzar fully king (assuming Nabonidus's death), or to observe the New Year's festival.[6] The identification of the occasion is not important to the author's purposes. Although the takeover by Media and Persia is not mentioned until 5:31, Belshazzar may have feared the worst. Even though Daniel's visions in chapters 7 and 8 occur, respectively, in 553 and 550 BC, there is no reason to assume that Belshazzar has knowledge of them in 539 BC.

5:2–4 *While Belshazzar was drinking his wine.* Because his table is set in a prominent place in the banquet room, the king is visible to the people, setting the stage for their involvement in the sacrilege. Some commentators see here a drunken king, yet the Aramaic *tᵉ'em* more likely connotes a routine "tasting the wine."[7] Though drunkenness is folly (Prov. 20:1; 31:4, 6), the issue here is

Table 1: Relation of Babylonian Kings to Nebuchadnezzar

Nebuchadnezzar (605–562) (mentioned 91 times in OT, most in Jer. 21–52; Dan. 1–5)
Awel-Marduk (562–560): son (2 Kings 25:27; Jer. 52:31)
Nergal-Sharezer (560–556): possible son-in-law; wife unknown (Jer. 39:3, 13)
Labashi-Marduk (556): possible maternal grandson (no biblical reference); murdered as a young boy
Nabonidus (556–539): perhaps son-in-law through daughter Nitocris (no biblical reference)
Belshazzar (550–539): perhaps maternal grandson (Dan. 5, 7–8); also son of, and coregent with, Nabonidus

intentional sacrilege, making Belshazzar's culpability all the more apparent.[8]

Nebuchadnezzar his father. Genealogically, Belshazzar was the eldest son of Nabonidus (see table 1 above). Yet the narrator (5:2), the queen (5:11), the king (5:13), and Daniel (5:18, 22) all reference Nebuchadnezzar as his "father." The Semitic terms for "father"/"son" can reference distant ancestors/descendants or unrelated predecessors/successors. This is the case with the Israelite king Jehu, who is called "son of Omri" (his unrelated predecessor) on the Black Obelisk of Shalmaneser III (ninth century BC).[9] In 5:2, the "grandfather"/"grandson" interpretation seems best.[10] Although three generations of kings ruled Neo-Babylonia's nearly seventy years as the ancient Near Eastern superpower (Jer. 27:7), Daniel focuses only on the first and the last—emphasizing the comparison with chapter 4 and alluding to Judah's nearly "seventy-year" exile.

they brought in the gold goblets that had been taken from the temple. Nebuchadnezzar's desecration of Yahweh's temple vessels to honor "his god" (1:2) foreshadows Belshazzar's action. That which God allows the former to take in Judah's judgment he now reclaims from the latter in Babylon's judgment. The king moves from treating holy objects as common to using the vessels to worship false gods—and his nobles share his culpability (cf. 5:3–4; Isa. 44:9–20).[11] The idols are made of gold, silver, bronze, and iron, recalling Nebuchadnezzar's statue (Dan. 2:31–45) and foreshadowing the continuing fulfillment of God's judgment. Though Belshazzar may be seeking his gods' protection, the focus is on his lack of humility—like that of Nebuchadnezzar (5:20, 22).

5:5–6 *Suddenly the fingers of a human hand . . . wrote on the . . . wall.* The abrupt appearance of the "hand" parallels the sudden changes in Nebuchadnezzar's circumstances (4:31, 33), intentionally linking the accounts. The "fingers" and "hand" are an anthropomorphic appearance of God, but they do not confirm the presence of angels (cf. Dan. 3; 6–12). God's "fingers" write the Ten Commandments (Exod. 31:18; Deut. 9:10) for Israel's instruction, and here, they prescribe Babylon's judgment. The adjacent lampstand adds vivid detail to the narrative. This pericope blends deathly terror and mocking humor. The arrogant king who has desecrated God's holy vessels in the cheerful security of his palace is now about to collapse in fear. Though the same term (*bᵉhal*; NIV: "frightened") is used to describe Daniel's "fear" at the site of God's revelations (4:19 [NIV: "terrified,"

"alarm]"; 7:15 [NIV: "disturbed"]), the loss of Belshazzar's bodily functions reveals extreme and obvious panic, intensified by the threat of the combined forces of Media and Persia (cf. Isa. 21:1–10).

5:7 *The king summoned the . . . wise men of Babylon.* The NIV's "summoned" might be paraphrased "screaming for help." Daniel's age (early eighties) and the changes of leadership explain his absence among the sages (see the sidebar "Wise Men in the Book of Daniel" in the unit on 1:17–21). The challenge to read and interpret the writing is similar to Nebuchadnezzar's requirement to recount and interpret his first dream (2:5–10, 26). Although the phrase "third highest ruler in the kingdom" could mean a privileged position "among three equals," Belshazzar's coregent status with Nabonidus makes "third in rank" more likely (cf. Esther 8:15; 10:3).

5:8 *all the king's wise men . . . could not read the writing or tell the king what it meant.* Because Aramaic (like Hebrew) was written without vowels and sometimes without word divisions, separating the words can result in different meanings, such as "Who caused Persia to stumble?" "What shall I weigh, a half mina?" or "Whoever you are, Persia is insignificant."[12] Alternatively, Jewish tradition suggests that these letters were written vertically as an anagram, creating an even more enigmatic letter puzzle.[13] The author never reveals the reason but focuses on the third recorded failure of the Babylonian cult and its representatives (2:1–10; 4:6–7).

5:9 *Belshazzar became even more terrified . . . His nobles were baffled.* The king's increased terror spreads to his guests, reinforcing their complicity in his sacrilege and its consequences (cf. 5:3–4) and setting the stage for the queen's (most likely "queen mother's") dramatic entrance in the next section.

Theological Insights

Although God is mostly behind the scenes in 5:1–9 at the outset of this pagan banquet, three insights are implicit regarding his work with unbelievers. First, intentional mistreatment of that which is sacred is a direct challenge to the Most High God. Second, God sometimes acts in a dramatic way to confront human pride. Third, wealth and power can inspire a false sense of confidence about controlling one's place in a world where God is sovereign.

Teaching the Text

1. *Profaning that which is sacred.* While we cannot expect unbelievers to live holy lives, we can learn from their failures. In this case, mistreating that which is holy is sacrilegious and offensive to the one true God. Although we may not venerate things and places, this text can legitimately have a broader application. From the giving of the law through Moses, God set his people apart as holy (Exod. 19:4–6) and expected them to treat him and his name as holy (e.g., Exod. 20:7; Lev. 19:12; Deut. 5:11). In today's religiously pluralistic, secularly relativistic, and sometimes blatantly pagan culture, treating the one true God as common, or taking his name in vain, amounts to sacrilege. Guide your listeners toward holy living as children of God who clearly stand out from unbelievers, realizing we should live lives set apart from, yet in witness to, our world (2 Pet. 3:8–16; 1 Tim. 2:1–4).

2. *God's confrontation of pride.* Although God often shows patience and grace, he may also intervene decisively at any time to confront human arrogance against him (cf. Nebuchadnezzar in 4:31, 33). Belshazzar's narrative does not teach that God regularly appears anthropomorphically (the "hand") or that we should understand all supernatural abnormalities as messages from heaven. Rather, God gets the attention of the king, his nobles, and his sages to make them consider their actions and to provide an occasion for the inspired interpretation that follows. Ask your listeners to be sensitive to the way God works through life's everyday events that give us pause, pushing us toward an understanding of who God is as revealed in Scripture. Warn them against the false assumption that God's patience means he does not care about apathy or prideful rebellion.

3. *False confidence and human arrogance.* Point to examples in your culture or context in which people use power, wealth, and prestige as either a substitute for or a means by which to manipulate, twist, or exploit godly wisdom. Such knowledge is not available at the whims of kings and sages. Use the interlude that ends this pericope (5:9) to allow your listeners to reflect on the emptiness of false religious systems (or secular philosophies) apart from God's Word and Spirit. Warn them against putting their confidence in the wrong sources of wisdom. Call those who are given positions of influence and power to guard their hearts against pride.

What not to teach. Do not build a sermon or teaching lesson from this passage on the foolishness of misusing alcohol or the dangers of partying with unbelievers. Other Old Testament texts caution us regarding such matters (cf. Prov. 20:1; 24:1). Keep your focus on the clearer issues of prideful rebellion against God, treating that which is holy with proper respect, and the failures of seeking wisdom apart from God.

Illustrating the Text

God is jealous for his own glory.

Quote: *Godly Jealousy,* by Erik Thoennes. The gravity of offense in profaning what is holy is best understood in light of the seriousness of God's holiness. In his book *Godly Jealousy*, Christian scholar and professor Erik Thoennes writes: "We have seen that God's primary goal in human history, a goal for which he is intensely jealous, is his own glory and honor. . . . God desires the fidelity of his people because he loves them, but ultimately because he is most glorified when they ascribe to him the honor that belongs to him alone."[14] God is a jealous God (Exod. 20:5; 34:14) who demands that he receive all glory and disdains all irreverence for his holiness. In the same way that God is jealous for his exclusive glory, we must also be jealous for his glory and consequently abhor the profaning of his holiness in all its forms.

modern history. In the same way, having an arrogant pride in our own power and political security—especially when it is set against God—can lead us to consequences and punishment of sin. Although we may be tempted to trust in our own strength, we only deceive ourselves. God opposes the arrogant boasting of mere mortals in whatever form it appears.

Boastful arrogance by mere mortals is foolishness before God.

History: On its maiden voyage from the United Kingdom to New York in 1912, the luxury passenger liner RMS *Titanic* stood as a monument to human engineering in its time and was immediately an international sensation. Moreover, it was deemed by many to be unsinkable. In retrospect, such pride and arrogance were clearly misplaced, resulting in a tragic collision with an iceberg, the sinking of the ship, and the loss of more than 1,500 lives. It is one of the deadliest peacetime disasters in

Trust in false wisdom is especially dangerous in those with influence.

Culture: The modern Scientology movement began with L. Ron Hubbard's self-help book *Dianetics* in 1952. Its beliefs, which include spiritual beings caught in human bodies with past lives from extraterrestrial cultures, have grown more popular partially due to endorsement from prominent actor and producer Tom Cruise. In particular, the financial resources required as "fixed donations" for participation in Scientology practices make it an attraction for those with greater power and influence. The false philosophies of this group, as well as others like it, are often popularized due to their bold claims of self-knowledge and wisdom. Yet these sources cannot meet people's true spiritual needs and instead give a false sense of confidence in using human wisdom as a substitute for God as the only true source of wisdom and answer to human emptiness.

Daniel Confronts Belshazzar

Big Idea *God is able and willing, through his Spirit, to gift and sustain those who honor him over years of faithful service.*

Understanding the Text

The Text in Context

See the unit on 5:1–9 for a discussion of the larger context, structure, and comparisons of this chapter, as well as a comparison of chapters 4 and 5. Against this backdrop, the second pericope in this chapter draws from chapters 1, 2, and 4, in which Daniel's God-given abilities and administrative successes lead to his interpretation of Nebuchadnezzar's dreams. Now Babylon's queen mother introduces him to the king, referencing the "spirit of the holy gods" (5:11; cf. 4:8–9, 18), which links the parallel accounts. Within this framework, 5:10–17 divides into three parts: the queen mother's appearance and announcement of Daniel (5:10–12), Daniel's appearance and

Belshazzar's offer (5:13–16), and Daniel's response (5:17).

Historical and Cultural Background

That the "queen" enters late, rebukes Belshazzar publicly, and appears separate from the "wives" suggests that she is the "queen mother" and wife of Nabonidus.

The "queen" mentioned in 5:10 who remembers Daniel is most likely the "queen mother," the wife of Nabonidus. Another example of a "queen mother" who exerted considerable influence is Nakija, the wife of King Sennacherib of Assyria (704–681 BC). She is shown here with her son Esarhaddon. Her power brought him and then later her grandson Ashurbanipal to the throne of Assyria, where they reigned in 680–669 BC and 668–627 BC, respectively.

Nabonidus's mother, Adad-Guppi, also fits this description, but she died seventeen years earlier. Herodotus's description of Belshazzar's mother, Nitocris, Nabonidus's wife (*Hist.* 1.185–88), supports this interpretation. She was the politically astute daughter of Nebuchadnezzar who aided in the ongoing construction of canals and bridges in Babylon after his death and lived to experience Babylon's siege by the Medes and Persians in 539 BC (Josephus, *Ant.* 10.11.2).[1]

The elaborate palaces of successive kings of Babylon were eventually merged into a palace complex that is now thoroughly excavated. The huge throne room (170 by 55 feet) stands adjacent to the largest of the palace's three courtyards, just inside the massive Ishtar Gate. This is, quite likely, the room used by Belshazzar for this banquet. Along one of the walls is a niche for the king's throne. Elsewhere, this room is adorned with brightly colored enameled bricks and white plaster.[2]

Interpretive Insights

5:10 *The queen . . . came into the banquet hall.* With the wives of Belshazzar already at the banquet (5:3), the chaotic uproar that had followed the appearance of the "hand" and the Babylonian sages' failure spreads quickly through the palace complex, drawing the queen mother into the king's presence.[3] The royal salutation "May the king live forever!" provides an ironic contrast to the king's death in this chapter's ending (5:30).[4] The older stateswoman risks breach of protocol in order to take control of the panicked situation. She comes unsummoned to rebuke and instruct her son in public, providing another

Key Themes of Daniel 5:10–17

- The Spirit of God in Daniel enables him to confront King Belshazzar.
- The God who gifts Daniel as a youth sustains and vindicates him throughout his life.
- Daniel recognizes his gifts as coming from God and is not willing to let them be corrupted by the king.

Queens and Queen Mothers in the Old Testament

The Hebrew *malkah* explicitly describes four "queens" in the Old Testament. First, the Queen of Sheba acts with independence and wisdom when she visits Solomon (1 Kings 10:1–13; 2 Chron. 9:12). Second, the wicked Athaliah (daughter of Jezebel) usurps rule of Judah for six years (2 Kings 11:1–3). Third, Vashti (first wife of Xerxes of Persia) is deposed and replaced by the fourth, Esther (Esther 1–9). Although she appears outside the Hebrew Old Testament, the Judean queen Salome Alexandra rules the Hasmonean kingdom of Judah for nine years (76–67 BC; Josephus, *Ant.* 13.11–12, 15–16). As consorts to a ruling monarch, queens in the ancient Near East usually did not engage in political matters while the king was alive.

However, the opposite was true for the most influential woman in the ancient Near Eastern palace, the queen mother. Both Bathsheba with her son Solomon (1 Kings 1–2) and Jezebel with her sons Ahaziah and Jehoram (1 Kings 22; 2 Kings 1–3, 8) function in this capacity in Israel. This is also likely to be the role of the unnamed queen who is "sitting beside" Artaxerxes of Persia when Nehemiah obtains permission to return to Judah (Neh. 2:6). In the ancient Near East, a king often had multiple wives, but he was raised by only one mother. Her position was more than honorary, and she often engaged in the affairs of state over which her son ruled. This provides an informative backdrop to the queen mother in Daniel 5:10.[a]

a *NBD*, 993; see Andreasen, "Role of the Queen Mother."

instance of his humiliation (cf. 5:6, 9). Moreover, her voice brings wisdom in the face of folly, like the woman of wisdom in Proverbs 31 (a passage also written by a queen mother speaking to a son).[5]

5:11–12 *a man in your kingdom . . . he will tell you what the writing means.* The specificity of "*your* kingdom" suggests Belshazzar should be aware of Daniel's value as a sage. Daniel may need such an introduction because he is less active (now in his eighties), or because new rulers want their own advisors, or because Belshazzar ignores Daniel as part of his rebellion and sacrilege against the God of the Jews. The last option fits this context best.[6] The formal introduction of Daniel to Belshazzar quickly points the reader to the source of Daniel's giftedness: from the queen mother's perspective, "the spirit of the holy gods." Daniel clarifies this to mean "the Most High God" in 5:18 (cf. 4:2, 17, 24, 32, 34). This gift of God's Spirit to Daniel is put first, providing a context for the seven also-familiar gifts to follow: "insight," "intelligence," "wisdom," "keen mind," "knowledge," "understanding," and "the ability to interpret dreams." In addition, two new gifts are added here, particular to this narrative: the ability to "explain riddles" (the wall writing) and "solve difficult problems" (Belshazzar's crisis inside and outside the palace). It is clear that God is in control.

5:13 *Are you Daniel, one of the exiles my father the king brought from Judah?* Every voice in this chapter (narrator, queen mother, Belshazzar, and Daniel) emphasizes the "father"/"son" relationship between Belshazzar and Nebuchadnezzar (see the

comments on 5:2–4). The constant repetition of this fact serves to indict Belshazzar—even by his own words (5:13)—for not realizing and appropriating the moral lesson learned by his grandfather of submitting to God's sovereign rule. Moreover, the king's words to Daniel are likely sarcastic: "So, you are *that* Daniel." Belshazzar's knowledge goes beyond the words of the queen mother. He may have heard of Daniel's reputation but by choice has not met him yet. Whereas the queen

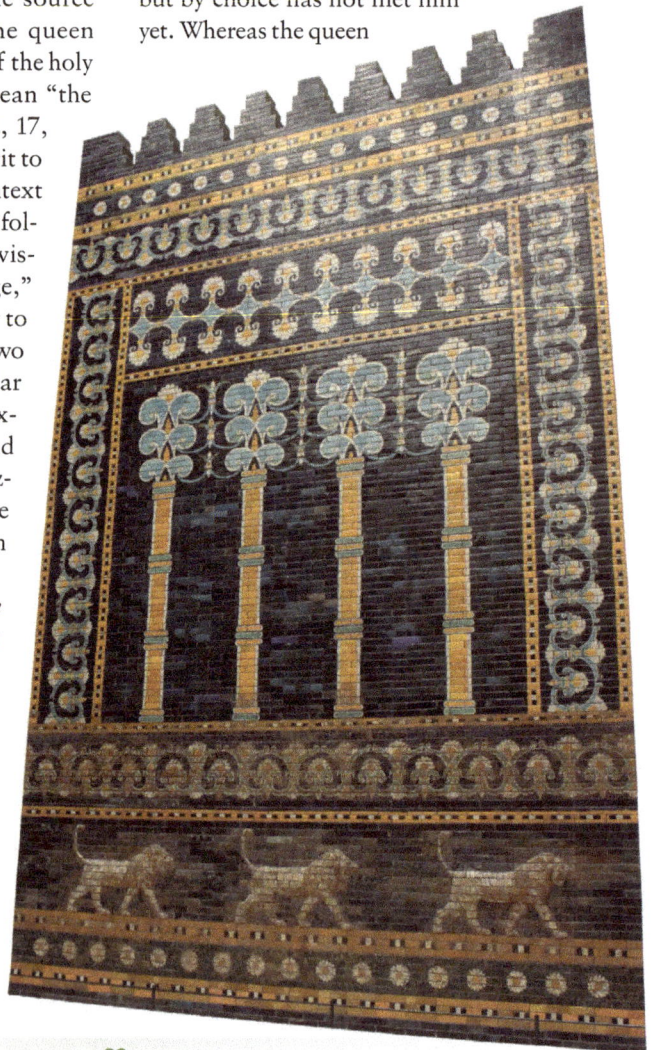

King Belshazzar's banquet may have been held in the throne room of the palace complex. This reconstructed glazed-brick facade is from the throne room of Nebuchadnezzar in Babylon.

mother emphasizes Daniel's appointments and giftedness, Belshazzar focuses on his status as an exile—implying an adversarial relationship.[7] The fact that Nebuchadnezzar names Daniel "Bel<u>te</u>shazzar" (perhaps a deliberate corruption by the author of "Belshazzar"; see the comments on 1:7) may offend the king. The reference "brought from Judah" is reminiscent of the temple vessels "brought in" at this time (cf. 1:2; 5:2).

5:14–16 *I have heard that the spirit of the gods is in you.* In the parallel narrative Nebuchadnezzar unambiguously states that "the spirit of the *holy* gods" is in Daniel and he *can* do what is needed (4:8–9, 18). This confidence is also evident in the queen mother's words (5:11–12). Here, however, Belshazzar speaks only by way of hearsay expressed in the form of a taunt, "if you can" (5:16). This reflects the tension in his relationship with Daniel and prepares the reader for the unsympathetic prophetic confrontation in 5:18–31. The king's omission of "holy" in his reference to "the gods" also subtly reflects his profaning of the temple vessels. For the third time the wisdom of the Babylonian sages is insufficient (cf. 2:1–13; 4:6–7). Offering the same ruling status to Daniel (cf. 5:7) prepares the reader for the contrast of Daniel and the Babylonian sages. The terms of the reward ("third highest ruler in the kingdom") reflect the lower status of Belshazzar—a coregent under Nabonidus—in contrast to Nebuchadnezzar.[8]

5:17 *You may keep your gifts for yourself and give your rewards to someone else.* The offer of a disproportionately great reward for services otherwise expected as part of his job would pressure any sage to return a favorable interpretation. But, as in chapter 4, Daniel once again takes the role of a prophet. The message given by the hand of God is sacred and therefore cannot be manipulated with human rewards (cf. Num. 22:18; Mic. 3:5–8). Though Daniel appears to accept gifts elsewhere (2:46–49), this one is offered in advance in order to affect the outcome of the interpretation. In response, Daniel shuns the sovereignty of Belshazzar in deference to the sovereignty of God. Also, the familiar and personal "you" language certainly offends the king.

Nevertheless, I will read the writing for the king and tell him what it means. The conjunction "nevertheless" (Aramaic *bᵉram*) carries an adversarial force: the interpretation comes in spite of the offer. This retort by Daniel sets the tone for the comparison and contrast with Nebuchadnezzar, and the judgment of Belshazzar to follow.

Theological Insights

In 5:10–17, the center section of this story, one can discern three character traits of the God who gives. First, he gives his Spirit to reveal what is needed for the challenges faced by faithful servants. Second, the nature of the gifts that God imparts reflects God's wisdom, knowledge, and ability to solve difficult problems. Third, the worthiness of the gift-giving God makes those gifts too valuable to be corrupted by human rewards.

Teaching the Text

1. *The Spirit of the Holy God.* The work of the Holy Spirit in the New Testament is foreshadowed here by the way God's Spirit is reflected in Daniel's life and ministry.

Although the king and the queen mother seem to understand "the spirit of the holy gods" in a pagan sense, God does not work that way. The critical gifts that Daniel possesses are the direct outworking of God's Spirit in his life. Encourage your listeners to become sensitive to the work of God's Spirit in their lives. Help them recognize that the gifts, abilities, and opportunities we are given as believers reflect the way God works through us, as we are faithful to him.

2. *The gifts reflect on the giver.* Daniel's gifts—insight, intelligence, and wisdom—are directly linked to his sphere of influence in the palace. These gifts are also discernible in the aged Judean's (now in his eighties) keen mind, knowledge, understanding, skills in interpretation, and ability to solve riddles and problems. Encourage your congregation or class to consider the many ways in which they have been prepared to serve God through the Spirit's working in their lives and to be careful to give God the credit for each of these gifts (cf. 2:27–30). It would not be inappropriate to speak specifically to the senior members in your audience, reminding them to give thanks for the way God has sustained them over decades of faithful service and godly living.

3. *The enticement of human rewards.* Daniel and his friends have been honored earlier in a tangible and public way after God had accomplished something special through them (2:48–49). However, the reward in chapter 5 is offered to Daniel, as well as to the other sages, as a conditional inducement before the fact, which might be understood as influencing the outcome. This kind of reward carries inherent dangers for corrupting the integrity of the message. In using the gifts God has given us, we must remain keenly aware of our inner motives and of the outward perceptions of corruption by others. This is not to say that believers should refuse payment for serving in professional ways. But we should carefully guard the opportunities God gives us so as not to tarnish his reputation before a watching world.

What not to teach. First, avoid parsing too finely the distinction between the ways in which God's Spirit works in the Old Testament as compared to the New Testament. In Daniel, the Spirit is consistently described as being "in him." Second, this passage is

If anyone can read the writing on the wall, he will be well rewarded. Belshazzar offers a purple robe, a gold chain, and the position of third highest ruler in the kingdom. A purple robe would have indicated both wealth and status because the dye used to create purple was very expensive, and usually only royalty could afford it. Shown here are the shells of the murex snail, from which the purple dye was obtained.

focused not on Daniel's faithful commitment to God for his lifetime but rather on God's gifting of, and faithfulness to, Daniel. Third, this passage does not teach that any specific gift is available, or not available, to believers today. Rather, it describes God's generous and relevant work through Daniel in a particular situation.

Illustrating the Text

The question is not how to use the Spirit but how the Spirit uses us.

Quote: **R. A. Torrey.** The working of the Holy Spirit in our lives is always a reflection of his character in us and should always point to him as the source. As R. A. Torrey has written,

> The Holy Spirit is a real Person, infinitely holy, infinitely wise, infinitely mighty and infinitely tender who is to get hold of and use us. . . . If we think of the Holy Spirit as so many do as merely a power or influence, our constant thought will be, "How can I get more of the Holy Spirit," but if we think of Him in the Biblical way as a Divine Person, our thought will rather be, "How can the Spirit have more of me?"[9]

These wise words should call us to humility and submission to the Spirit's work so that God can use us as testimonies to his greatness.

God equips us for the contexts he calls us to.

Children's Book: *The Lion, the Witch and the Wardrobe,* by C. S. Lewis. In Lewis's book, siblings Peter, Susan, and Lucy receive unexpected gifts when Father Christmas appears in their adventure. Though they are unaware of the purpose of the gifts when given, each item ends up being an essential tool on their journey. The sword given to Peter is used in his battle with the evil witch Jadis; the enchanted horn for Susan summons her brother to her aid when she is attacked by a wolf; and Lucy's magical cordial heals many wounded in battle, including their brother Edmund. None of the siblings could have known how these gifts would later be critical in these situations, yet each was intentionally granted exactly what he or she would need for the peril that lay ahead. In the same way, God in his foreknowledge knows exactly what his children need to be equipped for wherever he leads them.

Receiving human rewards should be a testimony to God's goodness.

Biography: **Ben Carson.** Born in 1952, pediatric neurosurgeon and author of six best-selling Christian books Ben Carson rose from humble beginnings to become a remarkably accomplished person. He became the youngest physician to lead a major division at Johns Hopkins, was the first to successfully separate conjoined twins joined at the head, and won the prestigious Presidential Medal of Freedom award from George W. Bush (2008). These awards were rightly bestowed on a man whose medical career is clearly worthy of its recognition; yet human recognition for Carson has served as an opportunity to testify to God's goodness through extensive philanthropic work, particularly in the service of children and education, as well as books encouraging the importance of persistent dedication and faith in God. While receiving human honors is not sinful, each accolade should be used as an opportunity to point others toward God as the giver of eternal reward.

Belshazzar's Judgment and Babylon's Fall

Big Idea *The God who sovereignly governs kings and kingdoms—for blessing or for judgment— also controls every breath a person takes.*

Understanding the Text

The Text in Context

See the unit on 5:1–9 for a discussion of the larger context, structure, and comparisons of this chapter, as well as a comparison of chapters 4 and 5. Against this backdrop, the third and last section of Daniel 5 provides the theological climax for the chapter. Daniel appears here again as a classical Old Testament prophet, as he did in chapter 4— the only two places this occurs in the book. This final narrative concerning Babylon signals the transition to the third of the four kingdoms seen in Daniel's vision of Nebuchadnezzar's dream in 2:31– 49. Within this framework, 5:18–31

divides into four parts: Daniel's retelling of Nebuchadnezzar's experience (5:18–21), Daniel's confrontation of Belshazzar (5:22– 24), Daniel's interpretation of the wall writing (5:25–29), and Belshazzar's death and Babylon's fall (5:30–31).

Historical and Cultural Background

Standard Babylonian monetary weights (although not yet coins in the ANE) include a mina, a shekel, and a half mina or a half shekel (a mina equals sixty shekels). Daniel converts these to verbs when interpreting the wall writing, a common wordplay in

> Babylonian weights were usually made of stone. Standard measures included a mina, a shekel, and a half mina or a half shekel. These barrel-shaped weights from the Old Babylonian period (2000– 1600 BC) include a full mina (the largest) down to a three-shekel weight.

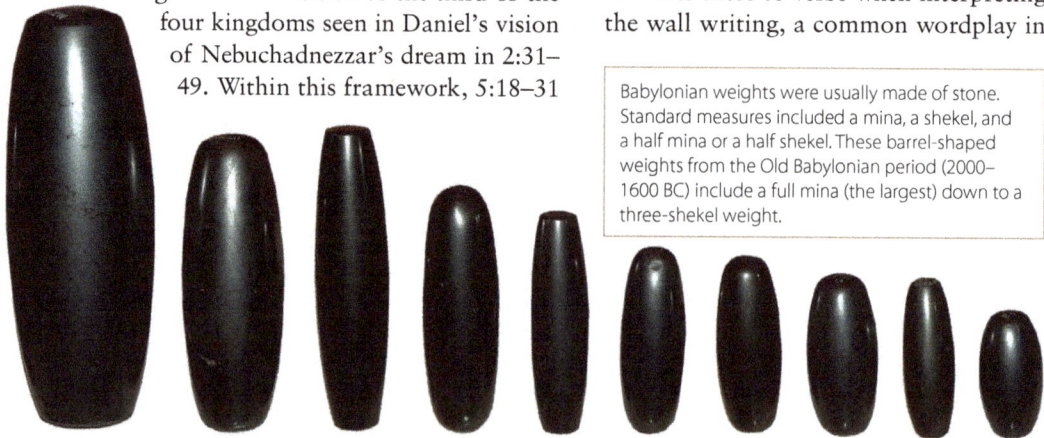

deciphering omens at this time. The imagery of being weighed on scales as a sign of divine judgment is also found in the Egyptian Book of the Dead. Not coincidentally, the fall of Babylon occurred on the sixth of Tishrit (October 12, 539 BC), a month linked in Babylonian tradition to the appearance of the constellation of "The Scales" (modern, Libra).[1] The court astrologers may see this as a sign confirming Daniel's explanation.[2]

The mention of purple clothing (purple was an expensive dye used mostly by royalty) and a gold chain (perhaps with an insignia of office) suggests that Daniel is offered the third position in rank under Belshazzar and his father, Nabonidus. If taken, such a position would put Daniel at risk when the Medes and Persians conquered Babylon.

Numerous Persian and Greek accounts of Babylon's fall have been preserved, ranging from the sixth to third century BC. They all attribute the conquest to Cyrus II of Persia, and some suggest it was without a fight (as was the case with the city of Sippar two days prior to Babylon's fall). Herodotus (*Hist.* 1.188–92, fifth century BC) claims that the Euphrates was diverted to allow access to the city through the canals. Xenophon (*Cyr.* 7.5.1–34) mentions a wicked Babylonian king, which may refer to Belshazzar. The exact fate of Nabonidus is unclear, although he was most likely either exiled or killed.[3] Regarding Darius the Mede, see "Additional Insights: Darius and/or Cyrus in Media and Persia" at the end of this unit.[4]

Interpretive Insights

5:18–19 *the Most High God gave your father Nebuchadnezzar.* The verb "gave"

Key Themes of Daniel 5:18–31

- God's establishing, judging, and restoring of Nebuchadnezzar should inform the way Belshazzar relates to God and governs Babylon.
- Belshazzar is called to honor the God who holds his life breath and ways in his hand.
- The handwriting announces Babylon's fall, Belshazzar's death, and the coming of a new kingdom.

(Aramaic *yᵉhab*) echoes Daniel's earlier declaration to Nebuchadnezzar (2:37), as well as God's "giving" that outlines Daniel's opening narrative (1:2, 9, 17; Hebrew *natan*). The "sovereignty" (Aramaic *malku*, "kingdom") given by God to Nebuchadnezzar (cf. Jer. 27:5–7), and held temporarily by Belshazzar, is divinely regifted to Darius the Mede (Dan. 5:31). This and its attendant "greatness and glory and splendor" are attributes elsewhere attributed to God as their true source (cf. 1 Chron. 29:11). Similarly, the power that accompanies these—life and death, promotion and humbling—also reflects divine prerogatives (Deut. 32:39; 1 Sam. 2:7–8).

5:20 *But when his heart became arrogant and hardened with pride.* The Aramaic literally concludes this clause, "and his 'spirit' [Aramaic *ruah*] became hardened." The language of "heart" and "spirit" captures the wide range of the inner, immaterial nature, including the mind, will, and psyche. This comprehensive self-exaltation is like the progressive hardening of Pharaoh's heart in Exodus 7–14 (cf. Hebrew *hazaq* and *kabed* in Exod. 7:13–14). The Aramaic text continues the use of *malku* in "the throne of his 'kingdom'" (instead of the NIV's "royal throne"), providing the connecting thread between the gift of the kingdom to Nebuchadnezzar and its loss under Belshazzar.

When Belshazzar was slain, he had been managing Babylon as co-regent with his father, Nabonidus. This father/son relationship is confirmed by the inscription on this clay cylinder recording a prayer of Nabonidus for himself and his eldest son, Belshazzar.

5:21 *until he acknowledged that the Most High God is sovereign.* The most striking contrast between Nebuchadnezzar and Belshazzar is neither their reigns nor their sins, although these differences are easily discerned. Rather, it is specifically the former's willingness and the latter's failure to repent.[5] Nebuchadnezzar recognized God's sovereignty over "all kingdoms on earth" (so the NIV; but the ESV preserves the literal sense, "kingdom of mankind," a corporate entity in contrast to God's kingdom).

5:22 *you, Belshazzar, his son, have not humbled yourself, though you knew all this.* The repeated reference to Nebuchadnezzar as the king's "father" throughout this passage reaches its climax in Belshazzar's complicit knowledge of his grandfather's judgment and subsequent repentance. Since Belshazzar is more accountable because of this knowledge, his sins of omission (not humbling himself and not honoring God) combine with his sin of commission (setting himself up against the Lord of heaven) to seal his fate. Though he knew firsthand what the Most High God had done with Nebuchadnezzar, he chose to honor false gods that "do not . . . know" (5:23 ESV).

5:23 *the God who holds in his hand your life and all your ways.* Job rightly acknowledges that God holds in his hand "the life of every living thing and the breath of all mankind" (Job 12:10 ESV). Here the metaphor of the "hand of God" is linked to the "hand" that writes on the palace wall in 5:5, which is sent by God to inscribe a declaration of his sovereign work among mortals. Elsewhere in Daniel, God's "hand" shapes kingdoms (2:45) while he does as he pleases without human hindrance (4:35).

5:25–28 *This is the inscription that was written:* MENE, MENE, TEKEL, PARSIN. The wall writing is a riddle that is first read (vocalized) as Babylonian weights: a mina, a shekel ("*tekel*"), and two halves of a shekel.[6] Then Daniel interprets these as verbs. "*Mene*" means "to be numbered" (cf. Ps. 90:10–12) and is most likely mentioned twice to emphasize God's active role in determining the now-elapsed days for the king's rule.[7] "*Tekel*" is the Aramaic form of "shekel," meaning "to be weighed," here in the sense of judgment (cf. 1 Sam. 2:3; Job 31:6). Belshazzar is found deficient on the scales in comparison both to Nebuchadnezzar and to what God required of him. "*Peres*" is the singular form of "*parsin*," which means, "to be divided" (into two halves)—although not necessarily in equal portions. The wordplay relates to the noun "Persia" (Aramaic *paras*; NIV: "Persians").[8] The closing reference to "the Medes and Persians" is literally "Media and Persia" (cf. Dan. 8:20); Cyrus the Great of Persia had by now subjugated the Median Empire. *Paras* is emphasized in the wordplay because "Persia" will become the enduring and comprehensive empire.[9]

5:29 *Daniel . . . was proclaimed the third highest ruler in the kingdom.* The NIV is correct in understanding Daniel's position to be one of rank under Belshazzar and Nabonidus (cf. Dan. 5:7; Esther 8:15; 10:3). He had refused this royal reward earlier (Dan. 5:7, 17), and the text does not say that he accepts it here. Perhaps Belshazzar forces it on him in fear of an even greater punishment or in hope that God will show mercy (cf. 4:36). Regardless, the reward is worthless at the best, and dangerous at the worst, in light of Babylon's imminent downfall.

5:30 *That very night Belshazzar, king of the Babylonians, was slain.* The immediacy of the king's judgment recalls that of Nebuchadnezzar's (4:31, 33), as well as the sudden appearance of the "hand" (5:5). Other Old Testament prophets explicitly predict Babylon's fall as well (Isa. 13:1–22; 21:1–10; Jer. 51:1–58), but the focus here is on the judgment of Belshazzar.

5:31 *and Darius the Mede took over the kingdom, at the age of sixty-two.* The Septuagint connects this verse with chapter 5 (so the NIV makes 5:30–31 one sentence), whereas the Masoretic Text reads it as the first verse of chapter 6.[10] Contextually and grammatically it makes sense either way. The mention of Darius's age, however, may intentionally conclude the wordplays in this pericope. If the identification of the weights above is correct, their monetary sum equals sixty-two shekels.[11] This historical marker is the second of four allusions to Babylon's fall in Daniel's narratives (1:21; 9:1–2; 11:1), although this significant event is not mentioned directly.

Theological Insights

In 5:18–31, the last pericope of this narrative, God's sovereignty confronts the reader in three ways. First, Scripture's redemptive history teaches mere mortals about the person and work of God in their lives. Second, God, the righteous judge of human sacrilege and blasphemy, holds the life breath and varied ways of all persons in his hand. Third, God sets up and takes down kings and kingdoms in this world to accomplish his purposes among humanity.

Teaching the Text

1. *Learn lessons from the past.* Knowing how God has worked with others in the past—especially in the Bible where inspired commentary is often provided—should teach us lessons of humility and repentance as we face our own failures and challenges. That God has blessed Nebuchadnezzar's repentance and judged his arrogance does not make him a hero or a villain but shows us how God works with flawed human beings. Belshazzar is expected to learn from these lessons, and so are modern readers of Daniel. Encourage your listeners to reflect on and learn from the examples of those believers who have preceded them or even their own experiences earlier in their lives. The greater our privilege and understanding of God's ways in the past, the greater our accountability is in the present.

2. *Sacrilege, humility, and the fragile nature of this life*. Because the Most High God is the giver of high positions, we should honor him if and when we receive such privileges. When acknowledging a person's efforts, achievements, and influence, always set these in the context of God as the giver. In contrast, it is sheer folly to set oneself up against the Lord of heaven. In Belshazzar's context this takes the form of desecrating sacred vessels from God's temple and using them to praise pagan gods. Today, we often fall prey to more subtle forms of dishonoring God, and as a result we are tempted to think that he overlooks such sins. Remind your congregation or study group that the sovereign Lord holds our best-laid plans in his grip—even the next breath we take! Keeping this truth before us can change the way we live and make us grateful for the gift of life itself.

3. *The changing of kings and kingdoms*. Belshazzar had only so much time to learn from the example of his grandfather and to choose sincere and lasting repentance before God instead of arrogance against him. Tragically, he came up light on the scales of justice, and his appointed days came to an end. These images remind us that we have only so much time to honor God and that this gift of life should not be wasted. In the bigger picture, the critical turn from this chapter to the next should also remind us that God sovereignly changes kings and kingdoms on the way to establishing his kingdom.

What not to teach. First, this neither is a place to heroize Daniel as a wise sage and courageous prophet nor a place to dwell on his prestigious reward for serving God

faithfully. Keep your focus on the God who humbles the proud regardless of their status, yet in response and proportion to their repentance. Second, the use of the numbers-and-scales metaphor does not teach that salvation comes from doing more good deeds than bad ones, but it does confirm that God cares about righteousness.

Illustrating the Text

Know your history to avoid the mistakes of the past.

History: Philosopher George Santayana (1863–1952) has observed, "Those who cannot remember the past are condemned to repeat it."[12] After winning military fame abroad, French general Napoleon Bonaparte returned home to arrange his own election as emperor of France. However, in 1812, he met a miserable end in his failed invasion of Russia, which led Napoleon deep into that country's harsh winter with dwindling supplies. Only a fraction of his army survived to return to France in defeat. Ignoring this lesson of history, German dictator Adolf Hitler attempted a similar strategy during World War II, besieging critical Soviet cities in 1941 but likewise running afoul of the same egotism and Russian winter that had ruined Napoleon. Learning from the past to avoid making the same mistakes is just as critical for believers as it is for world leaders. We are to learn from the work of God in the past, particularly in Scripture.

God, the righteous judge over all, opposes irreverent treatment of his holiness.

Bible: Throughout biblical history, sacrilege is considered a serious offense, whether against places or objects used in worship, or against the very name and person of God. In the Old Testament the Israelites in the exodus are sternly warned about coming too close to Mount Sinai, where God appears (Exod. 19:9–25). They are also told not to misuse God's name (Exod. 20:7). Later, the people of Beth Shemesh (1 Sam. 6:13–20), as well as a Levite named Uzzah (2 Sam. 6:1–7), are killed for mishandling the ark of the covenant. In the New Testament Jesus speaks against swearing an oath before God, going further to insist that it is better to simply keep one's word as it is spoken (Matt. 5:33–37). Similarly, Paul warns against taking communion in an unworthy manner (1 Cor. 11:27–32). Although Scripture does not speak of "sacred objects" after the advent of Jesus, we still serve a holy God whose person and work are profaned by our sacrilegious behavior. God is the judge over all, holds everyone's life in his hands, and therefore is deserving of our honor.

Beware of letting time slip away; live every moment for the Lord.

Quote: **Thomas Jefferson.** God is constantly at work bringing things to pass in his timing, and every day is an opportunity to serve God before our time comes to an end. United States president and founding father Thomas Jefferson wrote the now-famous adage "Never put off to tomorrow what you can do today."[13] We are often tempted to be lazy and procrastinate change in our spiritual lives, yet we do not know how long our time is. God has called us to serve faithfully each day, for we never know which breath will be our last. These wise words from Jefferson are a challenge to believers to follow their calling every day and never put off change for the better through godly service until the future.

The interpretation of the word "TEKEL" is that Belshazzar has been "weighed on the scales and found wanting" (5:27). This image of being weighed on scales as a method of divine judgment is also found in the Egyptian Book of the Dead. As this papyrus drawing shows, the heart of the deceased, in a container on the left scale pan, is being weighed. The Egyptian gods Anubis (jackal head) and Re (falcon head) judge its weight against a figurine of Maat, wearing the feather of truth (right scale pan) to determine whether the heart is to be devoured or whether the deceased can continue on the journey to the afterlife. Thoth (ibis-headed god) records the results (fourth to first century BC).

Daniel 5:18–31

Darius and/or Cyrus in Media and Persia

Darius and/or Cyrus

All accounts of Babylon's fall in 539 BC credit Cyrus II, the Great, of Persia (600–530 BC) with its conquest. No extrabiblical records have yet been discovered that mention a person named "Darius the Mede" (cf. Dan. 5:31; 6:1–28; 11:1). As a result, liberal-critical scholars consider him an "unhistorical character."[1]

Those who accept Daniel's narratives as historically accurate propose two ways of resolving this problem. The first understands Darius as a subordinate to Cyrus, possibly Gubaru/Ugbaru (Greek *Gobryas*), a general under Cyrus to whom the Nabonidus Chronicle attributes Babylon's conquest, and/or the one appointed afterward as governor in the city. It is not clear whether these are one or two persons, and whether his reign as "king of Babylon" is long enough to fit the account in Daniel 6. The statement that he "received the kingdom" (5:31; NIV: "took over") and "was made ruler" (9:1) could imply that a superior gave it to him. In this view, Cyrus would not have assumed the title "king of Babylon" until a year into his rule.[2]

The second way of resolving the problem, that "Darius the Mede" is an alternative name for Cyrus the Persian, is more likely. The linking of Darius with Cyrus in 6:28, which could be read, "Darius, *that is*, Cyrus the Persian" (see NIV footnote), suggests this theory. It also fits well with

Table 1: Key Events in Media and Persia in Relation to Darius/Cyrus

612–605	Darius/Cyrus's (D/C) great-grandfather Cyaxares (cf. "Xerxes" in Dan. 9) leads Media with Babylon against Assyria.	
605	Nebuchadnezzar's first year; Judah's first subjugation	Dan. 1
604	Nebuchadnezzar's second year; first four-kingdom vision	Dan. 2
600	**D/C born to Median mother and Persian father as prince of Anshan**	
562	Nebuchadnezzar's death; release of Judah's King Jehoiachin	2 Kings 25; Jer. 52
559	D/C king of Anshan (Persian tributary of Media) after his father Cambyses's death	
556	D/C revolts against Median rulers (Nabonidus's first year).	
553	Belshazzar's first year as coregent; second four-kingdom vision	Dan. 7
550	Belshazzar's third year; D/C defeats grandfather Astyages and controls Media.	Dan. 8
539	D/C's first accession year; defeats Babylon	Dan. 1; 5–6; 9; 11
538	D/C's first regnal year; releases Jewish exiles after approximately "seventy years"	
535	D/C's third regnal year; more precisely, seventy years after Daniel's exile	Dan. 10
535–530	D/C continues his expansion of the Persian Empire (paternal roots) until his death.	

Cyrus's mixed ancestry, which included a Persian father, Cambyses I, a vassal king in the Anshan province under Median control, and a Median mother, Mandane, daughter of Median king Astyages, and granddaughter of the powerful Cyaxares the Great, who united the loosely affiliated Median tribes into a kingdom. Both the Old Greek and Theodotion read "Cyrus" instead of the Masoretic Text's "Darius" in 11:1, and Theodotion names Cyrus as the king of the events parallel to Daniel 6 in his version of Bel and the Dragon (Bel 1). Herodotus notes that the name of Persia's founder, given to him at birth by his Median mother, was not Cyrus (*Hist.* 1.108–14). Darius/Cyrus was likely in his early sixties when he conquered Babylon. And the statements that Darius "received the kingdom" (5:31) and "was made ruler" (9:1) could refer to God as the giver of kings and kingdoms, as it was for Nebuchadnezzar (1:2; 5:18).[3]

Media and Persia

The proper nouns "Media"/"Medes" (*maday*) and "Persia"/"Persians" (*paras*) appear in close proximity in the Old Testament, yet always distinctly. Daniel speaks of God giving Babylon to Media and Persia (5:28), as well as of their laws (6:8, 12, 15) and kings (8:20; cf. Jer. 25:25)—listing Media first to emphasize historical sequence. Esther refers to military leaders (1:3), nobles (1:14), and laws (1:19)—putting Persia first, except regarding their kings (10:2). Isaiah notes the joint conquest of Babylon by Media and Persia (21:2; "Elam"

connotes "Persia"). Earlier, Media helped Babylon conquer Assyria; then Media became Babylon's rival after Nebuchadnezzar's death (562 BC). Cyrus became king of Anshan in 559 BC, and then he revolted against his Median overlords in 556 BC, winning a three-year battle against Astyages in 553–550 BC. With the combined forces of the Medes and Persians under his control, he took Babylon in 539 BC and began his rule as Darius the Mede, then as Cyrus the Great, king of Persia (Dan. 5:31–6:1). To be clear, Persia reflected "Medo-Persian" culture, and its legal system became known as the "law of the Medes and Persians," much like Rome later reflected "Greco-Roman" culture after it conquered Greece. However, there was no "Medo-Persian Empire" just as there was no "Greco-Roman Empire."

Daniel varies his usage of the names Cyrus (1:21; 6:28; 10:1) and Darius (5:31; 6:1, 6, 9, 15, 25, 28; 9:1; 11:1) but places a slightly greater emphasis on Darius. This serves a twofold purpose. First, it emphasizes the fulfillment of the prophecies of Isaiah and Jeremiah, who focus on the fall of Babylon to the Medes (Isa. 13:17; 21:2; Jer. 51:11, 28). Second, it helps to distinguish the rise of the inferior second kingdom (Media) from the expansive rule of the third kingdom (Persia) in Daniel's four-kingdom scheme (2:39).[4]

Cyrus II, the Great, of Persia (600–530 BC) is credited with the conquest of Babylon in 539 BC. The Tomb of Cyrus the Great, shown here, stands in Pasargadae, Iran, his capital city.

Daniel's Success and Darius's Decree

Big Idea *God may allow those who remain faithful to him and his word to experience jealous opposition from unbelievers in a hostile environment.*

Understanding the Text

The Text in Context

Daniel 6:1–28 is woven into the book's overall literary structure in two ways. First, it advances the narrative of chapters 1–6, in which the first four focus on Nebuchadnezzar (chaps. 1–2 with historical markers and 3–4 without) and the last two show the transition from Belshazzar of Babylon to Darius the Mede (chaps. 5–6). Second, it completes the second of three parallel pairs of chapters (3 and 6) in the book's concentric, Aramaic center section (see the comparison of these two chapters in "The Text in Context" in the unit on 3:1–12). Taken alone, 6:1–28 reflects a concentric structure with four pairs.[1]

 A Daniel succeeds in the kingdom (6:1–3).
  B Darius signs his first decree (6:4–9).
   C Daniel's accusers plan his death (6:10–15).
    D Darius hopes for Daniel's deliverance by God (6:16–18).
    D′ Darius witnesses Daniel's deliverance by God (6:19–23).
   C′ Daniel's accusers encounter their deaths (6:24).
  B′ Darius signs his second decree (6:25–27).
 A′ Daniel succeeds in the kingdom (6:28).

Against this backdrop, 6:1–9 recalls the previous accusations brought against Daniel's three Jewish friends and, at the same time, lays a foundation for his own crisis and deliverance to follow. In order to maintain the narrative flow of chapters 1–6, the author carries forward two ideas from Daniel 5: Belshazzar's dubious reward to Daniel is replaced by Darius's promotion of Daniel, and Belshazzar's wickedness is contrasted with Darius's goodwill.[2] Also, the interplay between God and Daniel unites the chapter: Daniel's observance of God's law, his routine of prayer and request of God, and his innocence before God and the king. Within this framework, 6:1–9 divides into three parts: Daniel's excellent service to Darius (6:1–3), the attempt of Daniel's colleagues to find him guilty (6:4–5), and the unwitting compliance of the king with their plot (6:6–9).

Historical and Cultural Background

The organizational work of Darius/Cyrus (see "Additional Insights: Darius and/or Cyrus in Media and Persia") reflects the administrative divisions of Persia into smaller regions governed by satraps ("administrators"). Herodotus mentions only twenty to thirty satrapies ("provinces") at most, although the Greek equivalent of the Aramaic term for "satrap" suggests smaller provinces are included (*Hist.* 3.89).[3]

Worship was reserved exclusively for the gods in ancient Persia—not for kings.[4] There was a struggle at this time, however, between adherents to monotheistic worship of Ahura Mazda (associated with Zoroastrianism) and the Magi enticed by an encroaching syncretism of religions. Also at this time, Cyrus was redistributing sacred images to their respective peoples, reversing the centralization of pagan idols by Nabonidus. One or both of these may explain Darius's first decree, in which he functions as a mediator for thirty days.[5]

The unchangeable nature of the laws of the Medes and the Persians is not referenced in extrabiblical sources. However, Diodorus Siculus (*Bib. hist.* 17.30) alludes to it regarding a case under Darius III in which an innocent man was sentenced to death.[6] The references at the time of Daniel and Esther may reflect a tradition of Hammurabi (eighteenth century BC) more than a ruling of law.[7]

Interpretive Insights

6:1–2 *appoint 120 satraps to rule throughout the kingdom, with three administrators over them.* The account of Esther and Mordecai attests to "127 provinces" under the rule of Xerxes (486–465 BC; Esther 1:1; 8:9; 9:30). If Darius and Cyrus are the same person, 120 satraps for the entire Persian Empire should be understood as a literal or rounded number rather than hyperbole. The mention of "three administrators" recalls the previous narrative, where Daniel is offered a high position as one of three (5:7, 16, 29). The Aramaic term used here for

Key Themes of Daniel 6:1–9

- God gifts Daniel with an extraordinary spirit and gives him favor with Darius in the new empire.
- Jealous administrators use Daniel's faithful, public commitment to the one true God to attack him.
- The God whom Daniel serves is set in opposition to the false gods of Media and Persia.

The decree suggested to Darius in Daniel 6, while politically motivated to harm Daniel, may have been favorably received by the king as a solution to the religious struggles between those who favored pure Zoroastrianism and those who were more syncretistic in their practices. At this time Magi, like the ones depicted offering sacrifices on this fifth-century BC relief fragment, served as priests in the Persian religious system.

"administrators" (*sarak*) is a Persian loan-word, reflecting the transition to a new regime. This unusual arrangement in Persian history may have been temporary following the death of Gubaru, the first governor of Babylon under Cyrus.[8]

6:3 *Daniel so distinguished himself . . . by his exceptional qualities.* The Masoretic Text credits Daniel's success to "an excellent spirit" (ESV; Aramaic *ruah yattira'*) within him, reflecting the "spirit of the holy gods" mentioned in 4:8–9, 18; and 5:11–12, 14. The NIV's translation, "qualities," better describes his aptitude and abilities (cf. 1:4; 5:14b), which were also given by God (cf. 1:4, 17). This is the third and final time a pagan king recognizes Daniel's giftedness and causes him to prosper (cf. 1:17–20; 2:46–49), which is his highest "promotion." Ironically, it is Daniel's pending appointment that contributes to his problems, just as it is Nebuchadnezzar's appointment of Shadrach, Meshach, and Abednego that angers their jealous colleagues (3:12).

6:4 *the administrators and the satraps tried to find grounds for charges against Daniel.* The two jealous administrators, supported by other satraps, seek to undermine Daniel's chances for success, although not by demonstrating his incompetence but rather by challenging his character. Ironically, their "corruption" is clearly implied, while Daniel's is explicitly denied. Moreover, their efforts to convict him only serve to vindicate him.

They could find no corruption in him, because he was trustworthy. The Aramaic *'aman*, "to trust in," appears strategically in the parallel statement of Daniel's deliverance, because he "trusted in his God" (6:23). The corresponding Hebrew term

is used elsewhere in the Old Testament to express God's trustworthy love for David (Isa. 55:3). In this way, the reader of Daniel is encouraged to look beyond the person to his God, who is always faithful.

6:5 *unless it has something to do with the law of his God.* The Mosaic law is set here in tension with the "law of the Medes and Persians" (6:8). By choosing this method of discrediting Daniel, his adversaries show blatant disregard for the law of God, just as Belshazzar blasphemes the sacred vessels of God's temple in the previous narrative. The plot of Daniel's accusers is based on their knowledge of his commitment to God. Earlier, Daniel had referred to his God privately with his friends (2:17–19), in his confrontation of Nebuchadnezzar (2:28; 4:25), and in his public rebuke of Belshazzar (5:23). Daniel may have revealed his beliefs and practices to the other administrators verbally or through his semipublic prayers (6:10).

6:6–7 *went as a group.* The NIV's "went" is too mild. The Aramaic term *regash* likely connotes "an angry, conspiring throng."[9] This is intensified by their assertion that they also have the full support of the "advisers and governors," implying virtually all of Persia's leadership besides the king. The standard ancient Near Eastern greeting of a monarch, "May King Darius live forever!" (cf. 2:4; 3:9; 5:10), prepares the reader for a dramatic wordplay that honors the "living God" at the close of this chapter (6:20–21, 26).

the king should issue an edict and enforce the decree. That Darius issues such an unusual religious edict suggests that he has the power of Cyrus the Great. However, the exact nature of the decree is puzzling,

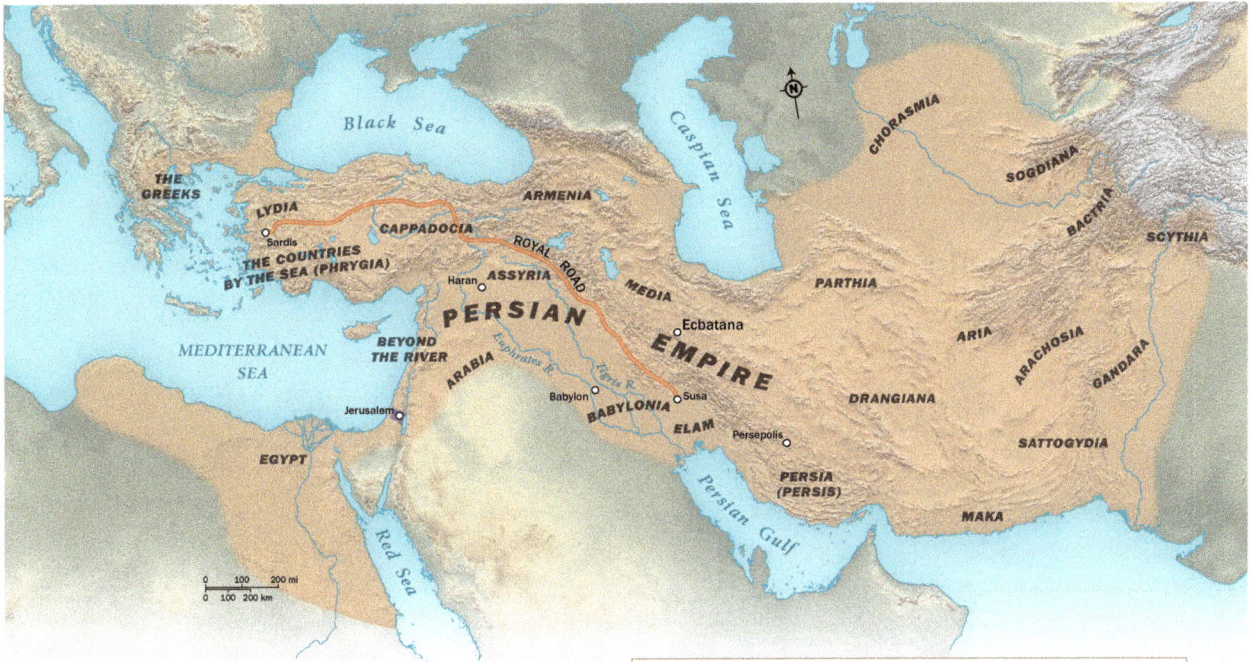

Map of the Persian Empire showing locations including Black Sea, Caspian Sea, Mediterranean Sea, Red Sea, Persian Gulf, The Greeks, Lydia, Sardis, Cappadocia, The Countries by the Sea (Phrygia), Armenia, Chorasmia, Sogdiana, Bactria, Scythia, Haran, Assyria, Media, Parthia, Aria, Arachosia, Gandara, Ecbatana, Beyond the River, Arabia, Jerusalem, Babylon, Babylonia, Susa, Elam, Persepolis, Drangiana, Sattogydia, Egypt, Persia (Persis), Maka. The Royal Road and Euphrates R. and Tigris R. are labeled.

because Persian kings were not deified. Perhaps the intent was to make Darius a priestly mediator between the people and the Zoroastrian deity Ahura Mazda.[10] Another explanation suggests that this reflects the approximately "thirty days" during which Cyrus redistributed sacred images previously centralized by Nabonidus.[11] Regardless, the edict presents Daniel with a totally unacceptable—albeit temporary—imposition. The edict includes the threat of execution by means of a "lions' den." The Aramaic *gob* connotes a "pit" carved out of the ground with an opening at the top that could be covered by a large stone. A catch of lions kept for hunting provides a weapon of opportunity on this occasion (cf. the furnace of Daniel 3).[12]

6:8–9 *the law of the Medes and Persians.* The account of Esther and Mordecai confirms that Persian kings were, to some degree, obligated to their own laws (Esther 1:19; 8:8). In Daniel's narrative, the custom accentuates the trap set by his adversaries to force Darius to serve their purposes. Once it has sprung, Darius is caught—and they think Daniel is as well. The Aramaic *'adah* ("to repeal") is also used in Daniel to speak of the God who deposes kings (2:21; 5:20 [NIV: "stripped"]), takes their authority from them (4:31; 7:12 [NIV: "stripped"]), makes their kingdoms pass away (7:26 [NIV: "taken away"]), and establishes his kingdom that never passes away (7:14).[13] There is a sense of finality when Darius becomes an unwitting accomplice to the plot of Daniel's adversaries by putting the decree in writing.

Theological Insights

Three attributes of God are discernible in 6:1–9 that contrast the schemes, failures, and laws of mere mortals. First, the extraordinary spirit by which Daniel distinguishes himself reflects the gifting of God's Spirit. Second, Daniel's trustworthiness in public service, while he is open about his faith, points to the God who is worth serving. Third, the revelation of God's person and purposes—here in his law—is meant to govern the daily conduct of believers, even in opposition to human laws.

Teaching the Text

1. *God's extraordinary Spirit in Daniel*. It is important to remind your listeners that the "exceptional qualities" by which Daniel distinguishes himself are the work of God's Spirit in his life (see the comments on 6:3, above). Ask your congregation (perhaps allowing brief times of silence for personal reflection) to consider times in their lives when they have distinguished themselves among their peers, and to reflect on the gifts and abilities that contributed to their success. Then encourage each person to consider and acknowledge God in silent prayer as the giver of every gift, aptitude, or ability. By keeping this truth before us we are better able to avoid false pride and embrace genuine humility as a testimony to God, who is the source and giver of our accomplishments.

2. *Daniel's trust in the worthy God*. This is a good text for teaching and preaching about being trustworthy in the varied opportunities we are given in service to others. Many times, Christians are poor witnesses to their professors, employers, and colleagues because of personal dishonesty or simple negligence, provoking appropriately negative and adversarial responses. Part of our proclamation of the gospel is that we

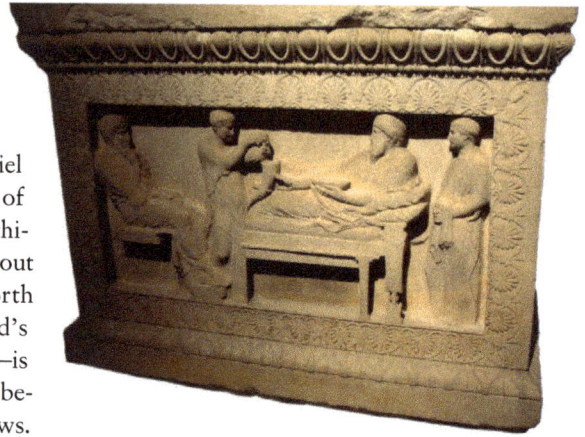

Darius appoints 120 satraps and 3 administrators to help him oversee the empire. They become jealous of Daniel's position in the royal court and take advantage of his faithfulness to God as they plot against him. This fifth-century BC sarcophagus, from the royal necropolis of Sidon, shows a satrap reclining at a banquet.

are called to live pure and holy lives, especially before those who know of our beliefs. Focus on being trustworthy as an appropriate response to the God who is worthy of trust—even in the face of adversity. Help your listeners to think of such behavior as worship (from the Old English "worthship") of the entirely trustworthy God.

3. *The law of Daniel's God*. Although believers today cannot, and should not, follow the Old Testament law of Moses in the same way Daniel does, God shows us how to live throughout the whole of Scripture. The New Testament, especially, gives believers liberty in certain areas of "disputable matters," which were strictly defined in the Old Testament (e.g., Rom. 14:1–18). Yet a pattern of godly behavior is easily discernible in Jesus's teaching and the New Testament letters. Challenge your listeners to examine their lives to see if such a pattern of biblical fidelity is evident in their lives and visible to those around them. As we live our lives before a watching world, we should do so in a way that draws others

to the God we serve, even though they may use such good intentions against us.

What not to teach. This is not a place to highlight Daniel's great accomplishments or lifelong faithfulness, but rather it is a place to focus on God's work through him. Daniel is able to remain faithful because God sustains and gifts him. This does not diminish Daniel's well-made choices but appropriately gives credit to the God who is worthy.

Illustrating the Text

God's gifts may distinguish us before people, but they ultimately give glory to God alone.

Biography: Johann Sebastian Bach. A German organist and prolific composer, Bach (1685–1750) is widely revered as one of the greatest composers of all time. His vast portfolio of compositions includes an immense number of chamber, organ, keyboard, and choral works, many of which are still instantly recognizable today. Bach was clearly gifted with an extraordinary talent for music, yet he was also a devoutly Christian man who remains to this day a true example of a person distinguished for his accomplishments yet testifying always to God as the giver of his abilities. To this end, Bach inscribed his compositions with the initials S. D. G. (*Soli Deo Gloria*: "Glory to God Alone"), pointing those who perform his works and admire his talent to the source of his giftedness.

Be a positive example of Christian faith in a world dominated by caricatures.

Film: Regretfully, popular media often satirizes faith and highlights caricatured, hypocritical Christians, like the condescending, judgmental Christian characters in such teen-comedy films as *Saved!* (2004) and *Easy A* (2010). This general perspective is all too common, and though no Christian life is perfect, sometimes a careless lack of integrity on the part of believers can reinforce this stereotype. In contrast, in director Adam Shankman's *A Walk to Remember* (2002), a teenage Christian girl named Jamie with terminal leukemia exercises faith in God, who gives her courage in the face of her illness to seek new experiences in the days that remain. This witness has a transforming effect on the popular troublemaker, Landon, who falls in love with her. Although negative perceptions of Christians are bountiful, being a believer with integrity who is a faithful witness can make an eternal difference to the lost around us.

Live faithfully under the authority of God's Word.

Church History: Having already been excommunicated from the church, leader of the Protestant Reformation Martin Luther stood trial at the Diet of Worms in 1521, where he was challenged to recant his convictions regarding justification by faith alone and his rejection of corrupt and unscriptural church practices. Though he faced condemnation as a heretic and subsequent arrest, Luther demonstrated that commitment to God's law as written in his Word must take precedence over any human law: "My conscience is captive to the Word of God. Thus I cannot and will not recant, for going against my conscience is neither safe nor salutary. I can do no other, here I stand, God help me. Amen."[14] We too must have this same conviction that Scripture is the final authority to be lived out every day, even when we are faced with opposition.

Daniel's Fidelity and Death Sentence

Big Idea *God is always worthy of faithful worship and obedience—no matter the consequences—and encourages those who trust him, although sometimes through unlikely persons.*

Understanding the Text

The Text in Context

See the unit on 6:1–9 for a discussion of the larger context, structure, and comparisons of this chapter. Against this backdrop, the sympathetic attitude of Darius toward Daniel forms a sharp contrast with the intentionally harsh actions of Nebuchadnezzar against Daniel's friends in Daniel 3. Yet these kings join voices in raising the question of God's ability to deliver his faithful servants at the center of their respective narratives, setting the stage for God's miraculous deliverances that follow. Within this framework, 6:10–18 divides into three parts: Daniel responds to the king's decree (6:10–11), Daniel's colleagues force the king's continued compliance (6:12–13), and the king expresses remorse over Daniel's apparent execution (6:14–18).

Historical and Cultural Background

People prayed three times a day in the traditional culture of Old Persia, whereas Zoroastrianism increased it to five. No laws existed in Jewish tradition at that time mandating a number of prayers per day or a direction for prayer—although later Jewish literature attests to both practices (Jdt. 9:1;

Lions were captured and then released to be hunted for sport in Assyria and Persia. In this Assyrian relief (645–635 BC), the door to a lion's cage has been opened so that the lion may escape to become prey for King Ashurbanipal.

Daniel 6:10–18

Mishnah, *Berakhot* 4:5).[1] Perhaps this custom developed among the Babylonian exiles, or Daniel acquired it when Persian rule began. If the latter is true, he most likely is using the Persian custom for his own purposes of fidelity to Yahweh, symbolized by his orientation toward Jerusalem.

Beginning around 2000 BC, lions were captured and confined in cages for sport, to be hunted by Assyrian and Persian royalty. There are no examples, however, of lions kept in this manner for executions, although the ancient Persians used equally horrible methods.[2] In earlier Assyrian literature, persons who break an oath are put into cages with wild animals to be devoured in public; and later texts (seventh century BC) use the metaphor of a lion's pit for a malicious person. In Babylonian wisdom texts, Marduk muzzles the lion's mouth, referring to the devouring tactics of an oppressor.[3]

Signet rings were routinely used along with stamp seals for the personal business of Persian kings, while cylinder seals were employed for official government purposes. During the time of Daniel, rings and stamps became more popular. A signet ring bears the official seal of the king, carved in chalcedony, and usually depicts a heroic accomplishment of the king under the protection of Ahura Mazda. In the unusual case in Daniel of the sealing of a lion's pit for execution, a rock is rolled over the opening, after which a clay seal is affixed with the impression of the royal signet ring, as well as those of the high administrators, so that it cannot be removed without being noticed.[4]

Interpretive Insights

6:10–11 *Daniel learned that the decree had been published.* This statement links

Key Themes of Daniel 6:10–18

- When Daniel hears of the edict, he continues his routine of semipublic worship of his God.

- Given the consequences of his choice, Daniel pleads with God for help but does not compromise his practice.

- Daniel is reminded by a pagan king of the one true God's ability to reward Daniel's faithful service by rescuing him from death.

the reader to the narrative of 6:1–9. Having an upstairs room with windows was associated with luxury and status in Israel (Judg. 3:20; 2 Kings 4:8–11; 9:30–33; Jer. 22:14), and the same may have applied to life in Babylon.[5] The practice of praying "toward Jerusalem" recalls Solomon's prayer, also "on his knees" (1 Kings 8:54), at the dedication of the temple, which foreshadows persons like Daniel praying toward Jerusalem, seeking God's mercy in the land of their exile (1 Kings 8:46–51). Praying "three times a day" may reflect Daniel's knowledge of Psalm 55:17–19, where David cries out "evening, morning and noon" for rescue from a battle waged against him, believing God will rescue him unharmed and humble his adversaries—much like Daniel's situation.[6]

prayed, giving thanks . . . praying and asking God for help. The first pair of participles ("praying" and "praising, giving thanks," 6:10) connotes worship, while the second pair ("seeking" and "imploring," 6:11) reflects an urgent plea (the NIV's rendering of the last two fails to capture the strength of Daniel's prayer). The phrase "just as he had done before" recalls a similar prayer nearly seventy years earlier in which the young Judean had found God equally responsive (2:18, 23). Through this spiritual discipline, he expresses confidence in God

Joseph and Esther Narratives

Whereas the book of Daniel presents four faithful Judeans in challenging times, the stories of Joseph and Esther depict Israelites struggling with their faith in their separate pagan contexts.[a] In these otherwise similar narratives, God graciously blesses these two individuals in spite of their questionable choices.

Joseph's personal exile (Gen. 37–50) reveals a struggle of faith evident in his choices. First, he always uses the generic 'elohim ("God," "a god," or "gods"; cf. 41:16). Second, he marries an Egyptian priest's daughter (41:45).[b] Third, he wants to forget his father's household (41:51). Fourth, he boasts about using his diviner's cup (44:5, 15). Though Joseph seems to return to faith in Yahweh at the end (50:20; 'elohim in private conversation with Israelites likely references their God), his story highlights God's grace to those who struggle.

Esther's narrative (Esther 1–10) raises similar concerns about the struggles she and Mordecai face. First, they voluntarily remain in exile long after the first return. Second, her pagan name, Esther, honoring the pagan goddess Ishtar, dominates the book (rather than her Hebrew name, Hadassah). Third, she marries outside the faith. Fourth, she initially refuses to risk her life to save her people, complying with Mordecai's orders only at the threat of death. Fifth, there is no mention of God, faith, or religious observance in the book.[c] This story highlights God's grace to a Judean remnant that has forgotten him.

[a] For a literary comparison of the three narratives, see Berg, *Book of Esther*, 123–65; for a critical, yet accessible, analysis of the book of Esther that develops these concerns, see Dunne, *Esther and Her Elusive God*.
[b] The apocryphal story of *Joseph and Aseneth* expands on Gen. 41:45–52, addressing this concern with Aseneth's conversion prior to their marriage.
[c] The Greek additions to Esther address these concerns with visions to Mordecai justifying Esther's actions and with their prayers to God for help.

in an otherwise unnerving crisis. Again, the administrators going "as a group" carries the force of an angry mob rather than an orderly group of associates (cf. 6:6).

6:13 *Daniel . . . pays no attention to you . . . or to the decree you put in writing.* The theological backdrop of the approximately "seventy-year" exile is continually kept before the eyes of the reader (see 1:3; 2:25; 5:13). Although Babylon had fallen several months earlier, the shadow of their exile

lingers over the Jews. The charge brought against Daniel is accurate because he knows of the decree yet continues his recently outlawed worship (3:10). This rhetoric is used in the accusation of Daniel's three friends in 3:12, further linking the parallel narratives. Their responses then demonstrate an intentional choice to be faithful to their God, who is worthy of such sacrifice.

6:14–15 *When the king heard this, he was greatly distressed; he was determined to rescue Daniel.* Darius could be upset with Daniel for ignoring the decree, or with his ministers for deceiving him, or with himself for getting caught in the middle.[7] Now, however, he is trapped under the "law of the Medes and Persians," which cannot be revoked even by the king. His efforts to rescue Daniel contrast sharply with Nebuchadnezzar's wrath in chapter 3, as well as with the persistence of Daniel's accusers here.

6:16 *May your God, whom you serve continually.* With the king's order the intended execution commences. Darius may be expressing a wish, or may be offering an implied prayer for Daniel's deliverance (NIV, ESV), or perhaps may be voicing a confident confession that this "will" happen (NJPS). Likely it is a wish in Darius's mind. Yet, in this context the repetition of the verb "to rescue" (*shezib*) from 6:14 contrasts the inabilities of the most powerful king in the world with the abilities of Daniel's God (3:17, 28–29). The reference to "whom you serve continually" reminds the reader of Daniel's "seventy years" of "a long obedience in the same direction."[8]

6:17–18 *A stone was brought . . . and the king sealed it with his own signet ring.* Daniel's seemingly unchangeable circumstances, symbolized in Darius's twofold sealing of the lions' den, provide the backdrop for the dramatic rescue to follow. This parallels the moment of his friends falling into the flames with no apparent sign of hope (3:23). Recalling the earlier narrative provides the reader with confidence that God will honor his servant's faithfulness. Moreover, the sleepless and abstinent behavior of the king this night expresses the concern of all who wish to see God rescue Daniel.[9]

Theological Insights

Daniel 6:10–18, the literary center of this beloved story, captures three important ideas about the God of Daniel. First, God is worthy of consistent, dedicated, and faithful worship, no matter how severe the consequences. Second, because worship goes beyond mere words in prayer, God sometimes calls believers to demonstrate outwardly their inner convictions through courageous acts of obedience. Third, God often reminds believers of his care in times of need through unexpected persons who point them to the God who is able to deliver.

Teaching the Text

1. *God is worthy, no matter the adversity.* Undeserved accusations by associates and unjust decisions by those in authority over us should not derail a well-established spiritual discipline of personal prayer or public worship. Daniel first resolves not to defile himself in a hostile environment during his midteens (1:8) and now remains unshaken in his regular practice of prayer and thanksgiving in his early eighties. Call your listeners to look beyond the example of the elderly sage to the motives for his behavior centered in the worthiness of the God he serves. Recount and reflect on the aspects of God's character that warrant such costly obedience: he is able to rescue because he is sovereign; he cares in our times of need because he is compassionate; he expects us to live holy lives because he is holy—to name only a few.

2. *"Worship" is an action verb.* Threatening words can quickly turn into imminent danger, taking us beyond worship as usual to a place of urgent petitions to God for help. Be careful here to emphasize God's unquestioned ability to rescue and save without implying that he always does so in this life. Do not underemphasize the genuine crisis Daniel faces. All evidence points to a no-way-out situation involving a horrific death within the day. Although a seasoned believer and consistently faithful servant of God, Daniel is human and

As Darius leaves Daniel to his fate, he says, "May your God, whom you serve continually, rescue you" (6:16). The carving on this ivory box (fifth to seventh century AD) depicts Daniel in prayer while surrounded by lions, an example of God's protection and deliverance.

to any individual through whom God chooses to glorify himself. Darius's wish, or prayer, challenges us to focus our hope on God alone.

What not to teach. First, the specifics of Daniel's practice of prayer (e.g., three times a day facing Jerusalem) are not prescribed for believers today, although there is nothing wrong with using a disciplined schedule or remembering the place where the greatest event in human history took place. Second, God does not always choose to deliver, but he is always able to do so. Our faithful service to him, therefore, should not be contingent on his reward or rescue.

Illustrating the Text

There is no greater reason to face adversity than the cause of Christ.

History: In the case of war, when the stakes may include losing one's life, the exhortation to support "the cause" often focuses on an ideal esteemed so highly that it is worth facing the adversity of battle. In the case of the American Revolutionary War, the call to war focused largely on freedom and the rights of all to "life, liberty, and the pursuit of happiness," as the Declaration of Independence puts it. These sentiments gave birth to Patrick Henry's exclamation, "Give me liberty or give me death!"[10] This kind of rhetoric seeks to touch the heart and stir courage even in the fearful. Though many causes (such as love, freedom, or patriotism) may move us to great sacrifice, no cause can be as great as the

therefore can experience fears and doubts like the rest of us. Encourage your listeners to process their fears through prayer, working toward a confidence in God's wisdom to determine best how to glorify himself and advance his kingdom.

3. *An unexpected word from the king.* We should always be mindful of encouragements God provides through others—even unbelievers—that show he cares for us and desires for us to remain faithful to him. Sometimes God asks us to face very difficult trials alone so that we can learn to trust him more deeply. In this passage the only voice of hope comes, strangely, from a pagan king. Take this opportunity to remind your listeners that God's sovereignty over the kingdoms of humanity extends

worthiness of God himself, who deserves our love and obedience—no matter the adversity we face.

Actions speak louder than words.

Literature: *Pride and Prejudice*, by Jane Austen. Though words are critical expressions of devotion, sometimes circumstances arise in which actions are the ultimate demonstrations of one's commitment. In the classic novel *Pride and Prejudice*, the principal characters Elizabeth Bennet and Mr. Darcy have a number of uncomfortable encounters and misunderstandings that result in an honestly meant marriage proposal by Mr. Darcy being pointedly turned down by Elizabeth, who refuses to believe that his words could be true. It is only after his selfless actions in seeking out Elizabeth's runaway sister and bearing the financial burden of her "necessary wedding" to the man she ran away with that Elizabeth believes his words and realizes she loves him. In the same way, though words are important, it is through actions—especially actions that require some level of sacrifice—that we truly show our devotion to God in worship, prayer, and service.

Help sometimes comes from unlikely sources.

Film: *The Emperor's New Groove*. The Walt Disney film *The Emperor's New Groove* (2000) depicts an unlikely friendship that grows between a vain, self-absorbed Incan emperor, Kuzco, and a humble village leader, Pacha. In the tale, the emperor is transformed into a llama by his aging advisor and her henchman and then accidentally taken by Pacha to his village. The two are an unlikely team, since the emperor plans to demolish Pacha's village to build a royal vacation home. Nevertheless, the challenges they face in traversing the wild and avoiding the pursuit of the emperor's advisor and her henchman end up bringing the two to understand each other. They even become friends, largely based on the help they give each other along the way. Each would have missed out on a great opportunity had they mistrusted each other, and both find an unlikely friend by the end of their journey.

God Rescues Daniel from the Lions

Big Idea *The living God is able to rescue his faithful servants and thereby reveal his person and kingdom to a needy world.*

Understanding the Text

The Text in Context

See the unit on 6:1–9 for a discussion of the larger context, structure, and comparisons of this chapter. Against this backdrop, 6:19–28 (this narrative's final section) reflects the structure of the first section, although in reverse order. The Judean exile Daniel, introduced in his midteens, is now an aged sage and prophet in his mideighties. In contrast to chapters 1–5, however, Daniel 6 provides no narrative segue to the one following it. Instead, its final historical marker (6:28) concludes the larger narrative portion of Daniel 1–6, which focuses on Judah's "seventy-year" exile. Daniel 7–12, in contrast, forms the apocalyptic second half of the book, which emphasizes Judah's suffering under Greece centuries later.[1] Within this framework, 6:19–28 divides into four parts: Darius's anxious arrival at the den (6:19–20), Daniel's deliverance and his accusers' punishment (6:21–24), Darius's counterdecree and praise of God (6:25–27), and a postscript regarding Daniel's prosperity (6:28).

Historical and Cultural Background

Trials by ordeal were common in the ancient Near East, usually employed when guilt or innocence was difficult to determine by reliable witness or evidence. In such cases, persons were put into the hands of a deity by exposing them to dangerous situations in which death would otherwise be likely. The assumption was that those charged with a crime were guilty until the gods intervened to prove them innocent. In Daniel's case, however, the ordeal is not intended to prove his guilt or innocence, although its surprising outcome does precisely that.[2]

Even though the custom of corporate responsibility was common in the ancient Near East, the cruel execution of the families of Daniel's accusers is unusual. In one instance, Herodotus (*Hist.* 3.119) notes that Darius I (late sixth century BC) executed a treasonous man along with most of his family—although they may have been suspected of conspiring with him. This is different—even though no more or less horrific—from the well-known practices of wiping out a dynastic line to limit future contenders for the throne or of attempting the genocide of a race of people.[3]

Interpretive Insights

6:19 *At the first light of dawn.* The urgency of the language carries forward from Darius's concern for Daniel's situation in the previous pericope, yet it introduces a new context for this narrative: a moment of truth in which God's power to rescue is dramatically revealed.

6:20 *Daniel, servant of the living God.* The king's acknowledgment of God as "living" separates God from the pagan deities, "which cannot see or hear or understand" (5:23). In contrast, Yahweh "sees" his servant's problem, "hears" his prayers, and acts with awesome power to rescue the faithful and judge the wicked. This theologically rich title for God occurs frequently in the Old Testament (Deut. 5:26; Josh. 3:10; 1 Sam. 17:26, 36; 2 Kings 19:4, 16; Isa. 37:4, 17; Jer. 10:10; 23:36).[4]

has your God, whom you serve continually, been able to rescue you from the lions? Darius's earlier wish, or prayer (6:16), now takes the form of a challenging question, which Daniel answers in the affirmative. Again, the faithful service of the elderly sage to his God is emphasized in the text, although here the Aramaic *pᵉlah* ("to serve, worship") carries more of

> "The men who had falsely accused Daniel were brought in and thrown into the lions' den, along with their wives and children" (6:24). The outcome they had envisioned for Daniel, much like the scene on this ivory plaque found at Nimrud (800–750 BC), became their punishment.

Key Themes of Daniel 6:19–28

- The living God is able to rescue Daniel, who serves him continually, is innocent before him, and trusts in him.
- God uses Daniel's courageous faithfulness as a witness to a pagan world through a pagan king.
- The kingdom of God is everlasting, demonstrated by his signs and wonders in heaven and on earth.

a religious tone in comparison to the noun *'abed* ("slave, servant") used earlier in this verse.

6:21–22 *May the king live forever!* Daniel's use of the standard protocol stands in bold relief with Darius's panicked demeanor. The use of "living"/"live" (*hay/haya'*) in the two greetings (6:20–21) contrasts the usual wish for the king's physical health with the reality of the only truly "living God," who "endures forever" (6:26).

My God sent his angel, and he shut the mouths of the lions. Daniel's identification

Bel and the Dragon

The Greek addition Bel and the Dragon is appended to the canonical book of Daniel as chapter 14 in the Septuagint (OG and Theodotion) and Catholic and Orthodox Bibles (see NRSV) but not in the Masoretic Text followed by Jews and Protestants.[a] The story (42 verses) begins with a theological debate between Daniel and Cyrus the Persian over whose god/God is a "living god." Daniel wins the first round by demonstrating that Cyrus's priests are actually consuming the food that his god Bel appears to consume. Cyrus then claims that a great dragon is a living god (Bel is pictured thus in Babylonian imagery). Daniel dispels this myth by slaying the dragon with poisoned food. Enraged Babylonians think the king has become a Jew, so they throw Daniel into the lions' den, where he remains until rescued by an angel—although after a visit by Habakkuk the prophet from Judea. This court tale draws themes from Daniel 6 yet adds nothing of theological significance to the canonical account.

[a] See C. A. Moore, *Daniel, Esther, and Jeremiah*, 23–38, 117–49; Collins, *Daniel*, 405–19.

of his rescuer as an "angel" (*mal'ak*) recalls Nebuchadnezzar's clarification of the "fourth person" in the furnace (3:28), again linking the narratives. These references also prepare the reader for the following visions (Dan. 7–12), in which such "messengers" play a more active role. The shutting of the lions' mouths most likely finds reference in Hebrews 11:33–34, in which it appears in juxtaposition with "quenched the fury of the flames" (referring to Dan. 3:25–27).

because I was found innocent . . . Nor have I ever done any wrong before you. References to Daniel's faithfulness to God occur repeatedly in this chapter: "trustworthy . . . law of his God" (6:4–5), "prayed . . . as he had done before" (6:10), "your God, whom you serve continually" (6:16, 20), "servant of the living God" (6:20), "because I was found innocent in [God's] sight" (6:22), and "because he had trusted in his God" (6:23). Scripture's primary concern

to reveal God's character includes both his call for faithfulness and his rewards for it.

6:23 *no wound was found on him.* Again, the examination proves the miracle, just as it has done with Daniel's friends, although the accusers are not implied as being among the examiners (3:27).

6:24 *the men who had falsely accused Daniel . . . along with their wives and children.* Community and family identity were highly valued in the ancient Near East. Sometimes in the Old Testament narrative texts this results in family punishment for a crime that an individual has committed (Num. 16:25–33; 2 Sam. 21:1–9; Esther 9:13–14). However, the prophets clearly speak against this practice (Jer. 31:29–30; Ezek. 18), and the judgment here comes from a pagan king. The instant consumption of the guilty by the lions underscores God's miraculous protection of Daniel.

6:25 *Then King Darius wrote.* The second decree comes from the king, without the coercion of Daniel's now-deceased accusers. As such, it carries the power of sincerity, preparing the reader for its rich theological content.

6:26–27 *people must fear and reverence the God of Daniel.* Two pagan kings, Nebuchadnezzar of Babylon (4:3) and Darius the Mede (6:26–27), each issue a royal decree—in strikingly similar poems—to honor the one true God. Not coincidentally these persons mark the beginning and the end of Judah's exile. Nebuchadnezzar also praises God in 2:47; 3:28; and 4:34–35, 37.[5] After reiterating the uniqueness of Daniel's God as the "living God," the king's words turn to God's sovereignty over earthly realms. The explicit language of God's "kingdom"/"dominion" in 2:44

Rembrandt illustrates a portion of chapter 14 in the Septuagint version of Daniel with his oil painting of Daniel and Cyrus before the idol Bel (1633).

and 4:3 occurs again in 7:13–14, 27. This contrasts with the clearly marked transfer of kingdoms from Babylon to Persia in 5:30–31. The reference to "signs and wonders" at the end of the declaration recalls the "rescue" of Daniel's friends from the furnace (3:24–27), as well as the judgment and healing of Nebuchadnezzar (4:1–3, 33–34). The idea of God performing "signs and wonders" easily applies to all three miracles.[6] The usual twofold parallelism of this poem is altered slightly: (1) rescues, (2) performs, (3) heaven/earth.[7] This emphasizes the God in heaven who works his will here on earth (contra the sages' assertion in 2:11).

6:28 *Darius and . . . Cyrus the Persian.* The Semitic conjunction *waw* can be explicative, meaning, "Darius, *that is*, Cyrus the Persian"; compare the NIV alternative reading in 1 Chronicles 5:26 regarding "Pul king of Assyria (that is, Tiglath-Pileser king of Assyria)."[8] This supports the identification of the two names with one person (see "Additional Insights" following the unit on 5:18–31).

Theological Insights

Three qualities of God's person dominate 6:19–28, the dramatic climax to this narrative. First, the living God is able to rescue and reward those who are trustworthy in their lives as witnesses in their world. Second, God is worthy of longtime, faithful service that goes beyond prayer to practice and sacrifice.

Third, the living God alone endures forever as sovereign over his never-ending kingdom.

Teaching the Text

1. *The living God is able to rescue.* Daniel's God is the only living God, in sharp contrast to the dead, false gods of the Median and Persian belief systems. Because of this quality, God is able to rescue faithful servants from impossible circumstances under powerful rulers. When preaching this familiar story, focus on God's ability to deliver, without presuming his intention to do so in every circumstance of our lives. Also, this narrative includes more information about Daniel's faithfulness than any other passage in his book. Without heroizing this elderly Judean exile, call your listeners to "trust" God, to serve God "continually," to be found "innocent" before God and other persons, if they wish to know God's blessing in their lives. Although Daniel is not presented as a model to emulate, he does serve as an example of how God is able to reward and rescue the righteous.

2. *Worship goes beyond words.* Realizing anew God's worthiness can revolutionize

our "worship" of God in our homes, churches, and societies. Although outward practice is the right place to end, it is not where we begin. Encourage your listeners to engage in a disciplined journey to know more intimately the God who calls us to serve him. Call your audience to search the Scriptures to know all they can about God and to search their hearts to know him better personally. Worship flows out of this kind of spiritual experience and relationship. Remind them that worship demonstrates in our lives that God is worthy and therefore extends beyond songs, prayers, and sermons to godly lives lived as a witness to God's person.

3. *God's character and work reflect his enduring kingdom.* Like Daniel, we are servants of the ever-living God in the redemptive act of establishing his never-ending kingdom "on earth as it is in heaven." From his youth, Daniel recognizes that his

> Even King Darius recognizes that God is able to deliver the righteous when he declares that God "has rescued Daniel from the power of the lions" (6:27). In his oil painting *Daniel in the Lions' Den*, Briton Rivière illustrates God's protection as the lions keep their distance from Daniel.

loyalties are to his God and not to the rulers under whom he lives (1:8). Moreover, God reveals to him that God's kingdom replaces all earthly kingdoms (2:44). Encourage your listeners to keep in sharp focus God's purpose and kingdom purposes. In doing so, exhort them to hold loosely their allegiances to political agendas of this transient world and to think first of their citizenship in God's kingdom.

What not to teach. Four mistakes should be avoided when teaching this familiar story. First, do not make the lions metaphors of problems that believers encounter today. Second, do not lessen the fearful situation that Daniel faces by making the lions cute and cuddly friends that talk with him. Third, this passage does not teach that each believer has a personal guardian angel to protect and rescue him or her. Fourth, Darius's decree does not prove a permanent conversion of him or his people.[9]

Illustrating the Text

God is always able to rescue—and sometimes he does so because of one's faith and obedience.

Bible: Genesis 6–9. In the biblical narrative regarding Noah (Gen. 6–9), righteousness is a reason for rescue. There, a depraved humanity grieves God to the point that he chooses to judge their wickedness by a great deluge, while Noah and his small family are spared (6:5–8). God instructs Noah after he completes the ark, "Go into the ark, you and your whole family, because I have found you righteous in this generation" (7:1). The emphasis on Noah's righteousness, resulting in his miraculous rescue from the flood, is confirmed in Hebrews 11:7, when Noah's faith is recorded as righteousness. God is always able to save, and in some cases, like those of Noah and Daniel, righteousness results in physical rescue from death—although this is not always the case. We are called to be righteous because God is worthy, whether he sovereignly chooses to deliver or not.

Worship is more than song, encompassing action, word, and attitude.

Quote: *My Utmost for His Highest*, by Oswald Chambers. We often have a limited perspective on worship. If asked to define it, one might consider examples of "music" or "song," or images of an emotionally charged auditorium filled with colored lights and a driving drumbeat. While worship may include these things, it is not nearly so limited. The modern English term derives from the Old English *weorthscipe* ("worth-ship"), meaning "acknowledgment of worth," which must be demonstrated by both word and deed. Oswald Chambers writes in his widely admired devotional *My Utmost for His Highest* of a more inclusive and holistic dimension of this important practice: "Worship is giving God the best that He has given you."[10] Knowing the God who is worthy and the goodness he has lavished on us turns us toward him in a loving response of praise that encompasses every aspect of our lives.

Our allegiance is to God's kingdom, regardless of our earthly context.

Popular Culture: People today are often fascinated with the danger and political intrigue popularly associated with international spies and the exciting espionage in the life of a secret agent. Examples of this abound in spy novels, films, and television shows, such as Ian Fleming's James Bond series, with films spanning fifty years. Much like an international spy, who lives discreetly in the context of another country by obeying its codes, all the while maintaining core allegiance to his or her homeland and agency, we also are "covert agents." As part of life on earth, we live within the context of human governments and powers and have other allegiances that are part of our daily lives, like voting, obeying the law, and paying taxes. Yet we must always remember that God's kingdom is everlasting and the place of our true citizenship and allegiance (cf. Heb. 11:13–16; 13:14; Phil. 3:20).

Ancient of Days and Son of Man

Big Idea *Envisioning the person and kingdom work of God through the Son of Man can bring comfort and assurance in a dark, unjust, and uncertain world.*

Understanding the Text

The Text in Context

Daniel 7:1–28 is woven into the book's overall literary structure in several ways. First, it resets the chronological narrative of chapters 1–6 by returning to Belshazzar's first year as its historical marker. Second, it completes the first of three parallel pairs of chapters (2 and 7) in the book's concentric, Aramaic center section. Third, as a parallel pair, Daniel 2 and 7 address the same four kingdoms. In addition, Daniel's "vision" in chapter 7 supplements the "vision" he receives regarding Nebuchadnezzar's dream (2:19, 28, 31–45), yet with additional information. Fourth, it is the first of four apocalyptic visions that end the book. Fifth, it is a "symbolic vision,"[1] like the corresponding chapter that follows it.

By this intentional shaping, the author connects the fourth kingdom of Daniel 2 and 7 with the Jewish suffering under Greece in the remaining apocalyptic visions (Dan. 8–12). Taken together, these features identify Daniel 7 as the book's pivotal center—inextricably bound to both halves of the book.[2] Providentially, this chapter in the book of Daniel also provides us with the clearest picture in the Old Testament of the coming of Jesus the Messiah in the New Testament as the Son of Man to inherit the kingdom of God (Mark 14:61–62).[3]

Daniel 7:1–28 is outlined by references to Daniel in the first person (7:2, 15, 28). Within this framework, 7:1–14 uses three identical phrases, "in my vision at night I looked" (7:2, 7, 13), to indicate this section's thought breaks: introduction and three beasts (7:1–6), the fourth beast's judgment by the Ancient of Days (7:7–12), and the appearance of the mortal from heaven receiving God's kingdom (7:13–14).

Historical and Cultural Background

The Median Empire sought to fill the power vacuum caused by Babylon's weaker

Table 1: Symbolic Visions of Daniel 7 and 8

Settings: Belshazzar's first and third years	7:1	8:1
Recipient/seer's firsthand report	7:2–14	8:2–14
Recipient/seer's need for interpretation	7:15–16a, 19–22	8:15–18
Angelic interpretation(s)	7:16b–18, 23–27	8:19–26a
Charge to recipient/seer	—	8:26b
Recipient/seer's reactions	7:28b	8:27

kings (562–539 BC), including Nabonidus, father of Belshazzar (Dan. 5, 7–8). Belshazzar became coregent in 553 BC, while Nabonidus was in Teima for religious reasons. Media remained independent until Cyrus (a vassal king with Median and Persian ancestry) rebelled against Astyages (553–550 BC), gaining control of Media on his way to establishing the Persian Empire (539–331 BC).[4]

Ugaritic literature depicts the Canaanite god El as "father of years," while the Mesopotamian goddess Mami is called "ancient one." Deity images were carried in religious processionals on wheeled thrones, and daily chronicles were kept in royal courts for reference and legal evidence. El and his son Baal were called "cloud riders"—"bringers of rain" and "cosmic warriors" riding on storm chariots.[5]

Daniel 7 reflects images from Mesopotamian religious literature and art in which cosmic wars stir up the sea and hybrid or deformed beasts appear. Although Daniel's vision is original to him, it utilizes materials

familiar to its exilic readers.[6] For a discussion of four-kingdom patterns in the ancient Near East, see "Historical and Cultural Background" in the unit on 2:31–49.

Interpretive Insights

7:1 *In the first year of Belshazzar . . . Daniel had a dream.* This historical reference (553 BC)[7] resets the book's chronology (cf. 6:28; see "Table 1: Chronological and Stylistic Literary Structure of Daniel" in the introduction), highlighting the beginning of Media's power bid before Cyrus's advances (553–550 BC). It also anticipates chapter 8 (550 BC), in which the last three kingdoms of chapters 2 and 7 are named. The Aramaic *hezu*, "vision," recalls Daniel's description of Nebuchadnezzar's first dream (2:28c), reinforcing the intentional parallel

The first beast that Daniel sees in his vision is like a lion with eagle's wings. This glazed-brick reconstruction of a portion of the frieze from the palace walls of Darius I in Susa (510 BC) shows a composite creature with the face and one pair of legs of a lion, the body and ears of a bull, the horns of a goat, and wings and one pair of legs like an eagle.

between chapters 2 and 7. At the same time, the apocalyptic genre and first-person report (7:2) connect this chapter with the following visions (Dan. 8; 9; 10–12). That Daniel "wrote down the substance of his dream" in a first-person dream report suggests his involvement in authoring his book.

7:2–3 *four winds of heaven . . . the great sea. Four great beasts.* Although the turbulent Great Sea could reference the Mediterranean (Josh. 9:1; Ezek. 47:10–28), the apocalyptic context here suggests the primordial waters known in the mythology of the broader Near East.[8] It dipicts the active presence of the Lord of creation, who brings order out of chaos. He controls the destiny of the four beasts that emerge in the darkness.

7:4 *The first was like a lion . . . wings of an eagle.* This image reflects the winged lion from Babylon's Ishtar Gate. Nebuchadnezzar is likened to a lion (Jer. 50:17) and an eagle (Ezek. 17:3–8, 12–15), and the language of "beast," "mind," and "eagle's feathers/wings" mirrors his experience in 4:16, 33. These references, read in the light of "head of gold" status in 2:37–38, represent Nebuchadnezzar's kingship (605–562 BC).

The title "Ancient of Days" alludes to God's existence over all time. Canaanites worshiped the deity El, to whom they gave the title "father of years." This figurine of El was found at Megiddo (1400–1200 BC).

7:5 *a second beast, which looked like a bear.* Being "raised up" suggests aggression (Hosea 13:8). The Aramaic *qum*, "arise," is used regarding the second kingdom in Daniel 2:39. Yahweh stirs up the "Medes" against Babylon (Isa. 13:1, 17–22; Jer. 51:1, 11–13). The "three ribs" (or "tusks") could represent three Median kings (Jer. 51:11, 28) or provinces (Jer. 51:27: "Ararat, Minni and Ashkenaz"). These references, read with the historical marker (Dan. 7:1), parallel "inferior" kingdom (2:39), and references to Media in Daniel (5:31; 6:1–28; 9:1; 11:1) represent Media's rise in power after Nebuchadnezzar's death (562–539 BC).

7:6 *another beast, one that looked like a leopard.* Scripture presents leopards as fast and fierce (Jer. 5:6; Hab. 1:8), like Cyrus's conquests, while "four heads" anticipate the four Persian kings after Cyrus (cf. 11:2). Persia ruled the then-known world (539–331 BC) following the rise of the inferior kingdom of Media (cf. 2:39), making Persia the most likely fulfillment of this beast.

7:7 *a fourth beast . . . different from all the former.* The "terrifying" and "powerful" fourth beast is separated from the previous by the beast's nondescript nature and the extended clause, "in my vision at night I looked" (cf. 7:2). The terms "iron" and "crush" reflect the fourth kingdom in 2:40–43. The "ten horns" anticipate the Hellenistic rulers chronicled in 11:3–39 (see "Table 2: Greek Kings in Daniel 11:5–35" in the unit on 11:2–20), and parallel the (assumed) ten "toes" of 2:41.[9]

7:8 *another horn, a little one.* "While I was thinking" slows the pace, drawing attention to the humanlike "little"

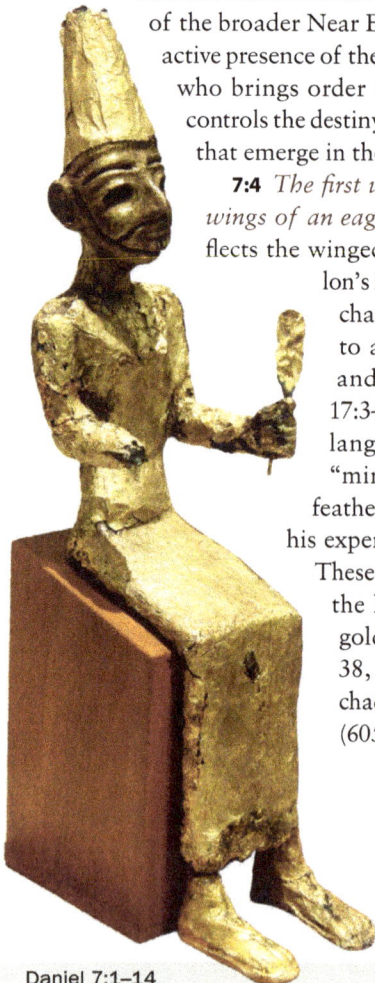

horn that uproots "three" from among ten. This extends the scope of 2:40–43, preparing the reader for an emerging, diabolical character (7:19–25; 8:9–12, 23–25; 11:21–35).

7:9 *the Ancient of Days took his seat.* A poetic description of God's holiness, purity, power, and judgment sets ablaze the dark prose setting (cf. 2:22). The Semitic metaphor "Ancient of Days" describes God's eternality and occurs only here in the Old Testament (Isa. 43:13 may allude to it).[10] The other symbols of God's character appear elsewhere: judgment thrones (Ps. 122:5), sins washed as white as snow/wool (Isa. 1:18), judgment and fire (Jer. 4:4; 17:27), and the symbolic "thousands" and "ten thousands" (Mic. 6:7). This scene takes the reader beyond Daniel's earlier vision (2:34–35, 44–45).

7:11 *the boastful words the horn was speaking.* The arrogant little horn reappears, framed by two God-focused poems (7:9–10, 13–14; the ESV correctly formats the latter). The slaying and burning of the fourth beast is contrasted with the loss of authority, but extended lives, of the previous three. Residual Babylonian, Median, and Persian realms still existed during the Greek era in the fourth to third century BC.

7:13–14 *one like a son of man, coming with the clouds of heaven.* The third repetition of "in my vision . . ." (cf. 7:2, 7) creates another pause in the narrative.[11] The apparent contradiction of a mortal (Aramaic *bar 'enash*) from heaven is striking and puzzling. Moreover, his standing before the Ancient of Days and inheriting his kingdom is recognized in some early Jewish sources as explicitly messianic (*1 Enoch* 46.1; 48.10; 2 Esd. 13).[12] His sharing of divine authority,

glory, sovereignty, worship, and kingship (cf. 2:34–35, 44–45) also strongly suggests a messianic interpretation, forming a remarkable conclusion to this pericope in Daniel's pivotal chapter.[13]

Theological Insights

Daniel 7:1–14 highlights three important dimensions of God's sovereignty over earthly kingdoms. First, God is actively in control of human history, moving toward the establishment of his kingdom. Second, in the end, the Ancient of Days will break forth into human history to judge his enemies and bless his people. Third, God has chosen to bring his kingdom blessings on humanity in the person of the Son of Man, Jesus the Messiah.

Teaching the Text

1. *God's kingdom replaces transient human kingdoms.* This passage is relatively straightforward when read on its own terms: temporal, earthly kings and kingdoms are sure to be replaced by the enduring work of God's kingdom. Focus

on the certainty of the establishment of God's kingdom on this earth, which alone brings order out of chaos and light into darkness. This message is central to the passage and can go a long way toward healing the damage caused by fear of the uncertain world around us. This assurance can unite believers in a strong sense of hope, rather than divide us over speculative details. Reiterated succinctly, it is enough to know that in the end God's eternal kingdom replaces all temporal, earthly kingdoms (cf. Rev. 19:6–22:21).[14]

2. *Appearance of the Ancient of Days.* This is one of the most striking theophanies in the Old Testament. Focus on the eternal God of judgment who, in his imposing purity, commands the heavenly armies while bringing justice to humanity. Explain how God's absolute purity and limitless power can comfort faithful believers as well as confront those living in opposition to God's word and will. Judgment and accountability are not the only aspects of God's character, but these are often neglected in favor of love and grace. Instill a sense of godly fear by inviting your listeners to imagine sitting in the courtroom of the eternal God on the day of reckoning.

3. *Appearance of the Son of Man.* This spectacular messianic image appears at the center of the carefully crafted structure of Daniel's book and is affirmed in the New Testament as an announcement of Jesus's person and ministry. Take some time to show your listeners how important

Ted Larson captures God's holiness, purity, power, and judgment in his depiction of the Ancient of Days from Daniel's vision.

this passage is for Jesus and the New Testament writers (see the sidebar "'Son of Man' Imagery in the Bible"). Contrast the clarity of this text and its New Testament counterparts with the vague depictions associated with angelic appearances in Daniel (e.g., 3:25; 10:5–6). Ponder the price Jesus paid by becoming human to complete God's kingdom purposes (cf. Phil. 2:5–8).

What not to teach. First, a sermon is not the place to debate the identities of the kingdoms. This is not the author's purpose. Express your opinion briefly, with humility, respect, and charity toward those who differ—then, move on. Second, avoid seeking to construct from this text a systematic eschatology regarding the when and where of the establishment of God's kingdom. Third, although the messianic reference is central, significant, and personal, there is no clear indication as to whether it speaks of Jesus's first coming or his return, or whether his kingdom is literal or spiritual—or a combination of both.

Illustrating the Text

We can be confident that God's ultimate victory is assured.

Human Experience: Most people do not want to know the final score of an important sporting event or the ending to a suspenseful novel before they watch or read it. Rather, we cherish the discovery, excitement, and drama of the journey, because we do these things for entertainment. But our experience with real life is different, especially when it involves the darkness and intensity of human evil and global strife. Will countries or religions that violently oppress Christians ultimately prevail? Will militant terrorism infiltrate and overrun even large and powerful countries like the United States? The good news is that while we cannot know the *stages* of history yet ahead of us, we can have a bold confidence because we know the *final outcome*. The redemptive drama of human history will conclude with God winning the victory over evil and fully establishing his eternal kingdom. Moreover, as believers, we will be part of that kingdom forever.

God's power and majesty as judge are beautiful and praiseworthy.

Literature: *Paradise Lost*, **by John Milton.** Though it deviates from Scripture's narrative, Milton's classic *Paradise Lost* depicts Satan's fall and judgment before creation, amply illustrating the glorious and terrible majesty of the Ancient of Days, while at the same time not losing sight of God's love and grace:

> . . . Him the Almighty Power
> Hurled headlong flaming from th' ethereal sky

> With hideous ruin and combustion down
> To bottomless perdition, there to dwell
> In adamantine chains and penal fire,
> Who durst defy th' Omnipotent to arms.
> . . . .
> With glory and power to judge both quick & dead,
> To judge th' unfaithful dead, but to reward
> His faithful, and receive them into bliss . . .[15]

Even the most poetic of human words used to describe God pale in comparison to the reality of his glory and might.

Son of Man imagery is a doorway to sharing the gospel.

Bible: Christ's depiction as the "Son of Man" (affirmed by all four Gospel writers) represents his person and work as God's unique and sole solution for humanity's plight. In Mark's Gospel alone the Son of Man "has authority on earth to forgive sins" (2:10); is "Lord even of the Sabbath" (i.e., the torah; 2:28); "must suffer many things and be rejected" by the Jewish leadership and "be killed and after three days rise again" (8:31); came "to serve, and to give his life as a ransom for many" (10:45); is seated "at the right hand of the Mighty One," and will return "on the clouds of heaven" with "great power and glory" (13:26; 14:62). The Son of Man, who was before time and was incarnated in time, will be the ultimate victor at the end of time. He alone is God's chosen means to establish his kingdom on earth.

Triumph of God's People and Kingdom

Big Idea *Although details remain mysterious and persecutions come, God defeats all forces of evil in the end and establishes his everlasting kingdom, in which his holy ones share.*

Understanding the Text

The Text in Context

See the unit on 7:1–14 for a discussion of the larger context, structure, and comparisons of this chapter. Within this framework, 7:15–28 is outlined primarily by three personal responses of Daniel that frame its question-and-answer core. First, the confused seer inquires about the vision and discovers that the beasts represent kings and kingdoms (7:15–18). Second, he probes more deeply regarding the fourth beast and the little horn, learning of a war against the "holy ones" that leads to the establishment of God's kingdom (7:19–27). Third, this section closes with Daniel's response to the vision and God's charge to him (7:28).

Historical and Cultural Background

Although interpreting angels appear in biblical apocalyptic literature (e.g., Zech. 1:6–6:8) from the sixth century forward, they find no counterpart in Mesopotamian texts. Daniel's visions are situated at the dawn of this age. "Holy ones" speaking on behalf of deities are usually identified as supernatural beings in Canaanite and Aramaic literature, as well as in the Dead Sea Scrolls. However, in other Jewish apocalyptic texts they are often called "angels" (Wis. 5:5; 10:10), or sometimes human beings, specifically, the Jewish people (Wis. 18:9; 3 Macc. 6:9).[1]

In *Enuma Elish* and the Anzu Myth, the "Tablet of Destinies" controls "times and laws," something the little horn attempts to do in Daniel 7:24–25.[2]

The text mentions ten kings plus one. However, more than ten appear historically in the relevant eras of Greece and Rome (the two candidates for the fourth kingdom), with no standard list of "ten" plus a significant "one."[3] For a discussion of the four-kingdom pattern in the ancient Near East, see "Historical and Cultural Background" in the unit on 2:31–49.

Interpretive Insights

7:15–16 *I, Daniel, was troubled in spirit.* In the second half of his book, Daniel is no longer the wise sage or courageous prophet as in earlier narratives (Dan. 2; 4–5). However, it is common in apocalyptic literature (like Dan. 7–12) for the seer-recipient of a vision to seek its meaning from a mediating angel ("one of those standing there"), to not fully understand what he has heard, and to be deeply disturbed by the traumatic events foreseen.[4]

7:17 *The four great beasts are four kings.* The beasts from 7:3–7 arise "from the earth," suggesting that this scene is not that of a heavenly courtroom. However, their designation as "kings" and "kingdoms" (cf. 2:39–42, 44) suggests these terms (Aramaic *melek* and *malku*) are sometimes used interchangeably (perhaps the first "king" represents each new "kingdom"). Ignoring the first three, the angel explains only the fourth beast/kingdom. Therefore, in order to identify the others one must rely on references to the first three in 2:37–43 and 7:3–8, as well as the inferences regarding kings from Media, Persia, and Greece in chapters 8 and 10–11.

7:18 *the holy people of the Most High will receive the kingdom.* The NIV translates the Aramaic *qaddish* (literally, "holy ones") as "holy people." This word and related Hebrew terms usually describe angels (Deut. 33:2; Ps. 89:5, 7; Dan. 4:13, 23; 8:13), although they also can refer to priests (Num. 16:7; Ps. 106:16 [NIV: "consecrated"]), and even Israel in general (Exod. 19:6; Ps. 34:9). The construct phrase "people of the holy ones" occurs in the mirror-image vision (Dan. 8:24 NRSV), perhaps connoting "people

Key Themes of Daniel 7:15–28

- When four earthly kingdoms have come and gone, God's holy people will share in his everlasting kingdom.
- An evil ruler from the fourth kingdom will oppose God and oppress his people for a short time.
- Daniel is deeply troubled by this new kind of vision, which he does not understand and therefore keeps to himself.

consisting of holy ones." The term here could mean "angels" or "people" (see the sidebar "Nondivine, Heavenly Beings in Daniel" in the unit on 3:24–30).[5] In reality, the earthly struggles of God's people under oppression are also spiritual struggles in which angels participate (cf. Dan. 10). And ultimately all of God's "holy ones" (saints and angels) will share his kingdom (Matt. 25:31–46). There may be an intentional ambiguity in this vision, alluding to both realms. However, the language of the struggle of the Jews in Daniel 11 implies that the "holy ones" are "people" in chapters 7 and 8.[6]

7:20–22 *the horn that looked more imposing than the others.* The vision in 7:9–14 is enlarged here to include "waging war against" and "defeating" God's people, which finds historic fulfillment in Jewish suffering under Antiochus IV (175–164 BC).[7] However, there is no

The horn with a boastful mouth, who wages war, defeats the holy people and "will speak against the Most High and oppress his holy people" (7:25), found its historic fulfillment in Antiochus IV Epiphanes, whose face is shown on this coin. He vented his frustrations with Rome on the Jews by ordering a Sabbath attack on Jerusalem, which resulted in the death or enslavement of most of its Jewish inhabitants. The city walls were destroyed, and pagan sacrifices were offered at the temple newly dedicated to Zeus. All Jewish religious practices were prohibited while he was in power.

Symbolism of Three and a Half Years in Daniel

References in Daniel to a three-and-a-half-year era of Jewish persecution by an evil ruler contain figurative terms, or numbers that are rounded or approximate. In 7:25 and 12:7 it is "a time, [two] times and half a time." Similarly, in 9:26–27, the desecration of the sanctuary occurs during the last half of seven years. In 8:13–14, the same event lasts for "2,300 evenings and mornings," which most likely means 1,150 days. Finally, the great "distress" at the end of the age will last approximately 1,290–1,335 days. None of these matches three and a half years exactly in a solar (1,278.38 days) or lunar (1,260 days) calculation, although each is close enough to be identifiable. The deliberate lack of precision is common in apocalyptic language.

consensus on when "the time came when they possessed the kingdom." This may point initially to the Hasmonean Kingdom (second century BC), or to a spiritual kingdom at Jesus's first coming (Luke 17:20–21), or to a kingdom more fully and literally established after his return (Matt. 25:34; Luke 19:11–12). Further, it may be that the conditionality of God's covenant with his people, combined with their unfaithfulness, pushes that time into the eschatological future.[8]

7:23 *The fourth beast is a fourth kingdom.* The reasons the angel does not interpret the first three beasts may be because the shift of power from Media to Persia is already in process (see the comments on 7:1), or it may simply be because he wants to focus on the fourth kingdom and its kings as he does in his explicit emphasis on Greece in chapters 8 and 10–12. Given these contexts, and in light of the descriptions of the second and third kingdoms in 2:37–43 and 7:3–8, the fourth kingdom is most likely Greece (331–146 BC; see "Additional Insights" following the unit on 2:31–49).

7:24 *The ten horns are ten kings . . . After them another king will arise.* Horns symbolize strength and power but also pride and honor for good (1 Sam. 2:10; Ps. 148:14) as well as evil (Jer. 48:25; Lam. 2:3). Here they describe the line of kings within the fourth kingdom that leads to a blasphemous and oppressive king. The exact referents for the numbering of the kings ("ten," including "three" that are "uprooted" by an eleventh "one," 7:7–8) are not explained in Daniel 7, although this text prepares the reader for the more explicit descriptions in chapters 8 and 11. The number "ten" represents the rulers of the Hellenistic Empire from Alexander the Great until the rise of Antiochus IV, while "three" indicates those from whom the latter stole the throne in 175 BC (see comments on 11:3–4; also "Table 2: Greek Kings in Daniel 11:5–35" in the unit on 11:2–20).[9]

7:25–26 *He will speak against the Most High . . . try to change the set times and the laws.* The first clause may be the source of "antichrist" language in the New Testament (see the sidebar "References to the 'Antichrist' in the Bible" in the unit on 11:21–39).[10] In its Old Testament context, such language points to second-century BC prohibitions against Jews observing Mosaic laws and the corollary requirements to observe pagan practices—with death penalties—under Antiochus IV (cf. 8:9–14; 11:30–35; 1 Macc. 1; 2 Macc. 6). Similar, yet varied, references to the symbolic expression "time, times and half a time" (Dan. 8:14; 9:27; 12:7, 11–12) suggest the meaning of approximately three and a half years. The last of the Jewish persecutions by Antiochus, including the desecration of Jerusalem's temple, lasted about this long (167–164 BC; 1 Macc. 4:54). After this, "his power" was "taken away," when Antiochus IV died from illness in 164 BC.

7:27 *His kingdom will be an everlasting kingdom.* The image of the "one like a son of man" inheriting the divine kingdom in 7:13–14 is rejoined here, adding the "holy people of the Most High," whom he represents. However, worship and obedience are appropriately connected only to "him."[11]

7:28 *I kept the matter to myself.* The chapter concludes with Daniel in the same state of mind described in 7:15.

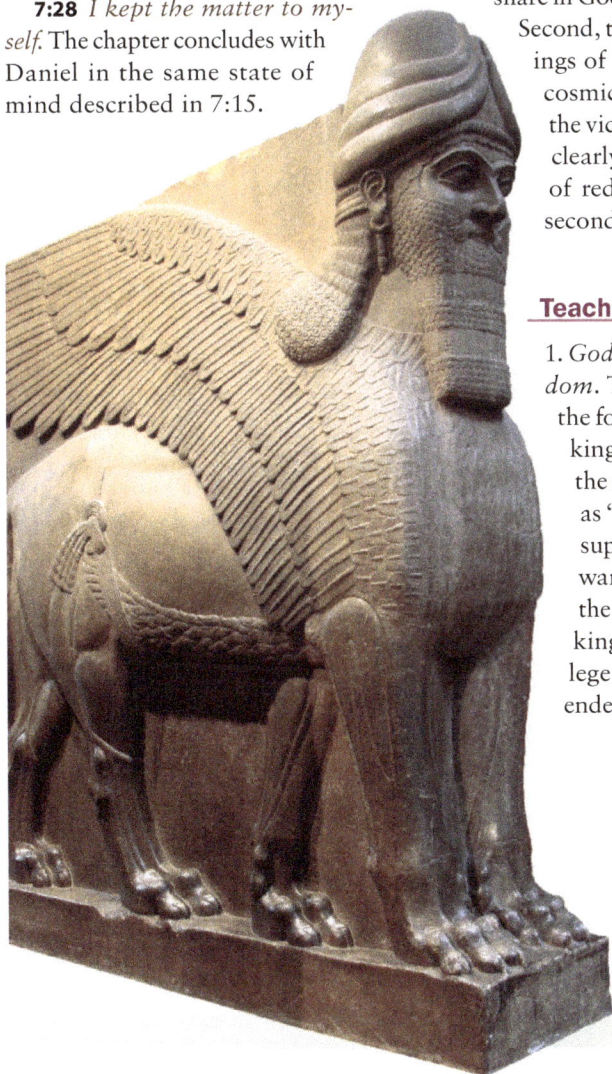

Although 7:1 speaks of his "writing down the substance of his dream," his keeping the matter to himself suggests that this information was not made public at that time.

Theological Insights

Daniel 7:15–28 presents the reader with three assurances about the establishment of God's kingdom. First, when the kingdoms of this world are gone, God's people will share in God's everlasting kingdom forever. Second, the earthly struggles and sufferings of the saints are part of a larger cosmic struggle in which God gains the victory for his people. Third, God clearly reveals the essential message of redemptive history, even though secondary details remain obscure.

Teaching the Text

1. *God's holy people share God's kingdom.* The writer passes over three of the four kingdoms to say that God's kingdom and people will prevail in the end. Assure believers today that as "people of the Most High," God supports them in times of spiritual warfare and suffering. Emphasize the certain establishment of God's kingdom in the end and the privilege of partnering with him in this endeavor. In a world of injustice, let

In Daniel's vision, the fourth beast has eleven horns. In the ancient Near East, horns were typically featured on the headgear of deities. The composite creature shown here, known as a *lamassu*, guarded the entrance to rooms in the Assyrian king's palace at Nimrud (865–860 BC). It has the body of a lion with wings and a human face. Three sets of horns, which represent strength and power, decorate its helmet.

them know the Ancient of Days will render judgment in favor of righteous saints and that the forces of evil will get the judgment they deserve in the same cosmic trial. In an uncertain world, help your listeners realize the eternal stability of God's sovereign kingdom in which they share.

2. *God's holy people share a cosmic struggle*. This passage reveals that the fourth kingdom will bring suffering for God's holy people, and that their earthly struggles and sufferings are part of a larger cosmic struggle in which God gains the victory on their behalf. Regardless of when one understands this vision to apply, it can assure believers today that we are not alone in our efforts to live lives that honor God. For a wicked, anti-God person to assault God's people is tantamount to setting oneself against the Most High God. Remind your listeners that their suffering for the sake of God's name will end at the appointed time, after which they will be delivered, vindicated, and rewarded in his kingdom.

3. *God's message is clear, even in the context of obscure details*. The essential message of this text is intended to be clear to the ancient and modern readers: God's kingdom replaces earthly kingdoms, and God cares about his people and grants them a share in his everlasting kingdom. Regretfully, an inordinate amount of time and effort is wasted, and a largely unnecessary

Daniel's visions show that earthly kingdoms will rise and fall, but ultimately God's kingdom will replace all earthly kingdoms. Daniel lived when the Babylonian Empire was at its height, and he saw the rise of the Persian Empire. From history we know that the Greek Empire next dominated the western world as a result of the conquests of Alexander the Great. This marble portrait of Alexander the Great is from the second to first century BC.

division is perpetuated, in an evangelical dispute over that which is not clear in this text. Legitimate discussions may occur between those interested in identifying these kingdoms, but these should not cloud the text's essential message. Daniel struggles with this new kind of vision, but most likely because it foresees the suffering of his people. In this sense, his concerns are personal and pragmatic, not esoteric and theoretical.

What not to teach. First, it is not necessary to insist that the "holy ones" are "angels" or "people." Either way, the essential message remains the same: we live in a world of spiritual struggle, and the forces of heaven are warring on our behalf. Second, the identity of kingdoms, including the timing of God's kingdom, is not clarified in this text. Help your listeners to live with the intentional mystery of apocalyptic visions. Acknowledge that something of kingdom significance began with Jesus's coming and will be fully realized when he returns.

Illustrating the Text

Believers are privileged members of God's heavenly army.

Lyrics: "The Battle Hymn of the Republic," by Julia Ward Howe. Howe (1819–1910) was a New York City abolitionist, social activist, and poet during the tumultuous American Civil War in the 1860s. She also penned the patriotic classic "The Battle Hymn of the Republic," an anthem proclaiming the victory of God's kingdom in the style of a Union Army hymn. Apart from a purely nationalist misuse, its repeating chorus, "Glory, glory, hallelujah!" and these familiar verses capture the privilege of sharing in the ultimate victory of God's *heavenly* kingdom at Christ's return and participating in his *spiritual* army now:

> Mine eyes have seen the glory of the
> coming of the Lord,
> He is trampling out the vintage where
> the grapes of wrath are stored;
> He hath loosed the fateful lightning of
> His terrible swift sword,
> His truth is marching on.
> . . . .
> He has sounded forth the trumpet that
> shall never call retreat,
> He is sifting out the hearts of men be-
> fore His judgment-seat;
> Oh, be swift, my soul to answer him,
> be jubilant, my feet!
> Our God is marching on.[12]

Even in the midst of severe oppression, God is working on behalf of his people.

Church History: The faithful witness of God's people throughout history as they have faced suffering and oppression with certainty of, and faithfulness to, the truth brings comfort to Christians in the twenty-first century. For example, Christian oppression by the totalitarian state of North Korea—perhaps one of the most challenging places to live as a believer—requires churches to operate underground. Many believers are imprisoned in labor camps, and in the spring of 2014, thirty-three were sentenced to death for receiving financial support to develop house churches—an attempted overthrow of the regime, in the government's eyes. Though this oppression is severe, the suffering inflicted upon Christians is part of the ultimate battle, which God has already won. No matter how great the sacrifice, suffering always has meaning, because God will vindicate us in the end.

We must never lose sight of the forest by staring at the trees.

Human Experience: We all have had experiences in which we have become so focused on what is before our eyes that we miss what is happening around us (such as using a smartphone while walking and suddenly running into a group of people). The conventional wisdom of the cautionary expression "I can't see the forest for the trees" is important for the reader of apocalyptic visions. While the study of such texts in their remarkable detail (the "trees") is a good thing, it must never overtake an understanding of the overall message of the context (the "forest"). A healthy balance is needed to explore the text fully and apply its truth meaningfully in our lives. Both the detail of each tree and the grandeur of the great forest depict the eternal beauty and might of God as Creator.

Spiritual Warfare and Jewish Suffering

Big Idea *Even though powerful, evil rulers oppose God and his angels, persecute his people, and defile his sanctuary, God emerges victorious in the end.*

Understanding the Text

The Text in Context

Daniel 8:1–27 is woven into the book's overall literary structure in several ways. First, it is the second of Daniel's four apocalyptic visions, as well as the second of two paired, symbolic visions (chaps. 7 and 8). Second, it advances the already reset chronology of chapter 7. Third, it begins the concentric Hebrew section of Daniel (chaps. 8–12) that parallels the book's Hebrew prologue (chap. 1). Fourth, it forms a chiastic pair with the literary unit of Daniel 10–12, sharing a common focus on Greek persecutions of Judea, while framing chapter 9, where the mysterious "seventy sevens" appear.[1]

The focus in 8:1–14 on two beasts (ram and goat, with the latter leading to a blasphemous little horn) provides an informative parallel to the previous vision (7:1–14) of four beasts (lion, bear, leopard, and nondescript, with the last leading to a blasphemous little horn). However, instead of concluding with God's kingdom like chapter 7, this chapter ends with the persecutions of God's people under the last kingdom and its little horn, giving only a hint of hope. This demonstrates the importance of the writer's connection of chapter 7 with the rest of the apocalyptic visions.

In 8:1–27, the resumptive "I, Daniel" marks the chapter's beginning, middle, and end (8:1, 15, 27), precisely as it did in the previous vision (7:2 [see NRSV], 15, 28). Within this context, 8:1–14 divides into four parts: the vision's setting and the appearance of the ram (8:1–4), the struggle between the ram and the goat (8:5–8), the struggle between the little horn and God's people (8:9–12), and a conversation between two angels (8:13–14).

Historical and Cultural Background

This text is set in Belshazzar's third year (550 BC), when Cyrus defeated Astyages, uniting the Medes and the Persians to conquer Babylon by 539 BC.[2] The focus of the chapter, however, is on the Greek Empire of Alexander the Great, who conquered Darius III of Persia (335–331 BC) to

replace Persian rule of Asia with Hellenism. Alexander died prematurely in 323 BC, leaving his empire to his four generals, with warring factions developing between the Ptolemies and the Seleucids. Antiochus IV Epiphanes (175–164 BC) arose from the latter to persecute the Jews in Judea.

Ancient Susa, where Daniel's vision is located, was the major city of the province of Elam, lying about two hundred miles east of Babylon. Nebuchadnezzar brought it under Babylonian control in his early conquests, and Darius I (522–486 BC) later made it Persia's administrative capital. The Ulai Canal is closely associated with Susa in Akkadian and classical sources.[3]

The host of heaven in the ancient Near East was commonly understood as the assembly of the gods, often represented as planets or stars. In the Akkadian myth Erra and Ishum, the starry host represents one

- Early in Belshazzar's reign, Daniel envisions the rise of three empires.

- A king from the last empire opposes God and his heavenly armies and persecutes God's people in Judea.

- After a short but intense time of Jewish suffering, Jerusalem's defiled sanctuary is reconsecrated.

side of a cosmic battle. The use of these phrases here puts an earthly struggle into a larger theological context.[4]

Interpretive Insights

8:1 *third year of King Belshazzar's reign*. Intentionally reflecting the historical marker in 7:1, this chapter marks the end of Media's power bid (553–550 BC), when Cyrus gains control over his grandfather Astyages to combine their forces against Babylon. It also forms the backdrop for the era of the uneven horns of the ram (8:3–4), which represent "the kings of Media and Persia" (8:20).

8:2 *In my vision . . . in the citadel of Susa in the province of Elam*. Geographical markers move the locus of the text from Media, with its capital at Ecbatana, to Persia (Hebrew *'elam*), with its capital at Susa. Daniel's visionary presence in Susa is not physical.

8:3–4 *a ram with two horns . . . charged toward the west*. "Horns" symbolized strength in the ancient Near East. Their growth here in differing stages and to differing lengths contrasts the realities of individual kings and kingships of Media and Persia. These forces are incorporated into a single animal, which eventually represents the enduring and all-encompassing Persian Empire.[5] The directions do not indicate sequence, as Cyrus moved northwest from

Susa toward Media and Lydia and then returned south toward Babylon.

8:5 *a goat with a prominent horn . . . came from the west.* The historical sweep of these verses is compressed. The narrator quickly moves from Babylon (8:1) to Media and Persia (8:3–4, 20), and to Greece two centuries later (8:5–14, 21). The single horn on the male goat represents the rule of Alexander the Great (336–323 BC), who rapidly extended Greek rule across Persia. The goat crossing the ancient world "without touching the ground" illustrates his strength and speed.

8:6–7 *I saw it attack the ram furiously . . . The ram was powerless.* Alexander's conquest of Persia was accomplished in four major military victories, in as many years, at Granicus, Issus, Gaugamela, and the Persian Gates (334–330 BC). The Persian "ram . . . beside the canal" at this time represents Darius III (335–331 BC).

8:8 *the large horn was broken off . . . four prominent horns grew up.* Alexander's young sons were murdered after his death (323 BC). Then the empire was divided between his generals "toward the four winds of heaven": Cassander (Macedonia and Thrace), Lysimachus (Asia Minor), Seleucus (Syria and Mesopotamia), and Ptolemy (Egypt). The Ptolemies (323–144 BC) and the Seleucids (311–164 BC) emerged as dominant, warring dynasties.

8:9 *Out of one of them came another horn, which started small.* The Hebrew terms *qeren* and *tsa'ir* (NIV: "another *horn*, which started *small*") are synonymous with the Aramaic *qeren* and *ze'er* (NIV: "another *horn, a little one*") in 7:8. This suggests

In Daniel 8, the goat with the horn represents Alexander the Great, and the ram it tramples represents the Persian ruler Darius III, whose armies were soundly defeated by those commanded by Alexander. This mosaic depicts a major battle between Alexander and Darius III.

that the last kingdoms in both chapters are the same: Greece (see "Additional Insights" following the unit on 2:31–49). The arrogant king remains Antiochus IV (175–164 BC). His three-directional growth reflects Antiochus's military campaigns targeting Egypt in the "south" (1 Macc. 1:16–19), Persia in the "east" (1 Macc. 3:31; 6:1, 5, 56; 2 Macc. 9:1–2), and the province of Judea, "the Beautiful Land" ("land" is implied; the full title *'erets hatsebi* appears in Dan. 11:16, 41). This title speaks of Judea's religious significance, not physical beauty.

8:10 *it reached the host of the heavens . . . some of the starry host.* The term *tsaba'* connotes "army" (NIV: "host").[6] Here, the language of "heaven" versus "earth," and "stars," suggests Antiochus comes against angelic forces. This lifts the eyes of the reader to see God at work to protect his people in times of persecution.

8:11 *the commander of the army of the LORD.* The Masoretic Text reads only "prince of the army" (*sar hatsaba'*). The NIV's insertion "of the LORD" with small capitals (also 8:12–13) is based on over two hundred occurrences of "LORD of hosts" (*yhwh tseba'ot*) in the Old Testament (e.g., Jer. 25:32). In Daniel, the covenant name Yahweh occurs only in chapter 9. The reference here could allude to the archangel Michael, who is called Israel's chief and great "prince" in 10:13, 21; and 12:1.[7]

it took away the daily sacrifice . . . sanctuary was thrown down. The vision refocuses on an earthly scene involving God's people. Antiochus not only bans Mosaic practices in Jerusalem but also desecrates the temple by erecting a bust of Zeus, sacrificing a pig on the altar, and burning Torah scrolls (1 Macc. 1:41–59; 2 Macc. 6:1–6). This renders the sacred precinct unfit (*shalak*, "thrown down")[8] for the morning and evening sacrifices (Exod. 29:38–41; Num. 28:3–8).[9]

8:12 *Because of rebellion, the* LORD's *people . . . were given over to it.* The NIV's "rebellion" (*pesha'*) is better translated as "transgression,"[10] a common Mosaic term for offenses against God and people (Lev. 16:16 [NIV: "rebellion"]; Gen. 31:36 [NIV: "crime"]). Even though the crimes of Antiochus IV precede this statement, the Jews also suffer because of their offense toward God.[11] Historically, many Jews compromised their faith to comply with Antiochus's Hellenizing policies (Dan. 11:32; 1 Macc. 1:11–15, 41–53).

8:13–14 *It will take 2,300 evenings and mornings.* If "evenings" and "mornings" are read separately—effectively making 1,150 days—the time until the sanctuary's reconsecration corresponds to the three and a half years mentioned elsewhere in Daniel (7:25; 9:27; 12:7, 11). This is consistent with two "daily sacrifices" made each day. But if a collective "evening and morning" connotes one day (cf. Gen. 1), this period

parallels the last "seven" (years) in Daniel 9:27. The latter might reflect the time beginning with Antiochus's murder of the high priest Onias III in 170 BC. Either way, the same general time of suffering is in view.[12] The temple's rededication occurred in 164 BC, when the holiday of Hanukkah was established (1 Macc. 4:36–59).

Theological Insights

Daniel 8:1–14 turns noticeably darker than the vision of chapter 7. Three facets of God's sovereignty are embedded in this pericope, calling to mind that which God reveals in the light. First, the Lord oversees the shifting of earthly kingdoms. Second, God is with his people in their struggle against evil, even as those forces assault the heavenly armies and even God himself. Third, regardless of how intense the struggle becomes, or whether others compromise, God sets a limit on his people's sufferings.

Teaching the Text

1. *God is in control.* Although God permits us to experience times when the instability of world powers darkens our perspective, we must remember that God remains sovereign over human history. At no time has it been easier to illustrate the many reasons for the fear, anxiety, and depression that trouble so many believers today. We have instant visual access to images that represent the sum of our fears. Draw from the theology of Daniel's narratives in which God establishes and removes kings and kingdoms as he pleases, and shine this light into the darkness of this vision, and into our world today. Remind your listeners

The reign of Antiochus IV brought great suffering to God's people living in Judea. In his frenzied attempt to Hellenize the Jewish population, he attacked Jerusalem, dedicated its temple to Zeus, and there sacrificed a pig on an altar built for the Greek god. Pigs were acceptable sacrifices in Greek and Roman culture, but as an unclean animal under Jewish law, it desecrated the Jerusalem temple. The painting on this drinking cup depicts two young men bringing a young boar as a sacrificial offering (510–500 BC).

your listeners that there is hope beyond despair. Sometimes our suffering comes because of the sin of our persecutors; sometimes it is because we, or others in our community, have sinned; and sometimes God simply does not reveal the reason we suffer. Regardless, God allows his people to suffer. Give your listeners hope that their suffering is not in vain, that it produces patience and godly character. Let them know that God's all-sufficient grace will not allow them to suffer beyond what the faithful can endure. Assure them that suffering will end when God's kingdom is fully established here on earth as it is in heaven.

What not to teach. First, refrain from seeking to identify the meaning of every detail of the symbolism in this vision. The text simply does not provide this information. Second, one need not decide whether the "2,300 evenings and mornings" approximate seven years or three and a half years. Either way, it fits into the same short time of suffering in Daniel. Third, a spiritual struggle against evil need not degenerate into a political agenda. Daniel distinguishes only between the kingdoms of this world and the kingdom of God.

that, as citizens of God's kingdom, we have a bright and enduring hope because the mortal from heaven (cf. 7:13–14) has come to receive the eternal kingdom of God and has won the battle necessary to secure it.

2. *God is with us.* God's people must remember that he shares our struggle against evil. Recognizing this truth can give us confidence to resist evil at a personal level. Emphasize the power of the Holy Spirit available to believers, and broaden their vision to see the community of believers who struggle with them. Scripture assures us that our struggle is spiritual, involving the powerful hosts of heaven, which are ultimately under God's command. Remembering this fact calls us to take up the cause of resisting evil. Challenge your listeners to refuse compromise as they engage in spiritual warfare.

3. *There is a time and purpose for suffering.* Although God allows significant times of suffering to come upon his people, assure

Illustrating the Text

Remember what you learned in the light as you live in a dark and needy world.

Bible: **Ephesians 6:10–13.** Imagine being held in a strange place of darkness under the control and evil intent of a hostile person—in part, because of your own failures. Just the thought of such an experience produces anxiety and fear. How could a believer face such an experience and survive?

The apostle Paul urges the Ephesians with these words:

> Finally, be strong in the Lord and in his mighty power. Put on the full armor of God, so that you can take your stand against the devil's schemes. For our struggle is not against flesh and blood, but against the rulers, against the authorities, against the powers of this dark world and against the spiritual forces of evil in the heavenly realms. Therefore put on the full armor of God, so that when the day of evil comes, you may be able to stand your ground, and after you have done everything, to stand. (Eph. 6:10–13)

God as our captain is both vanguard and rearguard.

Film: *We Were Soldiers.* Actor, director, and producer Mel Gibson's 2001 war drama, *We Were Soldiers*, follows the stories of a group of US Army brothers in arms in the first major battle of the Vietnam War at Ia Drang (1965). In it, Lieutenant Colonel Hal Moore (Gibson) pledges to his men: "This I swear, before you and before Almighty God, that when we go into battle, I will be the first to set foot on the field, and I will be the last to step off, and I will leave no one behind." He keeps this promise by always standing beside his men while leading them in crisis and staying in the fight until all are off the battlefield. God not only has entered into our spiritual battles against sin and death—and won the ultimate victory—but remains with us as we engage in such warfare daily.

Suffering, in part due to sin, requires repentance and faith.

Lyrics: **"I Still Believe," by Michael Been and James Paul Goodwin.** Popular Christian vocalist Russ Taff performed an inspiring pop-rock hit in 1987 titled "I Still Believe." The song reflects the intense struggles of Elijah (1 Kings 19:1–9) and Jonah (Jon. 2:1–9):

I been in a cave
For forty days
Only a spark
To light my way
I want to give out
I want to give in
This is our crime
This is our sin
. . . .
Through the pain
And the grief
Through the lies
Through the storms
Through the cries
And through the wars
Oh, I still believe
. . . .
Flat on my back
Out at sea
Hopin' these waves
Don't cover me
I'm turned and tossed
Upon the waves
When the darkness comes
I feel the grave
But I still believe
. . . .
Through the shame
And through the grief
Through the heartache
Through the tears
Through the waiting
Through the years
For people like us
In places like this
We need all the hope
That we can get
Oh, I still believe.[13]

The Rise of Media, Persia, and Greece

Big Idea *God reveals with measured detail a future that includes suffering for his people, but he assures them that he will triumph over the forces of evil.*

Understanding the Text

The Text in Context

See the unit on 8:1–14 for a discussion of the larger context, structure, and comparisons of this chapter. Against this backdrop, 8:15–27 begins and ends with the resumptive "I, Daniel" and another reference to the Ulai Canal (8:16). The explicit mention of the Medes, the Persians, and the Greeks in the interpretation—with an emphasis on the last—recalls the explicit identification of, and emphasis on, Nebuchadnezzar's Babylon in chapter 2. Also, the extended focus on the Greeks is consistent with this chapter's parallel in Daniel 10–12, as well as with the similar emphasis on the last kingdom in chapters 2 and 7. Finally, the sealing of the vision parallels Daniel "keeping the matter to himself" in 7:28.

Within this context, 8:15–27 divides into four parts: Daniel's encounter with the angelic messengers (8:15–18); the identification of the ram as the kings of Media and Persia, and the goat as Greece (8:19–22); the struggle between the little horn and God's people (8:23–26); and Daniel's reaction to the vision (8:27).

Historical and Cultural Background

Gabriel's interpretation of the vision's imagery aligns with Alexander's conquest of Persia in 334–330 BC. Shortly after Alexander's death in 323 BC, the Greek Empire, which extended south to Egypt and east to the borders of India, divided into four smaller kingdoms under the rule of his generals: Cassander, Lysimachus, Seleucus, and Ptolemy. From these the Ptolemies (Egypt, 323–146 BC) and the Seleucids (Syria, 311–164 BC) became the two warring factions within the Greek Empire (apart from Macedonia) that lasted into the second century BC. Regretfully, Judea was situated between them and suffered accordingly. The phrase "latter part of their reign" (8:23) foresees the severe persecutions of the Jews by Antiochus IV, as well as the Maccabean Revolts that led to the reconsecration of the temple in Jerusalem in 164 BC and the death of

Antiochus IV that same year (recounted in 1 and 2 Maccabees).[1]

The sealing of a scroll was common for Assyrian esoteric texts of this nature as early as the eighth century BC. This could be done by tying a string around the scroll, putting soft clay over the knot, and pressing it with a carved seal, or one could put the scroll in a jar and seal the lid. The purpose was to hide the secret text from the uninitiated.[2]

Interpretive Insights

8:15 *I, Daniel, was watching the vision and trying to understand it.* Daniel is no longer the wise sage as in earlier narratives (Dan. 2; 4–5) but the seer of a vision he does not understand, as in chapter 7. As such, he must obtain the meaning of this vision from a mediating angel "who looked like a man." The angelic messenger is described as a *geber*, "strong man" or "warrior." However, in Daniel the term also refers to Daniel and his friends (2:25; 3:12), as well as Babylonians (3:8; 6:24).

8:16 *Gabriel, tell this man the meaning of the vision.* A "human" (*'adam*; NIV: "man's") voice comes from over the Ulai Canal, calling to "Gabriel" ("warrior of God"), a play on *geber* in 8:15, identifying him as "the one who looked like a man." The voice may be directly from God[3] (cf. Ezek. 1:28) or from another angel.[4] In the Old Testament, only the book of Daniel names angels: Gabriel (8:16; 9:21) and Michael (10:13,

Key Themes of Daniel 8:15–27

- Gabriel identifies the three kingdoms as Media, Persia, and Greece—all known to Daniel.
- God brings a just end to the king who opposes him and his heavenly armies, and who persecutes his people.
- Although he is deeply impacted by the future vision, Daniel does not understand it.

21; 12:1). Both are "archangels" in *1 Enoch* (9.1; 20.1–7). Gabriel also appears in the Qumran War Scroll (9.15–16).[5]

8:17–19 *I was terrified and fell prostrate . . . in a deep sleep.* Daniel's reaction is not unusual for a person experiencing an angelic (Josh. 5:14) or divine (2 Chron. 7:3) encounter, although "falling on one's face" is also used before humans (2 Sam. 9:6). Falling into a trance usually involves

After the death of Alexander the Great, his kingdom was divided among his four generals. Judea became caught in the middle of the Ptolemaic and Seleucid struggle for power and territory. This map shows the extent of the Seleucid and Ptolemaic kingdoms (ca. 323–198 BC).

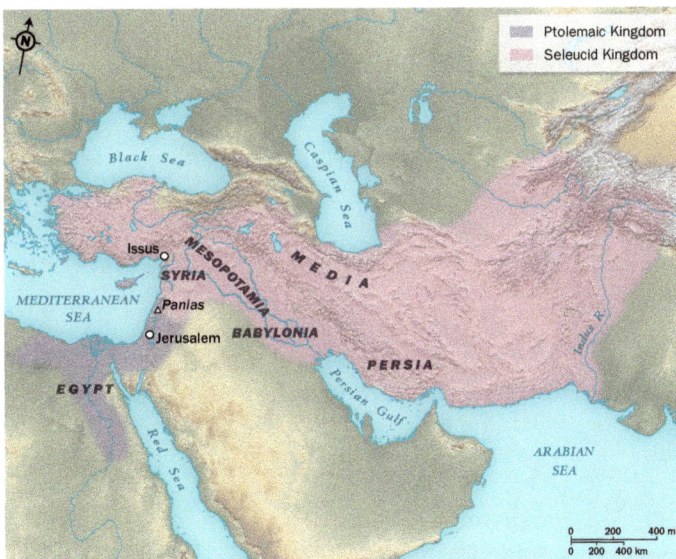

a theophany (Gen. 15:12). The Hebrew *ben 'adam* ("son of man") is synonymous with the Aramaic *bar 'enash* in Daniel 7:13, although Daniel is clearly the one in view here. "Later in the time of *wrath* [*za'am*]" connotes God's "indignation,"[6] which is described further in verse 23. The varied references to the distant future set the endpoint of this vision beyond Daniel's life, but not necessarily into the eschatological future. Instead, 8:20–25 identifies this time as that of the Greek persecution of the Jews in the second century BC.[7]

8:20–21 *kings of Media and Persia . . . the king of Greece.* The explicit identification here of the nations represented in 8:3–8 completes the book's list of four earthly kingdoms (including Nebuchadnezzar's reign over Babylon). This should be read as intentionally informing one's interpretation of Daniel's four-kingdom schema in chapters 2 and 7.

8:22 *four kingdoms . . . will not have the same power.* In Daniel's vision, Alexander and his four generals are described as "prominent horns" (8:5, 8) on the goat. However, the angel clarifies that the latter are less-powerful subdivisions of Alexander's domain.[8]

8:23 *when rebels have become completely wicked.* The vision moves quickly to the latter part of the four dynasties—specifically the Seleucids—where it further identifies the persecutions of God's people under the little horn (7:8, 11, 20, 24–25; 8:9–12). The "rebels" (better

"transgressors" [so ESV]; see the comments on 8:12), in this context, most likely references the sin of Antiochus and his followers, since it coincides with his rise to power.[9]

fierce-looking king, a master of intrigue. Antiochus's character is described in two ways. First, he is "strong-faced" (*'az panim*; NIV: "fierce-looking"),[10] a term used elsewhere to describe Babylon as a dispassionate, merciless nation that conquers Israel "without respect for the old or pity for the young" (Deut. 28:50). Second, Antiochus "understands riddles" (*bin hidah*; NIV: "master of intrigue"). Ironically, the Aramaic equivalent *'ahidah* is used in 5:12 to describe Daniel's ability to read the wall writing (NIV: "riddles"). Here, Daniel tries to "understand" (*bin*) this vision but fails (8:15, 27).[11]

8:24 *not by his own power.* This phrase in Hebrew is identical to the last words of 8:22, where it contrasts the greater power of Alexander with the lesser power of his generals. Here, it speaks of a source of strength beyond Antiochus that gives him success. Perhaps it refers to God as the

In Daniel 7:1, we are told that Daniel writes down the substance of his dream. In 8:26, Daniel is told to "seal up the vision." If Daniel recorded his visions on clay tablets, they would have been placed in a clay envelope, and a cylinder seal or stamp seal would have been used to indicate ownership and prevent tampering. Shown here is a clay envelope with its cuneiform tablet still inside. The seal impressions are still visible on the bottom left of the envelope (1720 BC, Alalakh).

source of both his rise and his fall (8:25); or it may speak of the spiritual forces of evil. Antiochus uses this ability to "cause astounding devastation" and succeeds for a short time. "Those who are mighty" may refer to the armies with whom Antiochus does battle, to "numerous" (another meaning of *'atsum*)[12] leaders among "the holy people" (Judeans), or to the other armies "and" the Jews—there is a conjunction between the two groups in the Masoretic Text.

8:25 *He will cause deceit to prosper.* This is the corollary to Antiochus throwing "truth . . . to the ground" (8:12) in his deception of the Jewish leaders who abandon their obedience to Mosaic law and embrace Hellenism. When they feel secure in their compromising covenant with Antiochus, he will turn on them, killing them and many other Jews in Jerusalem (cf. 1 Macc. 1:29–40).

consider himself superior . . . take his stand against the Prince of princes. In 8:11 the little horn claims equality with the "prince" (*sar*) of the heavenly armies; here Antiochus opposes the "Prince of princes" (*sar sarim*), meaning God as commander in chief of heaven's forces.[13] The futility of such arrogance is emphasized by Antiochus's destruction "not by human power." This phrase is similar to the rock cut out "not by human hands" (2:44–45). In fulfillment of the vision, Antiochus died in 164 BC, with no human being killing him (1 Macc. 6:1–16; 2 Macc. 9:1–28; Polybius, *Hist*. 31.11).

8:26 *The vision of the evenings and mornings . . . is true.* There is no further interpretation of this time period, only an assurance that the suffering will not last indefinitely. However, the news is bittersweet, in that Daniel is told to "seal up the vision, for it concerns the distant future." The darkness of the foreign oppression of Israel from Nebuchadnezzar's conquest to Antiochus's persecutions encompasses more than four centuries. It is not clear how long the scroll is to be "sealed," or how privately it is to be kept after Daniel's vision.[14]

8:27 *I, Daniel, was worn out.* This chapter's ending mirrors that of the parallel symbolic vision in 7:28. There the seer is "troubled" and "pale," whereas here he is "exhausted" and "appalled . . . beyond understanding." In each case, the vision remains private.

Theological Insights

In 8:15–27, three theological realities present themselves in the interaction between Daniel and Gabriel. First, arrogant, wicked rulers will arise who oppose God and his heavenly armies, and they will persecute his people. Second, God will ultimately triumph over such rulers, bringing them to their deserved end. Third, God knows the future and sometimes reveals small portions of this knowledge, embedding enduring principles in ancient history.

Teaching the Text

1. *God's goodness in an evil world.* Although God is just and good, we cannot always know why he allows evil ones to gain power over and oppress others—especially believers. However, affliction can call the unfaithful to repentance and

the faithful to greater obedience. When teaching this text, admit your limited understanding of God's ways when life seems unfair. Too often we bring simplistic answers to difficult questions, especially when the righteous suffer with the wicked, or under cruel tyranny. Help your listeners put themselves in the place of the Jews under Antiochus, asking how they might have responded to such circumstances. Even though our situation is different today, the choice of fidelity versus compromise remains the same.

2. *God's triumph over evil*. The righteous punishment of even one wicked ruler can illustrate God's victory at the end of the age. This gives us assurance that God remains sovereign over the finite power of mere mortals. The ancient world knew its share of terror-inspiring rulers. However, modern believers can be traumatized daily by terror-inspiring scenarios in our media—whether fiction, fantasy, or reality. More than ever we need to hear words of assurance that good will triumph over evil in the end, that faithfulness to God and his kingdom purposes is worth our allegiance as citizens of his kingdom, that the seemingly limitless power of rulers is insignificant in comparison to the power of God.

3. *God's knowledge of all history*. The essential message of this text is clear: God is sovereignly in control of history and able to deliver his people. However, the fact that Daniel does not understand all the details of this vision should give modern interpreters pause. Even though

The rise of the Greek Empire and its impact on God's people living in Judea are communicated to Daniel through Gabriel's interpretation. From our vantage point in history, we can recognize the impact that Alexander the Great's conquests had on this region of the world. This coin features Alexander the Great with a ram's horn, which associated him with the god Zeus-Ammon. It was minted by Lysimachus, one of Alexander's generals, as he tried to solidify his power base in the Greek Empire (306–281 BC).

God knows the future in its entirety, he reveals only small portions of it in texts like these. Humility demands that we acknowledge our limited understanding of apocalyptic passages. All interpreters agree that this passage and its chiastic parallel in Daniel 11 are about Judea under Greek oppression. Keep your listeners rooted in the text by giving them enough background to understand it, yet without overwhelming them with ancient history. Help them to see that this segment of Jewish history fits into the larger picture of God establishing his kingdom, even though we may not understand in detail how this will work.

What not to teach. First, do not use a sermon to debate the identity of the kingdoms. Again, share your opinion with respect and move on. Second, avoid speculation about typologies that may link this material to the end of the age. Rather, teach this text in its historical context. Third, the angel's explanation of the "evenings and mornings" is that the vision is "true" and "concerns the distant future" from the time of Daniel (8:26). Likewise, it is acceptable to leave your listeners with some unanswered questions, while assuring them of the certainty of God's Word.

Illustrating the Text

Persecution is the critical moment for choosing fear or faithfulness.

Church History: Correspondence between the Roman governor Pliny the Younger and the emperor Trajan (AD 53–117) reveals the grievous nature of Roman persecution of Christians. They were tortured and killed for refusing to deny Christ or were spared for cursing Christ and worshiping the emperor and his gods.[15] This "test of faith" was a critical moment for believers—a reminder of the seriousness of Jesus's words, "whoever disowns me before others, I will disown before my Father in heaven" (Matt. 10:33). Imagine facing such a moment and deciding whether to comply. Believers are called to remain faithful to the Lord no matter the cost and in times of severe persecution. We should remember and rejoice in God's goodness to reward the faithful, as Jesus also has promised: "Whoever acknowledges me before others, I will also acknowledge before my Father in heaven" (Matt. 10:32). We must remember that God's gracious gift of eternal life remains undeserved, even under these circumstances.

Diabolical rulers in this world will rise and fall.

History: The murder of six million Jewish people, plus countless others whom Adolf Hitler deemed inferior to Germanic "Aryans," is a nearly pure expression of evil. Moreover, the Nazi regime engulfed virtually all of Europe by 1941–42, from Morocco to Norway and from the Atlantic to the border of what was then the Soviet Union. This occurred mostly through military occupations and allegiances with sympathetic countries, but it also was tolerated by those states that chose to remain "neutral." Although this plague of oppression lasted just over a decade (1933–45), for those living in its grip it must have seemed like an eternity. Today survivors and their children still seek to make sense of this human tragedy, finding some ever-so-small comfort in the fact that the rest of the world finally exacted judgment on this unspeakable inhumanity and that the rise of the Third Reich ultimately culminated in its fall.

Sometimes we need not understand all the details.

Science: In many aspects of everyday life, the average person does not need to have scientific knowledge of how the world works to live productively within it. For instance, we do not need to understand computer programming, memory storage, or internal processing in order to use our computers and mobile devices productively and ethically. Similarly, we do not need to comprehend how introducing particulates and biological molecules into the Earth's atmosphere threatens the environment in order to ensure our children's future. Likewise, we do not need to fully grasp the chemical process that links bad eating habits with a heart attack or stroke in order to eat well. Rather, a basic awareness of how to operate a computer, what practices result in bad air quality, and how to construct a healthy diet are sufficient. So it is with apocalyptic visions—the basic contours of the text reveal the central message, from which we can draw principles for godly living.

Jeremiah's "Seventy Years"

Big Idea *Yahweh faithfully fulfills his prophetic word and keeps his covenant with his people, whether for blessing or for judgment.*

Understanding the Text

The Text in Context

Daniel 9 is woven into the book's overall literary structure in several ways. First, it advances the chronology of chapters 8–12. Second, it forms the middle of Daniel's final concentric Hebrew section, which is framed by the parallel units of chapter 8 and chapters 10–12. Third, it covers the same long-range time period as Daniel 2 and 7, aligning the "four kingdoms" with the "seventy sevens." Fourth, it is the third of four apocalyptic visions. Fifth, it is an "appearance" vision, like its parallel in Daniel 10–12 (see table 1).[1]

The Hebrew *mar'eh*, "appearance, vision" (9:23; 10:1)[2] differs slightly from the Aramaic *hezu* and Hebrew *hazon* (used in the earlier "symbolic" visions; 2:19; 7:1; 8:1)—the latter more broadly connoting a "vision." By this shaping, the author associates the "seventy sevens" of Daniel 9 with the Jewish suffering under Greece in the final "appearance" vision of Daniel 10–12.

Against this backdrop, 9:1–27 can be divided into three pericopes: the setting and beginning of Daniel's prayer (9:1–6); the remainder of Daniel's prayer regarding God's righteousness, Israel's sin, and a plea for mercy based on Yahweh's name (9:7–19); and the appearance vision proper (9:20–27). Within this context, 9:1–6 divides into three parts: a historical marker and reference to Jeremiah's "seventy years" (9:1–2), Daniel's response of mourning (9:3), and Daniel's confession of God's covenant and Israel's failure (9:4–6).

Historical and Cultural Background

The phrase "son of Xerxes" (9:1) most likely refers to Cyaxares, Darius's Median, maternal great-grandfather (see "Additional Insights" following the unit on 5:18–31), who unified his loosely affiliated tribes into a kingdom in 625–585 BC.

Table 1: Appearance Visions of Daniel 9 and 10–12

Settings: Darius's first year and Cyrus's third year	9:1–2	10:1
Recipient's/seer's fasting and prayer	9:3–19	10:2–3
Angel's appearance	9:20–21	10:4–9
Word of assurance	9:22–23	10:10–11:1
Recipient's/seer's vision proper	9:24–27	11:2–12:3, 5–8, 10–12
Charge to recipient/seer	—	12:4, 9, 13

Cyaxares's throne name can be abbreviated as Xerxes.[3]

Expressing one's grief through fasting, wearing sackcloth, and putting ash or dust on the head was practiced in ancient Canaan and Assyria. Fasting took away the pleasure of eating, sackcloth was coarse and uncomfortable to wear, and ash or dust reminded the mourner of the results of death or other occasions of grief.[4]

Daniel's appeals to God's covenant recall Hittite and Assyrian treaties (second–first millennia BC) between kings (suzerains) and vassals.[5] These agreements typically included a preamble, a historical prologue, stipulations, and a conclusion containing instructions, witnesses, and consequences for disobedience. The book of Deuteronomy reflects this format (see the sidebar "God's Covenants and Kingdom" in the unit on 2:31–49).[6]

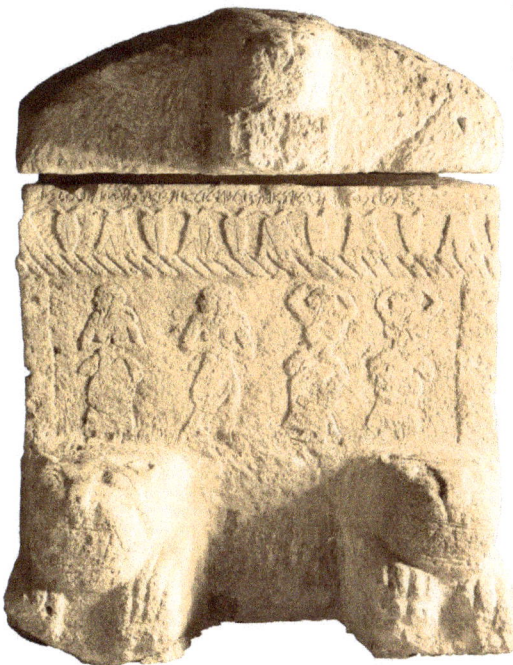

- Daniel realizes that Darius's rule ends the "seventy-year" exile predicted by Jeremiah.

- Daniel affirms that God keeps his covenant of love with those who love and obey him.

- Daniel confesses that the exiled Judeans have failed to keep God's commandments.

Interpretive Insights

9:1 *In the first year of Darius . . . who was made ruler.* The longer reference to Darius's Median ancestry (literally, "a son of Xerxes, a seed of Media") reinforces the importance of this kingdom in Daniel's theology. Mention of his first year is repeated in 9:2a to emphasize the end of Babylon's rule. Although the Hebrew verbal denominative *malak*[7]—literally, "was made king" (NIV: "ruler")—may suggest Darius was a subordinate under Cyrus, it might also refer to God's sovereignty over his appointment (Dan. 2:21).[8]

9:2 *I, Daniel understood from the Scriptures.* The emphatic first person occurs in each of Daniel's four apocalyptic visions. Although Daniel does not "understand" (*bin*) these visions (e.g., 8:27; 12:8), he does "understand" Jeremiah's prophecy. The NIV's "Scriptures" (*seper*) is more precisely "document, letter, or scroll,"[9] the same word used in Jeremiah 29:1 to describe the "scroll" (NIV: "letter") Jeremiah sends to the exiles announcing the "seventy years." Jerusalem's "desolation" (*harbah*) is also mentioned in Jeremiah 25:18 (NIV: "ruin") regarding the Babylonian

Daniel puts on sackcloth as he confesses the sins of the people of Israel. In the ancient Near East, wearing sackcloth was the conventional sign of mourning. This end panel from the sarcophagus of King Ahiram shows grieving women wearing sackcloth (tenth century BC).

Judah's "Seventy Years" of Exile

The temple's "seventy years" of desolations can be measured in two ways: from its destruction to its rebuilding (586–516 BC) or from the first exile to the first return (605–538 BC). The first calculation is well documented in the Old Testament (destruction: 2 Kings 25:9; 2 Chron. 36:19; Jer. 52:13, 17–23; rebuilding: Ezra 6:15; Hag. 1:4, 7–9; Zech. 1:12; 7:5). This time frame may also find support in Daniel's first and last Hebrew sections (Dan. 1; 10–12), which are dated to Nebuchadnezzar's first year (605 BC) and Cyrus's third year (535 BC).[a]

But the second computation, even though a rounded number, seems to be the focus in Daniel—especially in chapter 9. First, in Daniel 1, Nebuchadnezzar brings Daniel to Babylon in 605 BC. Second, in the same year, Jeremiah 25:11–12 predicts the exile's "seventy years." Third, in 597 BC, Jeremiah sends a letter containing this information to the Jewish exiles (Jer. 29:1–14). Fourth, during the Jews' return in Cyrus's first year (538 BC), 2 Chronicles 36:20–21 connects the "seventy years" with Israel's neglected sabbatical years (cf. Lev. 25:1–7; 26:33–35) as a fulfillment of Jeremiah's words. Fifth, Daniel 1–6 and 9 reflect the transition from 539 to 538 BC.

[a] See Grabbe, "End of the Desolations," 67–68.

exile, which begins as Jeremiah writes. The "seventy years" in Daniel 9:2 becomes the point of reference for the "seventy 'sevens'" of years in 9:24–27 (see the sidebar).

the word of the LORD. This phrase occurs nearly seventy times in the book of Jeremiah, signaling the authority of Yahweh's revelation to his prophet (Jer. 29:20). The divine name Yahweh ("LORD" [or "GOD"], using small capitals, in English translations) is the only personal "name" for God in the Old Testament. Special covenantal significance is attached to it in God's words to Moses in Exodus 3:13–15 and 6:2–5.[10] In Daniel, the name occurs only in this chapter (9:2, 4, 8, 10, 13, 14, 20). Yet its emphasis here provides a point of reference for God's covenant faithfulness during the struggles of Daniel 8 and 10–12.

9:3 *So I turned to the Lord God.* The title "Lord" (*'adonay,* "lord, master, sir")

speaks to God's sovereignty, a central theme in Daniel (cf. 1:2; 2:47; 5:23). It should not be confused with "LORD" (small capitals), which is the covenant name for God in this chapter. The phrase better translates as "my Lord, the [one true] God," emphasizing the personal nature of Daniel's plea. The irony of Daniel's reaction is striking. Understanding from Jeremiah 25:1–14 and 29:1–14 that the exile is to end with Babylon's fall, one would expect praise, thanksgiving, and festive celebration. Instead, Daniel's pleading, prayer, petition, fasting, sackcloth, and ashes suggest that he is concerned, rather than relieved, by this knowledge.[11] His adoption of these habits of crisis and mourning sets the tone for his prayer in 9:4–19.

9:4 *I prayed to the* LORD *my God and confessed.* The reader is also surprised by Daniel's passionate confession, begging the question of the nature of his remorse. Even though he is a "mere mortal" (8:17; NIV: "son of man") with shortcomings like anyone else, none of these appear in his book.

Lord . . . who keeps his covenant of love with those who love him. A strong particle of entreaty (*'anna',* "ah now!")[12] appears before "Lord" (omitted in the NIV), accentuating the fear of the Lord reflected in "great and awesome God." Further, the two terms for "love" (NIV) reflect different Hebrew words. The first (*hesed*) denotes "mercy, kindness, steadfast love, loyalty," while the second (*'ahab*) is related to "affection, friendship."[13] This theologically balanced declaration appears in Exodus 20:4–6; Deuteronomy 5:10; 7:9; and Nehemiah 1:5—all regarding God's "steadfast mercy" pledged to Israel in the Mosaic covenant. The identical wording suggests that Daniel is citing Deuteronomy 7:9. The explicit conditionality of this statement, in relation to the Judean exiles at this time, troubles him.[14]

9:5–6 *we have sinned.* Six verbs expose Israel's failure: sinning, doing wrong, acting wickedly, rebelling, turning away, and not listening. Five more complete the list in 9:7–14.[15] The mention of the torah gives this comprehensive indictment its point of reference. Reading these charges with the statement about God's covenant (9:4) reveals the question implied in Daniel's petition: Will God restore Israel after exile in spite of their overwhelming failure? Reference to God's "servants the prophets" points to Jeremiah, whose ministry was characterized by rejection (Jer. 25:3). The repetitive "we" and the form of the verbs suggest that Israel's failure has persisted until the day of Daniel's plea. The history of their disobedience encompasses every stratum of Israelite society: kings, princes, ancestors, and people of the land (cf. Jer. 1:18; 44:21).

Theological Insights

Daniel 9:1–6 exposes three facets of God's revelation to, and relationship with, his people. First, God fulfills his prophetic word spoken through his faithful prophets. Second, the sovereign Lord Yahweh is faithful to keep his covenantal promises and to show both mercy and justice toward his chosen people. Third, God's people of the covenant are, in turn, responsible for loving God and keeping his commandments, if they wish to know the personal blessings of his covenant.

Teaching the Text

1. *God fulfills his prophetic word.* Much emphasis is placed on the visions of Daniel that point to a distant future. However, it would be equally helpful to draw your listeners' attention to the predictions of Jeremiah that point to this moment in Judah's exile. Help your audience to understand the significance of Israel's corporate sin for centuries and how this led to the separate exiles of Israel and Judah—especially the latter with its focus on Jerusalem, the temple, and David's dynasty. Point your listeners' attention to the unusual response

Daniel also comes before the Lord with fasting and ashes. To sprinkle dust or ashes on the head was a way to publicly express grief and mourning in the ancient Near East. In this Egyptian tomb painting, a mourning woman puts dust on her head as a sign of her sorrow (Tomb of Nebamun, ca. 1350 BC).

Rembrandt's oil painting titled *Jeremiah Lamenting the Destruction of Jerusalem* shows Jeremiah mourning as Jerusalem burns. Although Jeremiah spent much of his life prophesying this event, he also brought words of hope and mercy from the Lord. Jeremiah 24:5–7 says, "This is what the Lord, the God of Israel, says: 'Like these good figs, I regard as good the exiles from Judah, whom I sent away from this place to the land of the Babylonians. My eyes will watch over them for their good, and I will bring them back to this land. I will build them up and not tear them down; I will plant them and not uproot them. I will give them a heart to know me, that I am the Lord. They will be my people, and I will be their God, for they will return to me with all their heart.'"

of Daniel as the "seventy years" are drawing to a close. Encourage them to identify with his concerns. Paying close attention to this chapter's introduction informs our understanding of the essential message of its enigmatic conclusion.

2. *God's covenantal mercy.* God's promises assure us that we can trust him to show us mercy as his people. Daniel understands the promise of the "seventy-year" exile that Jeremiah predicts, and he lives to see its fulfillment. The exile ends with Judah receiving God's covenantal mercy in their partial return to the land. Use either Jeremiah 25 or 29 as an example of God's promise regarding the exile's end. When applying these texts to Daniel 9:1–6, focus on the aspect of the promise Jeremiah emphasizes: the fall of Babylon at the end of the "seventy years" and Judah's restoration. Remind your listeners that wicked empires eventually receive a just punishment for their failure to acknowledge God, and that God does his part in bringing covenantal blessings to his people.

3. *God's covenantal accountability.* God's promises also warn us that he will keep his people accountable regarding their fidelity to him. Refer your listeners to Jeremiah 29:11–14 to show this aspect of

God's character. There, Jeremiah's promise of restoration is inseparably linked with the people seeking God with all their heart. Daniel reminds his readers of the original stipulation in the torah to love and obey God if they wish to know his blessing (Deut. 7:9). By way of application, avoid the temptation to emphasize God's promise in a way that marginalizes our human responsibility—or vice versa. While assuring your listeners of God's faithfulness, remind them that obedience before God is essential to knowing his blessing.

What not to teach. First, avoid the temptation to discuss in too much detail the identity of King Darius in comparison to King Cyrus. His mention here is intended to mark the setting of this chapter, which is clearly the first year after Babylon fell. Second, this is not a place to debate Calvinism versus Arminianism. Instead, acknowledge that this text teaches God is sovereign and humans are responsible before him.

Illustrating the Text

God's promise to fulfill his prophetic word is like a parent's promise to a child.

Human Experience: Those who have had the privilege, responsibility, and challenge of raising children appreciate the importance of keeping their word. It builds for children such life-shaping virtues as trust, discipline, integrity, dependability, honesty, and respect. Sometimes promises are freestanding, such as responding to a child's wish for a special gift on her or his birthday. But sometimes promises are more complex and connected with achievements or behavior. For example, college students might be promised a special trip upon graduation *if* they maintain their GPA. Here, the promise is twofold: (1) if the grade is made, parents are bound by oath to deliver the goods; but (2) if the grades are insufficient, the "promise" still must be kept—*no* trip. The virtues learned from parents keeping both positive and negative aspects of their "word" are the same—and God always keeps his word.

The Old Testament roles of priest and prophet illustrate God's mercy and justice.

Bible: Jeremiah. A simple, twofold biographical sketch of Jeremiah's life can be easily reconstructed from his book. From his conception he is destined by God to serve as both priest and prophet, though he is trained as a priest from birth and called as a prophet much later (Jer. 1). The Old Testament role of priest—a generational inheritance—speaks of God's mercy, as priests intercede with God on behalf of the people. But Jeremiah's radical calling as an Old Testament prophet diametrically opposes the family tradition. Prophets speak to the people on God's behalf, often bringing words of impending judgment for sin. The latter role dominates Jeremiah's life, resulting in his rejection by his own people, in addition to much personal trouble, sorrow, and shame—even tempting him to forsake his prophetic calling (Jer. 20). This instructive tension reveals the broken heart of God in bringing exile on Judah and Jerusalem.

God's blessing in covenantal relationship implies the obedience of his people.

Culture: In the history of political theory, the concept of the "social contract" (argued in different nuances by seventeenth- and eighteenth-century philosophers, including Thomas Hobbes, John Locke, and Jean-Jacques Rousseau) asserts that "a contract" (much like a biblical covenant) is formed when one party consents to relinquish some freedoms and submit to an authority, receiving in return the protection of that authority. For example, in American government, citizens consent to certain stipulations on their part (such as obedience to the law), and they implicitly receive with their obedience the benefits provided by the state (such as foreign defense or the building and maintenance of roads). However, disobedience is a failure to follow through on the agreement and results in consequences (for example, fines or imprisonment). God's interaction with his people is similar in that the protection and blessing of God imply the expectation of obedience from his people as inherent to their covenant relationship.

Daniel's Prayer for Israel and Judah

Big Idea *Even when God in his righteousness judges his people's sin, they may seek God's mercy for his name's sake.*

Understanding the Text

The Text in Context

See the unit on 9:1–6 for a discussion of the larger context, structure, and comparisons of this chapter. Against this backdrop, 9:7–19 divides into two parts: the remainder of Daniel's prayer regarding God's righteousness and Israel's sin (9:7–14) and a plea for God's mercy based on his covenant name (9:15–19). In this section, Daniel adds five more charges against Israel to the six mentioned in 9:5–6: acting unfaithfully, not keeping the law, transgressing, not seeking God's favor, and not turning from sin.[1] This litany of indictments raises questions about Israel's restoration.

Historical and Cultural Background

Daniel references kings of Israel and Judah, several of whom are known outside the Bible. Omri is mentioned on the Moabite Stone (840–830 BC), Jehu on the Black Obelisk of Shalmaneser III (825 BC), Hezekiah in the Taylor and Sennacherib prisms (701 BC), and Jehoiachin in Awel-Marduk's rations lists (562–560 BC).[2] International treaties from this time, similar to the covenant treaty of Deuteronomy alluded to in this section, delineate responsibilities for keeping those covenants. The deities, in whose names they are made,

In his prayer Daniel acknowledges that "we and our kings, our princes and our ancestors are covered with shame, Lᴏʀᴅ, because we have sinned against you" (9:8). Starting with Jeroboam, the kings of Israel did not keep the law of the Lord. Instead they worshiped at Dan and Bethel, where Jeroboam had erected golden calves. Shown here are the archaeological remains of the tenth-century BC altar foundations and high place at Tel Dan.

will carry out the blessings and curses. For Israel and Judah, God is the suzerain, with Israel as his vassal, who makes a covenant in his name with Israel. The divine name Yahweh appears outside Scripture on the Moabite Stone (840–830 BC), inscriptions from Khirbet el-Qom (Judea) and Kuntillet Ajrud (northeast Sinai Peninsula; both about 800 BC), the Arad Ostraca (about 600 BC), and the Lachish letters (shortly before 586 BC)—to name a few of the most prominent occurrences.[3]

Interpretive Insights

9:7 *Lord, you are righteous, but this day we are covered with shame.* God's righteousness contrasts with Israel's sin in a legal sense of innocence and guilt (cf. Ezra 9:15; Neh. 9:33).[4] Because of Israel's public indictment and conviction made evident in the exile, they are (literally) with "shame of face" (a phrase borrowed from Jer. 7:19).

all the countries where you have scattered us. Jeremiah uses this broad geographical reference frequently (Jer. 16:15; 23:3, 8; 32:37). Before Judah's deportations to Babylon (605–586 BC), Assyria conquered the northern kingdom of Israel (722 BC). At this time, the majority of the people were scattered around the Fertile Crescent, while other people groups were brought to Israel—all for the sake of assimilation (cf. 2 Kings 17:1–6; Ezra 4:1–2).

9:9 *merciful and forgiving.* Two characteristics of God contrast with his righteous judgment. Both are plural nouns in the Masoretic Text, suggesting repetition or intense expression of these attributes.[5] "Mercies," in singular form, refers to a mother's "womb," picturing tender compassion for a child.[6] "Forgiveness" often

- Daniel affirms that Yahweh remains righteous and is justified even when judging Israel and Judah.

- Daniel acknowledges the persistent sin of Israel and Judah, for which they deserve exile.

- Daniel pleads with God to forgive and restore his people for the sake of his name.

Deuteronomic Theology of Exile and Return

The contrast between God's righteousness and Israel's sin in Daniel 9:7–19 reflects a theology of exile and return first appearing in Deuteronomy. Two texts, Deuteronomy 4:25–31 and 30:1–10, bracket the book's large covenantal center, which predicts Israel's scattering among the nations because of their idolatry, as well as their restoration from exile if they sincerely seek God. The Hebrew Bible's "Former Prophets" (Joshua, Judges, Samuel, and Kings) is often called the "Deuteronomic history," because it recounts Israel's failure during the judges and kingdom eras. In it, Solomon fashions a pattern of idolatry (1 Kings 11:1–13), perpetuated by most of the kings of Israel and Judah after him. Jeremiah reflects this theme in his prediction of the "seventy-year" exile (Jer. 25:1–14; 29:1–14), which serves as the theological backdrop for Daniel 9.[a]

[a] See discussion in Miller, *Daniel*, 243–49; Pierce, "Covenant Conditionality," 33–35.

appears in the Old Testament parallel to "atonement" (Num. 15:25) and always occurs with God as subject (Jer. 50:20 refers to Babylonian exile).

9:10–11a *the laws he gave us through . . . the prophets.* Torah (usually translated "law") is better understood as "instruction." Moses began Israel's prophetic tradition (Deut. 34:10–12), followed by schools of prophets under Samuel (1 Sam. 19:20), and later classical literary prophets like Isaiah. Here, Daniel has Jeremiah in mind (9:2).[7]

9:11b *Therefore the curses and sworn judgments.* The NIV's "therefore" is interpretive, as the Masoretic Text has only the conjunction *waw* ("and"). The Hebrew terms are singular and definitive, suggesting "the curse, even the sworn oath." This recalls Moses's "curses of the covenant written in this Book of the Law" (Deut. 29:20–21). Deuteronomy 28:14–68 elaborates on these in a collection of "curses" for disobedience, predicting exile under foreign domination (especially 28:47–52, 64–65).

9:12 *nothing has ever been done like what has been done to Jerusalem*. When Israel was a kingdom, Jerusalem was home to Solomon's temple with its sacred vessels. These symbols are alluded to often in Daniel 9 (see also 1:2; 5:2–3; 6:10; 11:31).[8] The ark of the covenant, however, was conspicuous by its absence after Jerusalem's fall, last seen before Josiah's death in 609 BC (2 Chron. 35:3; Jer. 3:16). Exile opened a spiritual wound among the Jews that never fully healed, destroying a kingdom that was never fully restored.

9:13 *Just as it is written in the Law . . . all this disaster has come*. The opening phrase becomes common parlance in the New Testament (Luke 2:23; Heb. 10:7) and in later rabbinical literature.[9] It reinforces the argument of Daniel 9:11 that Deuteronomy's warning is adequate justification for God's actions in the exile. "Giving attention to your 'truth'" refers to the torah, including the larger theology regarding the conditionality of the covenant.[10]

9:14 *The Lord did not hesitate to bring the disaster*. Literally, God "kept watch over" the disaster, again showing Daniel's familiarity with Jeremiah (Jer. 1:12; 31:28; 44:27). The contrast of God's "righteous"

The curses written in the law of Moses and recited by Joshua from Mount Ebal when the Israelites entered the promised land had come to pass because of their sin. In this photograph, Mount Gerizim is on the left and Mount Ebal on the right with the modern town of Nablus (ancient Shechem) in the valley between them.

acts with Israel's sinful disobedience mirrors the opening words of this section, emphasizing its essential message.

9:15 *Now, Lord our God, who brought your people out of Egypt.* Daniel uses *'attah* ("now, at this time") twice in his passionate plea for God's immediate action (see 9:17).[11] His intensity grows until he is suddenly interrupted by Gabriel's appearance in verses 20–21. Mention of the exodus sets Daniel's final petition in the theological context of God's explanation of his covenantal name, Yahweh (Exod. 3:13–16; 6:2–5). There, God acted on the basis of his covenant with Abraham and brought Israel to the land of promise. Now, Daniel begs God to do the same, based on his covenant through Moses (Deut. 4:25–31; 30:1–10).[12]

9:16 *Lord, in keeping with all your righteous acts, turn away.* Daniel acknowledges that Israel's punishment is consistent with God's righteousness (9:7, 14). But here, he also implies that the exile's appointed time is complete and that God should act righteously by showing mercy and bringing restoration.[13] Daniel's concern that the exile makes Yahweh's city and people an "object of scorn" among the nations recalls Moses's argument with the Lord in Exodus 32. There, Yahweh's angry intent to destroy Israel is countered by a plea that the Egyptians might accuse him of "evil intent," scorning his name. Moses implores God to "relent"—that is, to show compassion instead of anger by canceling his judgment. And Yahweh does exactly that (32:12–13).[14] Daniel is hoping for the same response in his situation.

9:17–18 *Now, our God, hear the prayers and petitions of your servant.* A string of imperatives follows Daniel's second statement of immediacy, tying together the final verses of his prayer (9:17–19): "hear," "look with favor" (literally, "cause your face to shine"), "give ear," "open your eyes," "listen," "forgive," and "act." He insists that the temple and city still reflect God's name, even in their desolation.[15] Although Daniel acknowledges and even appeals to God's righteousness, he bases his plea solely on God's "great mercy." This is echoed in Daniel's urgent request for God to act for his name's sake, which concludes this section (9:19b). Within months after Daniel prays, the Judeans return to their homeland (2 Chron. 36:22–23; Ezra 1:1–4; 2:1, 64). However, the full "restoration" of what was lost in exile (Jer. 29:14) is far less than what was desired by Jeremiah and Daniel. Jerusalem and the temple are rebuilt (538–516 BC), but without the former splendor, autonomy, land occupation, Davidic kingship, ark of the covenant, and return of the other tribes of Israel.

9:19 *Lord, listen! Lord, forgive! Lord, hear and act!* The repetition of God's title of sovereignty punctuates the threefold climax of Daniel's prayer, which takes the form of an immediate demand. This literary tension prepares the reader for the dramatic intrusion of Gabriel with news that God's answer to Daniel's concern "went out" at the start of his prayer.[16]

Theological Insights

Daniel's passionate prayer to Israel's covenantal God in 9:7–19 confronts and encourages the reader in three ways. First, God's righteousness stands in sharp contrast to humanity's sin. Second, persistent disobedience to God's revealed will in Scripture may result in a just punishment.

Third, for his name's sake, our merciful and forgiving God may choose to extend his grace instead of the judgment we deserve.

Teaching the Text

1. *God's righteousness and our sin.* The righteous, covenant-keeping God demands righteous living from his people. God calls his people to holiness because he is holy. Exhort your listeners to avoid the theological and practical trappings of cheap grace and to rededicate themselves to serious discipleship. Encourage them to begin with an honest examination of their lives, asking how much they have become accustomed to tolerating their own sinful behavior under the excuse of being "just human." Point out that God is our standard, not so-called biblical heroes. Challenge them to new goals for living godly lives. Warn them that this must be done by depending on the power of God's Spirit, but remind them that they also must remain faithful.

2. *Consequences of persistent sin.* When God's people make choices that are against his revealed will, they often pay a price for those bad decisions. This does not mean that all sufferings or failures are the result of sinful behavior. On the contrary, innocent people sometimes suffer with the wicked. Help your listeners to examine their behavior in the light of God's Word, rather than in relation to bad experiences. Having done that, we should also take a second look at our personal choices when life is challenging. Encourage your listeners, when facing difficulties, to be sensitive to the Spirit's guidance, while comparing their lives to Scripture's teaching about living in obedience to God's revealed word.

3. *Mercy for his name's sake.* God's mercy and forgiveness are always available to those who sincerely repent of, and turn away from, sinful behavior. However, in the end, Daniel's priestly prayer does not bring the complete restoration of Judah from exile. This is because the larger remnant at this time is not repentant. The portrayal of the returnees in the postexilic books suggests this conclusion (Hag. 2:14; Zech. 1:3–4a; Mal. 1:1–3:15). After reminding the members of your congregation of God's righteous requirements and calling them to self-examination, assure them that God responds to sincere repentance and forgives our failures. The strikingly similar prayer of Ezra (nearly a century after Daniel) illustrates what can happen when God's people repent (Ezra 9:1–10:15).

What not to teach. First, do not teach this prayer in isolation from its context. It flows out of verses 1–6 and lays a foundation for verses 20–27. Second, Daniel's prayer should not be taught as a "model prayer" in the way that the Lord's Prayer is presented in the Gospels (Matt. 6:9–13; Luke 11:2–4). It does not necessarily reflect the form of "true" or "mature praying."[17]

Illustrating the Text

The gracious gift of covenant with a righteous God demands our obedience.

Quote: **Dietrich Bonhoeffer.** The perfectly holy and righteous God paid the ultimate price for our sin. Such an amazing sacrifice demands our awe and worship and also compels us to obedience. God's righteousness is a call to believers to live in obedience, for we have been bought with a price (1 Cor. 6:20). Remember the danger of "cheap grace," as famous pastor and theologian Dietrich Bonhoeffer (1906–45) has written:

> Cheap grace is not the kind of forgiveness of sin which frees us from the toils of sin. Cheap grace is the grace we bestow on ourselves. Cheap grace is the preaching of forgiveness without requiring repentance, baptism without church discipline, communion without confession, absolution without personal confession. Cheap grace is grace without discipleship, grace without the cross, grace without Jesus Christ, living and incarnate.[18]

Persistent sin disgraces God's people and damages their global witness.

Church History: An ongoing scandal in the Roman Catholic Church from 1950 to 2002 revolved around thousands of sexual abuses of minors by clergy—more than 6,700 cases were discovered in the United States alone.[19] Numerous world news stations, as well as critically acclaimed films like *Doubt* (2008), have helped catalyze more-effective efforts by governments as well as the church to prevent the perpetuation of this heinous crime. However, the persistent sin of Christian priests—many of whom are repeat offenders—as well as the sin of bishops and church authorities who ignored or covered up the problems, has created mistrust and criticism by Christians and non-Christians alike and a looming shadow of shame over the church.

God responds as he chooses to a plea based on divine mercy alone.

Bible: Exodus 32:1–14. The encounter between Moses and God in Exodus 32:1–14 clearly influences Daniel's prayer. While Moses is with God atop Mount Sinai, God hears the idolatrous revelry of his people below in the camp as they worship the golden calf, which Aaron the high priest fashions. In response, God threatens to wipe out Israel and begin anew with Moses's descendants. Moses objects to the severity of the punishment and appeals to God for pure mercy based on God's covenant with the Israelites' ancestors and his reputation in delivering them from Egypt. In the end, Yahweh "relents" (literally, "changes his mind") and does not judge the nation as he has threatened. Sometimes God grants such requests, although this is not the case for Daniel.

Daniel entreats God to allow the Israelites to return to Jerusalem not because they are righteous but because of God's great mercy. This small cast-bronze bull from the twelfth century BC was found at Samaria and is a reminder of the golden calf incident recorded in Exodus 32:1–14, one example of God responding in mercy in spite of well-deserved judgment.

Daniel 9:7–19

Gabriel Brings an Answer to Daniel's Prayer

Big Idea *Despite the prayers of a faithful servant, the persistent sin of God's people can bring serious consequences before their punishment is completed.*

Understanding the Text

The Text in Context

See the unit on 9:1–6 for a discussion of the larger context, structure, and comparisons of this chapter. Against this backdrop, 9:20–27 is the appearance vision proper. It can be divided into three parts: Gabriel's arrival to answer Daniel's prayer (9:20–23), the announcement of "seventy 'sevens'" (9:24), and an explanation of its divisions (9:25–27).

Historical and Cultural Background

Ancient Near Eastern literature attaches symbolic significance to the numbers seven and seventy in the Sumerian royal inscriptions (twenty-sixth century BC) and the Egyptian Amarna letters (fourteenth century BC), the latter emphasizing vengeance and repentance.[1] In Babylonian astrological texts, sevens figuratively represent regnal and dynastic years, whereas in the Black Stone of Esarhaddon (seventh century BC) Marduk allows Babylon to lie in ruins for "seventy years" after Sennacherib destroys it.[2] The symbolic use of "weeks" or "sevens" to portray history also occurs in the Apocalypse of Weeks (*1 Enoch* 91; 93), which uses ten "weeks" composed of sevens and threes. Similarly, the *Testament of Levi* 16–18 refers to "seventy sevens," while the book of *Jubilees* mentions ten Jubilee cycles ("seven sevens"). Such schemas are best understood as chronographies (rather

The numbers seven and seventy have symbolic significance in ancient Near Eastern literature. In this inscription on the Black Stone of Esarhaddon (670 BC), seventy years is the time decreed for the desolation of the city that Marduk has destroyed.

than chronologies): a symbolic way of expressing the significance of history.[3]

Interpretive Insights

9:20–21 *while I was still in prayer, Gabriel.* These words connect Daniel's vision proper (9:20–27) to the chapter's larger context, through his ongoing confession and petition, and by referencing Yahweh's "holy hill" (Jerusalem). "Gabriel" also appears "in the earlier vision" (8:16), may be among the angels in 7:16 and 23, and may be the "man dressed in linen" in 10:5–6. Daniel's successive references to earlier visions (8:1; 9:21) provide continuity and connectivity between these literary units.[4]

came to me in swift flight . . . evening sacrifice. The first clause may connote "touched me" or "reached me" (*naga'*)[5] in "extreme *weariness*" (*y^e'ap*)[6]—referring to Daniel instead of Gabriel (cf. NASB footnote; see also Daniel's weariness after fasting in 10:2, 8). Daniel's routine of praying "three times a day" (6:10) includes a twilight session remembering the temple's "evening sacrifice" (Dan. 8:11; Num. 28:3–8).

9:22 *I have now come to give you insight and understanding.* The appearance vision proper (9:20–27) differs from the "symbolic" visions in chapters 7 and 8 (see "The Text in Context" in the units on 7:1–14 and 9:1–6), in which angels explain previously received visions. Rather, Gabriel addresses Daniel's concern in 9:2 about Jeremiah's "seventy years."

9:23 *As soon as you began to pray, a word went out.* The apparently preemptive answer to Daniel's petition does not imply divine indifference. Rather, it demonstrates God's eagerness to respond to a "highly esteemed" servant.[7]

Masoretic Punctuation in the Hebrew Bible

Today's academic version of the Hebrew Bible (*Biblia Hebraica Stuttgartensia*) is based primarily on medieval manuscripts crafted by the Masoretes of Tiberius. Among other things, these Jewish scholars added punctuation (or "accents") to the consonantal text of earlier manuscripts, reflecting an oral tradition from the Second Temple period. In addition to indicating cantillation for public reading, these markers reveal grammatical syntax, giving the sense of a verse. Masoretic punctuation includes both "disjunctive" and "conjunctive" accents that separate and connect words, respectively. Disjunctive accents are especially helpful for exegesis of a text. The two strongest, *'atnah* and *silluq*, mark the logical midpoint and end of each verse (respectively) in the Hebrew Bible—although this varies slightly in Psalms, Job, and Proverbs. It is important for the translator and interpreter to pay close attention to this ancient guide to determine the main thought breaks in each verse.[a]

[a] See Khan, *Short Introduction to the Tiberian Masoretic Bible*, 37–41.

9:24 *Seventy "sevens" are decreed.* "Sevens" is sometimes translated "weeks" (ESV; the Hebrew can mean either). Jeremiah's "seventy years" (9:2) are based on Israel's sabbatical cycles (70 × 7 years; 2 Chron. 36:21–23) yet may also be calculated as Jubilee cycles (10 × 49 years). Failing to observe sacred seasons results in God's judgment (Lev. 25:1–17; 26:33–35). This symbolic period originally reflected Israel's failure from Solomon to the exile (970–586 BC; cf. the content of 1 and 2 Kings, and the division between 1 and 2 Chronicles).[8] In Daniel 9:24–27, the former sabbatical "seventy 'sevens'" are judged by "seventy 'sevens'" of extended, foreign domination. All these eras consist of rounded or symbolic numbers.[9]

to finish transgression . . . to anoint the Most Holy Place. Six infinitives (three positive, three negative) describe this period's purpose. Yet the first four are separated from the last two by the Masoretic Text punctuation (see the sidebar). Contextually, God's "righteousness" contrasts with Israel's "transgression," "sin," and "wickedness." These four terms frequent Daniel's prayer (9:4–19) concerning Judah's future (9:7). The last two, "seal up" and "anoint," however, do not occur in his prayer, yet they accent the conclusion to this extended judgment (9:25–27). To "seal up" connotes "ratifying" Daniel's visions about extending Jeremiah's prophecy (Dan. 9:2). Anointing "the Most Holy Place" anticipates the temple's reconsecration after its desecration (cf. 8:13–14; 11:31–35).[10]

9:25 *From the time the word goes out.* The NIV correctly reads *dabar* as "word." Although it may connote "decree" (NASB) when used of a king (Esther 1:12 [NIV: "command"], 19), its nearest antecedent here is the prophetic "word" of Jeremiah regarding the "seventy years" (Dan. 9:2).[11] Restoring that which has been lost in exile includes rebuilding Jerusalem.

until the Anointed One, the ruler, comes, there will be seven "sevens." The NIV's rendering of 9:25–26 is based on Theodotion's Greek translation. In contrast, this commentary follows the Masoretic Text punctuation of the text: "from the going out of the word . . . to the coming of an anointed one . . . seven sevens" (cf. ESV, which reads instead, "seven weeks"). There is no definite article attached to the adjective *mashiah* ("anointed"), and Hebrew has no capital letters. Further, the strongest punctuation mark within a verse ('*atnah*) follows "seven 'sevens,'" indicating the thought break.[12] Therefore, this "anointed leader" comes "49 'years'" after Jeremiah's word goes out (605 BC [Jer. 25], 597 BC [Jer. 29], or 587 BC [Jer. 30–31]). This may be Cyrus, Yahweh's "anointed" (Isa. 44:28–45:1, 13; cf. Josephus, *Ant.* 11.1–18), who rises to power in 556 BC and releases the Jews in 538 BC.[13] Or, it may be Joshua, the "anointed" high priest during Judah's return (538 BC; Ezra 2:2; Hag. 1:1; Zech. 3:1; 4:14).[14] Symbolically, these "seven 'sevens'" form a Jubilee cycle, which is a fitting backdrop for Judah's redemption from bondage and return to the land (cf. Lev. 25).

and sixty-two "sevens." It will be rebuilt . . . in times of trouble. This number begins a new sentence: "And for sixty-two 'sevens' it will be rebuilt. . . ." Its

"And at the temple he will set up an abomination" (9:27). Many think this "abomination" refers to a statue of Zeus since the temple was dedicated to Zeus and sacrifices were offered there on an altar to Zeus during the reign of Antiochus IV Epiphanes. This marble statue of the supreme god Zeus is from the second to first century BC.

significance is to connect the Jubilee cycle ("seven 'sevens'") and the sabbatical cycle ("one 'seven'") in 9:27. In this way, it symbolically represents the rebuilding following Cyrus's release of the Jews and Joshua's anointing (538 BC), during which they experience "times of trouble" (Ezra 4; Neh. 1; 4; 6). Antiochus IV of Greece (175–164 BC) persecuted them at the end of this time. Such a focus is clear in the visions that bracket this chapter (e.g., 8:21–25; 11:30–35) and makes the best sense of 9:26–27.

9:26 *After the sixty-two "sevens," the Anointed One will be put to death.* The Masoretic Text literally translates, "an anointed one," who must be a different person than the "anointed leader" living four centuries earlier. Most likely, he is the Jewish high priest Onias III, who was murdered in 171 BC, shortly after Antiochus began his rule (2 Macc. 4:23–28).[15]

The people of the ruler who will come will destroy. Antiochus's troops vented his fury against Jerusalem from 169 to 164 BC after being defeated by the Ptolemies (Dan. 11:30–31; 1 Macc. 1:29–40; 2 Macc. 5:11–14). In the visions that bracket this chapter, the sanctuary is "thrown down" (*shalak*; 8:11) and "desecrated" (*halal*; 11:31). Although *shahat* can mean "destroy" (NIV), the verbal form used here connotes "spoil, ruin, or corrupt."[16] As foreseen, "war" and "desolations"—like a "flood" (cf. 11:10, 40)—mark the end of the "seventy 'sevens.'"

9:27 *confirm a covenant . . . for one "seven."* One sabbatical cycle (seven years) represents the last division of the symbolic "seventy 'sevens,'" paralleling the Jubilee cycle (forty-nine years), which these time periods begin. Although *bᵉrit* refers to

God's "covenant" with his people in 11:28, 30, and 32, here it describes the "alliance" (cf. 11:22) between Antiochus and the Jews who forsake the "holy covenant" to embrace Hellenism (1 Macc. 1:11).[17]

In the middle of the "seven" . . . an abomination. Just as 9:26 marks the beginning of the last "seven" with Onias's death in 171 BC, this verse marks its midpoint with the temple's desecration in 167 BC. Daniel variously refers to this half of a "seven" as "a time, times and half a time" (7:25; 12:7), "2,300 evenings and mornings" (8:14), and 1,290 and 1,335 days (12:11–12). During this time, Antiochus has entered the temple, offered an unclean animal on the altar, and erected a bust of Zeus (cf. Dan. 11:31; 12:11; 1 Macc. 1:54–59).[18]

until the end that is decreed is poured out on him. Elsewhere, Daniel describes Antiochus's death (164 BC) as occurring "not by human power" (8:25) and at a time when no one helps him (11:45). It is God's appointed time for his judgment.

Theological Insights

Three insights into the person of God can be seen in the cryptic vision in 9:20–27. First, God is eager to answer the prayers of his beloved, although his answer may not be what we expect. Second, because of his righteousness, God takes seriously the persistent sin of his people and brings an appropriate judgment in his appointed time. Third, God holds accountable those who persecute his people, bringing their judgment in his time.

Teaching the Text

1. *A prompt yet bittersweet answer.* Since God answers prayer, we may come to him

humbly confessing our sin and passionately pleading for mercy—yet being content with his answer. Daniel's lengthy prayer and Gabriel's response should not be presented as a formal model for how we should pray or how God always responds. Nevertheless, the interaction reflected in this passage is consistent with instructions in the Old Testament and the New Testament regarding humanity's sin and God's justice. Moreover, Daniel's actions are affirmed by his description as "highly esteemed" (9:23). Encourage your listeners to come eagerly and boldly before God in prayer, yet to be prepared for, and content with, the answer God gives. Warn them that God does not always give all that we ask or comply with our requests in ways we might expect.

2. *"Seventy 'sevens'" are decreed*. Knowing that God is righteous and that he holds his people accountable for sin should cause us to take our fidelity to him more seriously. Daniel appeals on behalf of Israel on the basis of God's name, not their righteousness. Yet God's answer includes both grace and justice. On the one hand, a partial restoration comes in a relatively short time. On the other hand, persistent sin results in extended punishment. Help your listeners to keep these two aspects of God's character in balance, knowing that sometimes his response will reflect one of these more than the other. Call them to be people of righteousness who are, at the same time, thankful for his mercy.

3. *Times of trouble*. Persecution by ungodly people may cause us to question God's justice and fairness. But knowing that God will judge such people in his time can help us endure faithfully. Trying to understand why God allows the wicked to prosper can be a fruitless pursuit. Although our sin may likely be involved, the sin of our persecutor is equally visible before a watching God. Encourage your listeners to trust God through the darkness of suffering and to stay focused on their witness to the God who cares about their pain. Remind them that there is a future and hope for those who seek God with all their hearts (Jer. 29:10–14), that God keeps his covenant of love with those who love him and keep his commandments (Dan. 9:4), and that God will exact justice against the ungodly in his time (Ps. 37).

What not to teach. Since the New Testament nowhere appeals to this passage to confirm the time of Jesus's coming, we should avoid this emphasis in our general preaching and teaching. Further, technical debates over Old Testament typology of the New Testament "antichrist"—especially as these relate to systematic eschatology—should be reserved for more academically focused settings.

Illustrating the Text

God's answers to our prayers may not always be what we expect or desire.

Bible: David's cry in Psalm 51 is a useful example of penitence that is genuine, yet does not turn God from his just punishment of sin. Though he is forgiven, David suffers significant family and national tragedies as the consequence of his sin with Bathsheba (2 Sam. 11–19). This same principle holds true for Israel on the corporate level. In 1 Kings 8:46–51, Solomon preemptively pleads on behalf of the people of Israel that when their nation falls into sin and exile, God will hear their prayers. Yet, when this occurs, God tells Jeremiah, "Do not pray for the well-being of this people. . . . I will destroy them with the sword, famine and plague" (Jer. 14:11–12). God may not always answer our prayers as or when we wish, but he acts according to his sovereign will, which is ultimately for our good and his glory.

Grace and justice must go hand in hand.

Quote: **Rowan Williams.** Exercising grace and forgiveness toward those who have wronged us must remain interwoven with the enactment of justice. Rowan Williams, archbishop of Canterbury, in a 2011 interview warns against letting forgiveness run rampant without a complementary commitment to justice: "If forgiveness is easy it is as if the suffering doesn't really matter."[19] To singularly emphasize grace for those who have done wrong minimizes the gravity of sin. While grace is the calling of all believers, justice must accompany it—otherwise, forgiveness can be self-destructive and enable further sin. Restorative justice bears the merciful and forgiving love of God yet does not separate love from justice when appropriate consequences must be borne by the offender. Rather than seeing these two aspects of God's character as competing with each other, we must consider the two equally part of God's work, as well as a paradigm for forgiveness in our own lives.

We should handle difficult and controversial prophetic texts prophetically.

Ethics: God calls us to do "what is good," that is, "to act justly and to love mercy and to walk humbly" with him (Mic. 6:8). These eighth-century BC prophetic words should challenge preachers and teachers of Daniel 9:24–27 today. Opinions vary so widely within the evangelical community that unnecessary polarization and unfair treatment of fellow interpreters often result. In response, imagine how the conflict regarding this text might become more civil—indeed, more Christian—if we "justly" represented the others' views, even as they would present them. If we must speculate on the motives of those whose views differ from our own, we need to do so with genuinely demonstrated Christian love for our opponents—assuming their best intentions. Finally, the consensus in biblical scholarship regarding the difficulty of this text should evoke a sincere posture of humility in the way we write and speak.

> God mercifully orchestrates the return of his people to rebuild the temple and the city of Jerusalem, providing leadership in men like Zerubbabel, Ezra, and Nehemiah and encouragement through the prophetic voices of Haggai and Zechariah. Archaeological excavations have exposed these layers of stone, and the topmost portion is thought to be the remains of Nehemiah's wall built in the middle of the fifth century BC.

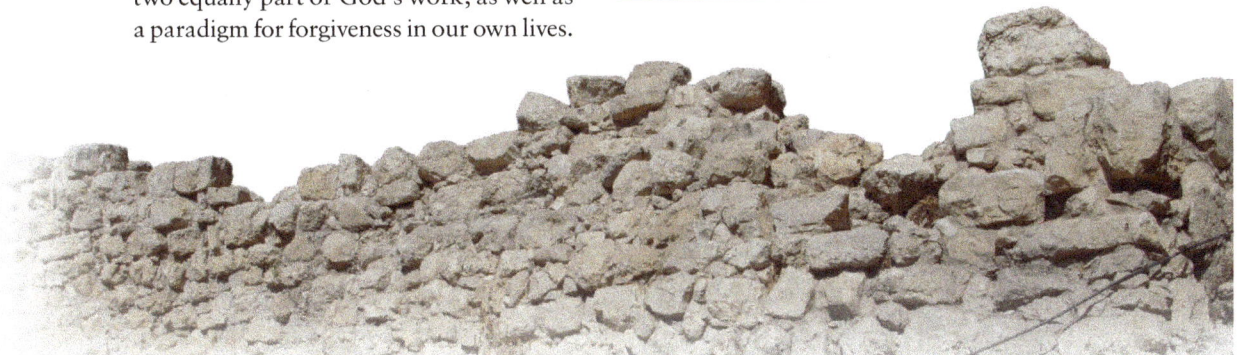

Daniel 9:20–27

The "Seventy 'Sevens'" of Daniel 9:24–27

The history of conflicting interpretations of this passage suggests it is among the most enigmatic texts in Scripture. Two general categories of views dominate the current discussion: Messianic (Jesus the Messiah) and Antiochene (Antiochus IV Epiphanes).

Messianic Interpretations

Most conservative Christian scholars[1] follow the Septuagint punctuation (contra the Masoretic Text) and add the "seven 'sevens'" and "sixty-two 'sevens'" to make a single unit of sixty-nine "sevens." This era extends from "the word [that] goes out" until "the Anointed One," who is Jesus (9:25 NIV; cf. NASB, NKJV). Although the church has held some version of this view throughout its history,[2] there remains no consensus on four key issues: which "word . . . goes out" to begin this period, which coming of Jesus ends the sixty-nine "sevens," when does the last "seven" occur, or what is the identity of the "ruler who will come" (9:26). Messianic views divide according to covenant and dispensational systematic theologies.

Covenant theology further divides into traditional and typological views.[3] In the *traditional messianic* view the "seventy 'sevens'" culminate in Jesus's first coming in this way: The "sixty-two 'sevens'" are the longer time of "great trouble and disgrace" (Neh. 1:3) for the Jews from Nehemiah to Jesus, four centuries later. The "one 'seven'" is a very short time, including Jesus's life and ministry, as well as Rome's destruction of Jerusalem and the Jewish Diaspora (first–second centuries AD). The "ruler who is to come" may be Jesus or a Roman general. In the *typological messianic* view the "seventy 'sevens'" culminate in Jesus's second coming in this way: The "seven 'sevens'" are the shorter time from Cyrus's decree (sixth century BC) to Jesus's life and ministry (first century AD). The "sixty-two 'sevens'" are the longer "times of trouble" (9:25) for Christian believers throughout history (from the first century AD until the return of Jesus). The "one 'seven'" is the very short tribulation under

In the traditional messianic view of covenant theology, the "one 'seven'" is a very short time and includes the life and ministry of Jesus, the siege of Jerusalem by the Romans in AD 70, and the Jewish Diaspora. This relief on the Arch of Titus at the southern entrance to the Roman Forum shows items taken in plunder after the destruction of the temple in Jerusalem including silver trumpets, the table for the shewbread, and a menorah.

the "antichrist" (the "ruler who is to come") in the end times, just before Jesus returns.[4]

Dispensational theology arose in the nineteenth century with the works of John Nelson Darby.[5] Its proponents understand the numbers in 9:24–27 as literal, while maintaining a strict distinction between ethnic/national Israel and the church. In this view, the "seven 'sevens'" (49 years) extend from a royal decree ("word") of one of the Persian kings (Cyrus to Artaxerxes) to some significant moment in Judea's rebuilding process. The "sixty-two 'sevens'" (434 years) continue from that time to sometime near the end of Jesus's earthly ministry. But the last "seven" is disconnected from the previous sixty-nine and is relocated in the eschatological future. This creates a two-thousand-year (and counting) gap between the sixty-ninth and seventieth "seven," during which God works only with the church. Finally, the last "seven" (seven years) brings tribulation for Israel after the church has been raptured, just before Jesus returns to earth. Although there is agreement on the larger structure of the "sevens" within this view, there is considerable disagreement on the details within that structure.[6]

Antiochene Interpretation

Most liberal Christian and secular scholars, along with a growing number of evangelicals,[7] follow the reading of the Masoretic Text, giving exegetical value to its punctuation in 9:25. This means the "seven 'sevens'" and "sixty-two 'sevens'" are read separately, distinguishing "an anointed ruler" in 9:25 from a different "anointed one" who comes "sixty-two 'sevens'" later in 9:26 (NRSV,

ESV, NJPS). This interpretation first appeared in the third and fourth centuries AD[8] and then reemerged in the nineteenth century with the rise of modern scholarship. The numbers are generally understood as figurative or symbolic,[9] and the combined era mirrors that described in Daniel 8 and 10–12: the persecutions of Antiochus against the Jews in Jerusalem. This view addresses the key issues raised above in the following way: The "seven 'sevens'" are the short time that extends from Jeremiah's "word" to Cyrus's rise to power (sixth century BC). King Cyrus or Joshua the priest is the first "anointed ruler." The "sixty-two 'sevens'" cover the "times of trouble" for Judea under Persia and Greece (sixth–second century BC). The priest Onias III is the second "anointed one" (171 BC). The last "seven" represents Judea's persecution under Antiochus IV (171–164 BC), who is the "ruler who will come." This last "seven" finds its midpoint in Antiochus's desecration of the temple (167 BC) and ends with its rededication (164 BC). Daniel's vision sets the "seventy 'sevens'" here in juxtaposition to the "seventy 'sevens'" of neglected sabbatical cycles that led Israel into exile (2 Chron. 36:21–23).[10]

In sum, the widely divergent messianic views agree on their christological understanding of this passage but are deeply divided regarding the combination of events that connect the sixty-nine "sevens" to Jesus as Messiah. In contrast, the Antiochene view is a nonchristological—although much more unified—reading of these verses, primarily in their literary and historical contexts.

Daniel's Final Revelation

Big Idea *God reveals the essential, though sometimes overwhelming, reality of spiritual warfare behind his purpose and plan for humanity.*

Understanding the Text

The Text in Context

The literary unit of Daniel 10–12 is woven into the book's structure in several ways. First, it is the last of Daniel's four apocalyptic visions: chapters 7 and 8 in "symbolic" form, and chapters 9 and 10–12 in "appearance" form (see "Table 1: Appearance Visions of Daniel 9 and 10–12" in the unit on 9:1–6). Second, it concludes the concentric Hebrew section of Daniel 8–12, which parallels the book's Hebrew prologue (chap. 1). These sections frame and inform the book's Aramaic core (chaps. 2–7). Third, it completes the chronology of chapters 8–12, as well as that of the book as a whole, extending it to Cyrus's third year.

Daniel 10–12 divides into four sections: the first (10:1–11:1) introduces the vision; the second (11:2–20) moves the scene from Persia to Greece; the third (11:21–39) focuses on Antiochus IV Epiphanes; and the last (11:40–12:13) reveals the struggle and resurrection at the end of the age. Within this framework, 10:1–11:1 consists of this vision's historical setting (10:1), Daniel's fasting and prayer (10:2–3), the angel's arrival (10:4–9), and the word of assurance (10:10–11:1).

Historical and Cultural Background

Fasting and mourning to receive a vision occur frequently in 2 Esdras and 2 Baruch. In the ancient world, oils healed and refreshed dry skin and hair, while perfumed oils and lotions provided a fragrance that made social interaction more pleasant. As a sign of penitence and sincerity, one would forego such amenities when mourning or fasting.[1] In the Babylonian wisdom poem of Ludlul Bel Nemeqi, a righteous sufferer undergoes an extended period of fasting and mourning before seeing the mysterious man in new raiment.[2]

In intertestamental literature Gabriel, one of eight holy angels, is set over paradise, serpents, and cherubim, whereas Michael, one of six holy angels, is a "prince" over the "best part of mankind" (Israel) and over chaos (*1 Enoch* 9–10; 20; 24). These two observe humanity's behavior and lament to God about their sin. Both are sent to wage war against perpetrators.[3]

The "Book of Truth" brings to mind the Old Babylonian "Tablet of Destinies" mentioned in *Enuma Elish* and the Anzu Myth—both likely familiar to Daniel.[4] This tablet contains cosmic decrees about "times and laws" dictating world history and gives power to whoever holds it.[5]

Interpretive Insights

10:1 *the third year of Cyrus.* The historical marker, read with its corollary in 9:1–2, links the "appearance" visions in chapters 9 and 10–12, in the same way the "symbolic" visions are linked in chapters 7 and 8. Moreover, this date extends the book's chronological scope to a full "seventy years" for Daniel (605–535 BC), going beyond Babylon's fall and the implied Jewish return in 538 BC (9:1–2). The assertion that the vision is "true" not only highlights its chiastic parallel with Daniel 8 (cf. 8:26) but also anticipates the "Book of Truth" in 10:21. The cryptic announcement of "a great war" anticipates this vision's dramatic conclusion in chapters 11–12.

10:2–4 *At that time . . . On the twenty-fourth day of the first month.* The phrase "three weeks" literally translates, "three weeks of days" (cf. ESV). The latter distinguishes this number from the "weeks" (NIV: "sevens") of years in 9:24–27 and connects it to the "twenty-one days" in 10:13. Daniel's fast would have included the festivals of Passover and Unleavened Bread (fourteenth to twenty-first of Nisan), setting the more precise end of the seventy years in

Key Themes of Daniel 10:1–11:1

- At the end of Daniel's life, God responds to the prayers of a faithful and highly esteemed servant.
- This intense revelation of God's person and plan, even through a mediator, overwhelms Daniel.
- God's angels wage war against spiritual forces behind kings and kingdoms that dominate his people.

the context of deliverance from bondage (Exod. 12:14–18).[6] Daniel may be mourning over and praying about the incomplete restoration a couple of years earlier. His abstinence from "choice food" suggests he does not make a regular practice of his special diet from seventy years earlier (1:11–12). His location on the Tigris parallels the mention of the Ulai Canal (8:2, 16).

10:5–6 *a man dressed in linen.* A comparison of these verses to Ezekiel 1:4–28 and Revelation 1:13–16[7] raises questions about the identity of this "man." Some scholars see here a preincarnate visitation of Jesus,[8] while most understand the theophany as involving "Gabriel, the man" who appears in Daniel's other visions (cf. 8:16; 9:21).[9] This is suggested by the angel's assuring words, Daniel's reaction, and the context of the final visions (see the sidebar "Nondivine, Heavenly Beings in Daniel" in the unit on 3:24–30).

In mourning for three weeks, Daniel eats no meat and drinks no wine. Wine strainers, similar to our modern household strainers and sieves, were used to remove the sediment before wine was served. This strainer, whose central area of small holes has eroded away, is from the sixth to fourth century BC and is decorated in the Persian style.

Daniel 10:1–11:1

John's Use of Daniel in the Book of Revelation

In addition to the many references to the "Son of Man" in the Gospels (see the sidebar "'Son of Man' Imagery in the Bible" in the unit on 7:1–14), the apostle John employs a wide variety of images and phrases from Daniel throughout his apocalypse.

Correlation of the Language of John (Revelation) and Daniel

"Four winds"	Dan. 7:2	Rev. 7:1
"Ten horns"	Dan. 7:7, 20, 24	Rev. 12:3; 13:1; 17:12
"Ancient of Days" court scene	Dan. 7:9–10	Rev. 1:14; 5:11; 20:4, 11–12
Blasphemous little horn against the holy ones	Dan. 7:11, 21	Rev. 11:7; 13:5a, 7
"One like a son of man . . . clouds of heaven"	Dan. 7:13	Rev. 1:7, 13; 14:14
Three and a half years	Dan. 7:25	Rev. 12:14; 13:5b
Starry hosts of heaven	Dan. 8:10	Rev. 12:4
"Seal up the vision"	Dan. 8:26	Rev. 10:4
Theophany	Dan. 10:5–6	Rev. 1:14; 2:18; 19:1, 12
"Time of distress"	Dan. 12:1a	Rev. 7:14
Names written in the book	Dan. 12:1b	Rev. 3:5; 13:8; 20:12

At the time of John's writing, the annual remembrance of Antiochus's persecution of Judea in the celebration of Hanukkah stirred messianic expectations for Jews under Roman oppression (John 10:22–24). These eventually led to Jewish revolts, the destruction of the temple and Jerusalem, and the Jewish Diaspora. Although there is no focused interpretation of any one passage from Daniel in Revelation, John uses Daniel's imagery by way of secondary application to a similar persecution of both Jews and Christians under Rome. Like Daniel, he blends a historic situation with the ultimate struggle and triumph of God's kingdom at the end of the age.[a]

[a] See Beale, "Influence of Daniel."

10:7–9 *I, Daniel, was the only one.* Daniel's associates vanish as quickly as they appear, creating a frightening aloneness for the seer. Again, as in 8:17–18 and 27, Daniel is completely overwhelmed by the revelation. The intentional parallels in this vision accent the chiastic structure of chapters 8 and 10–12 in the concluding Hebrew section of the book—the latter significantly expanding on the former.

10:10–12 *A hand touched me . . . highly esteemed.* This gesture begins the words of assurance that continue through the end of this section, reflecting the language of 8:18. The angel's kind words (repeated in 10:19) also match the positive description of Daniel and God's eagerness to hear his prayer in 9:23. These ideas further connect the appearance visions. Like the one in 9:24–27, this message is difficult for Daniel to hear—yet he is assured the outcome is not his fault.

10:13–14 *the prince of the Persian kingdom.* Daniel's time in prayer (10:2–3) corresponds to the "twenty-one days" Gabriel is detained by the Persian "prince." Most likely this term connotes "angels" (good and bad) with spiritual powers on behalf of nations (cf. "prince" in Josh. 5:14; Dan. 8:11; NIV: "commander").[10] The NIV's "king of Persia" is actually plural and probably should be identified with this "prince," meaning "spiritual powers." The allusion to spiritual warfare (also in 10:20–11:1) paints a theological backdrop for the "great war" to follow. Michael, the second named angel in Daniel, assists Gabriel in his struggle. The reference to the "future" (literally, "the latter days") of Daniel's people corresponds to the announcement of the "great war" (10:1), anticipating the vision's dramatic conclusion (11:21–12:13).

10:15–19 *I bowed with my face toward the ground.* These verses further describe Daniel's reaction to this vision, though they add little additional information. When taken together, 10:7–12 and 15–19 expand

and emphasize the cryptic statements in 8:17–18 and 27.

10:20–11:1 *I will return to fight.* The idea of spiritual warfare, introduced regarding Persia in 10:13, also includes the wars of Greece, the persecution of the Jews, and the final apocalyptic struggle at the end of the age. The "Book of Truth," alluded to in 10:21 and 11:2, corresponds to the vision's content, which concludes this section and the book as a whole. The mention of "the first year of Darius the Mede" further connects the appearance visions of Daniel 9 and 10–12. The Masoretic Text and the Septuagint agree on connecting the sentence regarding "Darius" to the verses that follow it (ESV)—no doubt influenced by this historical marker. The immediate context, however, favors the NIV's parenthesis around 10:21b–11:1. Even though Darius is the nearest antecedent to the direct object "him" at the end of 11:1, Michael is more likely supporting Gabriel in his spiritual warfare (10:21b).[11]

Theological Insights

The aged seer's angelic encounter in 10:1–11:1 reveals three things about how God works with his people. First, God graciously responds to the prayers of the faithful. Second, an intense revelation of the person of God, even through a mediator, reveals the frailty of mere mortals. Third, God sends angels to contend against demonic forces in the spiritual warfare that often lies behind the struggles of his people.

Teaching the Text

1. *God hears our prayers.* God listens to mournful prayers of beloved servants today

The archangels Gabriel and Michael are depicted on this Byzantine icon (tenth to eleventh century AD).

and eagerly responds, although not always in the way we desire. God wants believers to engage with one another in the dynamic fellowship of prayer, sometimes while we mourn or fast. When teaching this passage, warmly invite the members of your congregation or study group to come to their heavenly Father with confidence and assurance that he welcomes them. Help them understand, however, that they must temper their expectations with the larger reality of God's will. This is especially important when their prayers involve intercession for others where they have no control over the repentance, or lack thereof, on the other's part.

2. *Mere mortals encounter God.* An intense realization of the awe-inspiring

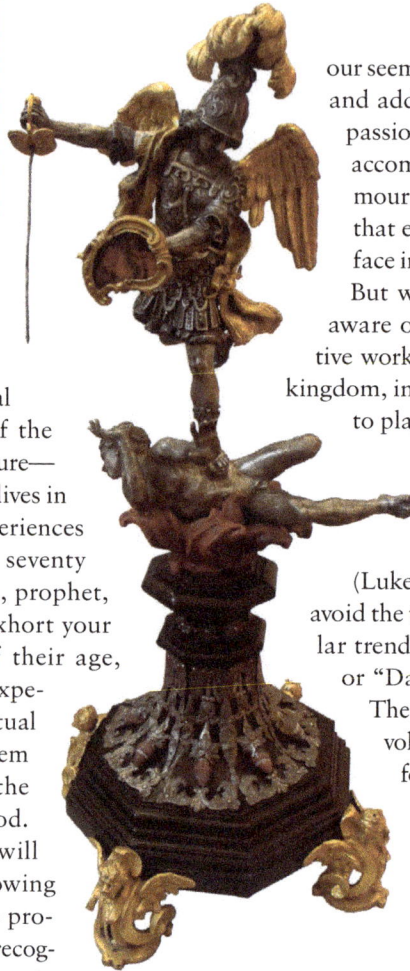

person of God continues to remind us as believers of our human frailties. Knowing God in a deeper and more personal way—yet in the light of the clear teachings of Scripture—helps us to put our own lives in perspective. Daniel experiences this most acutely after seventy years of service as sage, prophet, seer, and intercessor. Exhort your listeners, regardless of their age, spiritual maturity, or experiences, to pursue spiritual disciplines that help them to know more deeply the person and work of God. Assure them that this will also result in them knowing themselves better in the process. Encourage them to recognize and accept their humanity in contrast to God's sovereignty and to yield to his wisdom and will in this context.

3. *Spiritual warfare.* The struggles we face as God's people today exist in a larger context of spiritual warfare. This can give us hope and focus. In Daniel's narratives and visions, evil human beings set themselves against God and his people (cf. 8:25; 9:26), and evil spiritual beings oppose the angels sent to protect God's people. Therefore, we should recognize the spiritual dimension of our seemingly "earthly" struggles and address them with sincere, passionate prayer—sometimes accompanied by fasting and/or mourning. This does not mean that every human problem we face involves spiritual warfare. But we should be constantly aware of the ongoing redemptive work of God to establish his kingdom, in which we are privileged to play a role.

What not to teach. Whereas fasting and praying are presented positively in Scripture (Luke 2:37; Acts 13:2; 14:23), avoid the temptation to join popular trends toward "Daniel fasts" or "Daniel diets" (see 1:8–16). These practices for Daniel involved special circumstances for special occasions and were neither intended by him as enduring models nor practiced by him as a general lifestyle.

Illustrating the Text

God's ear is always turned to the earnest prayers of those who love him.

Lyrics: "Come, Ye Weary Sinners, Come," by Charles Wesley. Wesley (1707–88), a central figure in the Methodist movement and author of over six thousand hymns, wrote "Come, Ye Weary Sinners, Come" (1747).

Come, ye weary sinners, come,
   All who groan beneath your load,
Jesus calls His wanderers home,
   Hasten to your pardoning God!

Come, ye guilty spirits oppressed,
    Answer to the Savior's call,
"Come, and I will give you rest.
    Come, and I will save you all."

Jesus, full of truth and love,
    We Thy kindest word obey;
Faithful let Thy mercies prove,
    Take our load of guilt away;
Fain we would on Thee rely,
    Cast on Thee our sin and care,
To Thine arms of mercy fly,
    Find our lasting quiet there.

Burdened with a world of grief,
    Burdened with our sinful load,
Burdened with this unbelief,
    Burdened with the wrath of God;
Lo! we come to Thee for ease,
    True and gracious as Thou art,
Now our groaning souls release,
    Write forgiveness on our heart.[12]

Looking too far into the future of our world can be fearfully overwhelming.

Personal Testimony: Over nearly forty years of teaching Daniel, I have observed many very different responses from my students to apocalyptic texts—at least three are relevant here: being obsessed, dismissive, or fearful. The first recalls the evangelical prophecy conferences of the twentieth century—still popular in some places today. These students obsess over confirming every detail of the end times and how these relate to their own time in history.

Opposite this is the dismissive approach, which assumes the dark apocalyptic visions cannot be understood and should be ignored. These students merely want a quick-and-easy principle to apply to their lives. In contrast to these diametrically opposed reactions, a third group has dared to sense the fearful reality that confronted Daniel: his people would suffer greatly in an even greater conflict many years in the future. This response engages the heart of the text.

Spiritual warfare is an everyday reality for believers, whether we realize it or not.

Film: *The Visitation.* Robby Henson's 2006 film adaptation of Christian novelist Frank Peretti's 1999 novel, *The Visitation*, dramatically cautions its viewer to be aware of, and spiritually equipped for, encounters with the forces of darkness. In Antioch, Washington, Pastor Travis Jordan, who has lost faith in God after his wife's murder, ends up caught in a spiritual battle when a mysterious stranger named Brandon Nichols begins to take the town by storm with his miraculous healings worked through demonic powers. Peretti's story depicts the danger of ignorance through the townspeople's spiritual fervor that is carelessly devoted to this false teacher as well as the importance of courage in the face of demonic forces that are real and at work in our world even though we may not always be aware of them.

From Persia to Greece

Big Idea *Often working behind the scenes, God foresees and oversees the struggles of his people with hostile world forces.*

Understanding the Text

The Text in Context

See the unit on 10:1–11:1 for a discussion of the larger context, structure, and comparisons of chapters 10–12. Against this backdrop, 11:2–20 (the extended unit's second section) divides into two parts: a summary of the transition from Persia to Greece (11:2–4) and a description of key events in the Ptolemaic and Seleucid wars

Table 1: Kings of Persia

Kings	Reigns (BC)	Mentioned in Scripture
Cyrus	539–530	2 Chron. 36; Ezra 1; 3–6; Isa. 44–45; Dan. 1; 6; 10
Cambyses II	530–522	—
Gaumata	522	—
Darius I	522–486	Ezra 4–6; Neh. 12; Dan. 5–6; 9; 11; Hag. 1–2; Zech. 1; 7
Xerxes I	486–465	Ezra 4; Esther 1–3; 6–10
Artaxerxes I	464–423	Ezra 4; 6–8; Neh. 2; 5; 13
Darius II	423–404	—
Artaxerxes II	404–359	—
Artaxerxes III	359–338	—
Arses	338–335	—
Darius III	335–331	—

(11:5–20). Because the unnamed persons in this passage are difficult to follow, an interpretive paraphrase appears in the "Additional Insights" following this unit.

Historical and Cultural Background

Akkadian apocalypses from the twelfth to third century BC reveal a literary relationship with the astrological omen texts, which fall in the realm of Daniel's expertise. Like Daniel 11, these include a series of unnamed kings who come in the future, including brief references to their accomplishments. The series ends with the last king being greater than all the lesser kings that preceded him. Most likely the last king has commissioned the writing of these texts in the form of a prophetic apocalypse. The literary style of Daniel 11 is quite similar to these texts, although Daniel's vision condemns the last king rather than honoring him.[1]

Interpretive Insights

11:2 *I tell you the truth.* This assertion reflects the similar statement at the beginning of this vision (10:1), making the "Book of Truth" the source of the vision (10:21).

Three more kings will arise in Persia, and then a fourth. This "three . . . four" idiom appears in Proverbs 30:15–31 and Amos 1–2. Although several identifications of these kings are suggested,[2] two factors seem compelling. First, because this vision comes in Cyrus's third year (10:1), he should not be counted among the four. Second, the description of the fourth as wealthy and as stirring up everyone against Greece best fits Xerxes I (see the four rows shaded together in table 1). This interpretation includes Gaumata (Pseudo-Bardiya/Pseudo-Smerdis), who usurped the throne during the six months between Cambyses II and Darius I.[3]

11:3–4 *a mighty king will arise . . . his empire will be broken up.* Alexander the Great receives this title because of his swift and extensive conquest of Darius III of Persia (last shaded row in table 1). Alexander's death at age thirty-two, however, resulted in the division of his empire among his four generals at first, an arrangement that is then consolidated between just two: Ptolemy and Seleucus (see the comments on 8:5–8).[4] In table 2, the succession from Alexander to Antiochus IV (on the Seleucid side only) might be numbered with regard to the "ten horns" of chapter 7:7, 20, and 24. Following the initial reference to Alexander, the table parallels the Ptolemaic (left) and Seleucid (right) kings. One of the sons and would-be heirs to Seleucus IV, "Antiochus" (Seleucus's infant son) would have been titled "IV" if "Antiochus IV Epiphanes" had not arranged his murder and seized the throne first. An alternate interpretation of reckoning the ten might include Ptolemy VI and VII among the "ten horns" (instead of Seleucus's sons), in

Key Themes of Daniel 11:2–20

- The angelic messenger reveals the transfer of world power from Persia to Greece.
- The Ptolemies of Egypt and the Seleucids of Syria arise as two warring factions within the Hellenistic Empire.
- Jerusalem is caught in the middle of the civil war, threatened by a powerful king of the North.

that Antiochus IV "uproots" these "horns" as well (7:20, 24).

11:5 *The king of the South will become strong . . . one of his commanders . . . even stronger.* Daniel 11:5–12 highlights key persons and events during Ptolemaic dominance over Judea (323–200 BC). Ptolemy I, a general under Alexander, began this rule, until a contender dethroned Seleucus I, forcing him to seek refuge in military service under Ptolemy. Together, they restored Seleucus's rule as "king of the North" in 312 BC. Within a decade, Seleucus's kingdom became the largest division of Alexander's Greece (Arrian, *Anab.* 7.22.5), giving rise to conflicts with the Ptolemies.[5]

11:6 *The daughter of the king of the South will . . . make an alliance.* Around 250 BC, Ptolemy II agreed to a marriage alliance with Antiochus II of Syria (Antiochus I plays no role in this passage). Ptolemy's daughter

The description of the fourth king of Persia fits King Xerxes, shown here in relief with his attendants at the remains of his palace at Persepolis, Iran.

Berenice was given to Antiochus, who left his wife, Laodice. Four years later, Antiochus took Laodice back and mysteriously died shortly thereafter. With her husband out of the way, she arranged the murder of Berenice, Berenice's child, and "her royal escort." Berenice's father Ptolemy ("the one who supported her") died in Egypt the same year.[6]

11:7–9 *One from her family line . . . will attack . . . the king of the North.* Berenice's brother Ptolemy III assumed Egypt's throne in 246 BC, plotting his revenge. He captured Syria's capital at Antioch and killed Laodice, leaving her son Seleucus II in control of the North. Idols taken by Cambyses from Egypt were among Ptolemy's spoils of war.[7] Returning to deal with revolts in his kingdom, Ptolemy left Syria unattended for two years. Consequently, Seleucus regained power and attacked Egypt, but he quickly retreated without a victory.[8]

11:10 *His sons will prepare for war.* Seleucus III succeeded his father as king of the North (226 BC) but died in a military venture three years later. His brother Antiochus III took his place and quickly gained control of Media and Asia Minor. After Ptolemy IV took Egypt's throne (221 BC), Antiochus's army spread "like an irresistible flood" through Phoenicia and Judea. Coming "as far as his fortress" could mean Antiochus's fortress at Gaza on Egypt's border.[9]

11:11–12 *the king of the South will march out in a rage.* Ptolemy IV responded with a counteroffensive at Raphia (217 BC), where he slaughtered thousands within Antiochus's "large army" (Polybius, *Hist.* 5.79). He did "not remain triumphant," as rebellions at home forced him to redirect his efforts—like his father once did (cf. 11:8).

11:13 *the king of the North will muster another army.* This verse marks the turning point for Judea from Ptolemaic domination (11:5–12) to that of the Seleucids (11:13–20). Antiochus III reestablished control over the eastern extent of his empire (212–205 BC), earning the title "the Great." A year later, Ptolemy IV and his queen died, leaving their kingdom under guardianship to their five-year-old son, Ptolemy V. Antiochus seized this opportunity and assembled a "larger [army] than the first"

Table 2: Greek Kings in Daniel 11:5–35

Alexander the Great (336–323 BC)—Daniel 11:3–4					
South: Ptolemies in Egypt			**North: Seleucids in Syria**		
Ptolemy I	323–285	11:5	Seleucus I	311–280	11:5
Ptolemy II	285–246	11:6	Antiochus I	280–261	—
			Antiochus II	261–246	11:6
Ptolemy III	246–221	11:7–9	Seleucus II	246–226	11:7–9
			Seleucus III	226–223	11:10
Ptolemy IV	221–204	11:10–12	Antiochus III	223–187	11:10–19
Ptolemy V	204–181	11:13–19	Seleucus IV	187–175	11:20
Ptolemy VI	181–146	11:22–27	[Would-be heirs Demetrius & Antiochus]		
Ptolemy VII	169–164, 147–144	11:25–27	Antiochus IV	175–164	11:21–35

to retake southern Syria and Samaria/Judea. The decisive battle occurred at Paneas (NT Caesarea Philippi) in 200 BC.

11:14 *In those times many will rise against the king of the South.* The opening phrase accents the increase of Seleucid dominance and prepares the reader for "times" to come (cf. 11:21–39). Egypt's troubles under Ptolemy V continued unabated. In addition to local seditions, Philip V of Macedon allied with Antiochus against Ptolemy. The "violent among [Daniel's] own people" are militant Judeans who became involved in the surrounding war—some Jews favored the North, and others, the South. Their efforts were "without success." The most apparent meaning of "the vision" is that recorded in Daniel 10–12.[10]

11:15–16 *the king of the North . . . will do as he pleases.* After his defeat at Paneas, Egypt's general Scopas retreated to Sidon. In turn, Antiochus III besieged the city, forcing the surrender of troops who had no "strength to stand" due to famine. In his well-established rule, Antiochus did as he pleased (cf. 4:35; 11:3, 36). Judea is "the Beautiful Land" (8:9; 11:16, 41), which Antiochus now controlled.

11:17 *He . . . will make an alliance with the king of the South.* Although the power and wealth of Antiochus inclined him to attack Egypt again, the rise of Rome caused him to seek a marriage treaty instead. In 197 BC, he gave his daughter Cleopatra I to Ptolemy V, hoping to retain her loyalty. But she sided with Egypt, and after her husband's death, she led the South until her son Ptolemy VI took the throne in 181 BC.[11]

Antiochus III, also known as Antiochus the Great, is one of the kings of the Seleucid Dynasty. His exploits begin in Daniel 11:10, since he is one of the sons who assembles an army. This gold octadrachm (223–187 BC) bears his image.

11:18–19 *he will turn his attention to the coastlands.* Thwarted in the South, Antiochus launched campaigns in the west, taking Aegean islands and attacking Thrace in 196 BC. The Roman commander Scipio, however, reversed Antiochus's momentum in the battles of Thermopylae and Magnesia (191, 190 BC). Two years later, Antiochus became a Roman vassal, surrendering twenty hostages—including his son Antiochus IV. Turning "back toward . . . his own country," the broken Seleucid ruler met an ignominious death while pillaging a temple in Persia to pay tribute to his new western overlord.[12]

11:20 *His successor will send out a tax collector.* Antiochus III's other son, Seleucus IV, assumed Syria's throne in 187 BC. To honor his obligations to Rome, he sent the "tax collector" Heliodorus to Jerusalem to draw from the temple's wealth (2 Macc. 3). Seleucus was assassinated in 175 BC.

Theological Insights

Three truths about God and his work are evident in 11:2–20. First, God knows the future precisely and, in his wisdom, reveals measured portions of this knowledge to his people. Second, God keeps his covenant by bringing a just punishment, requiring an extended and hostile foreign domination of his people. Third, it is futile for God's people to seek safety in the violent plans of powerful kings that die with them, rather than in God's work and kingdom.

Teaching the Text

1. *God has sovereign foreknowledge.* The Lord's knowledge of the future, together with his sovereign rule over human kingdoms, should give us confidence that he is in control. This chapter is unique in the Old Testament with its sixth-century BC view of second-century BC events, making it an appropriate place to note the foreknowledge of God. Draw from the theologically rich statements in previous chapters, which confirm that God sets up and takes down human kingdoms to establish his kingdom. Remind your listeners that this vision is an expansion of God's answer to Daniel's prayer in the previous vision. Keeping this big picture in mind can help us face often-frightening current events within a greater theological framework.

2. *Persistent sin has consequences.* God's covenant with his people has two contrasting dimensions: his love and his righteousness. It is easier for believers to relate to the first than the second. The era described in this pericope is long and dark. Moreover, it includes the subjugation of God's people because of their persistent sin that lasts several generations. Contemplating such a scenario should cause us to do two things. First, we should remember in the darkness what God has revealed to us in the light. Drawing from earlier passages in

Daniel can be helpful in doing this. Second, we should keep in mind that persistent sin results in serious consequences. Because of this, we should not take lightly God's tender mercies or his warnings of discipline.

3. *Perspective on earthly rulers.* It is sometimes tempting to put too much stock in political or personal power. God's kingdom is eternal, while the kingdoms of this earth will die with their rulers. The brief allusion to God's land and people in this passage speaks negatively regarding the Judeans' attempt to fulfill this vision through violent political efforts. The frailty of human kingdoms should give us pause when we are inclined to rely too heavily on them. Although they serve a purpose in God's plans, their power is limited. Moreover, the suffering we may experience under their rule is, in the long run, temporary—even though it may go beyond our lifetimes. Encourage your listeners to invest themselves beyond the temporal circumstances that attend this life.

What not to teach. Resist the temptation to skip this section of Daniel because of its tedious character. It is part of God's

Earthly kingdoms rise and fall with the power of their rulers, but God's kingdom is eternal. This map shows the Seleucid and the Ptolemaic kingdoms in 188 BC, after the death of Antiochus III.

Antiochus III defeated by Romans, 191 BC

MACEDON THRACE

BITHYNIA PONTUS
GALATIA

Thermopylae

Magnesia CAPPADOCIA

Sparta CILICIA

Antiochus III defeated by Romans, 190 BC

LYCIA

Cyprus Antioch

SELEUCID TERRITORY

Sidon

Antiochus III defeated by Ptolemy IV, 217 BC Damascus Babylon Susa
Paneas

Alexandria Raphia Jerusalem Antiochus III victorious at Paneas, 200 BC

EGYPT

Daniel 11:2–20

Word and should be addressed in teaching the text. This is not, however, merely a place to teach Persian and Greek history. Keep the theological backdrop constantly before your listeners, and provide relevant examples of how God's sovereignty guides human history.

Illustrating the Text

Future visions of mere mortals pale in comparison with the God who knows all.

Culture: Throughout human history, predicting the future has been attempted by many and with varying degrees of detail. Some have tried to describe in explicit detail events purportedly taking place years in the future (and failed), and still others have taken vague and general prophecies, like those of the French seer Nostradamus (1503–66), and retroactively attempted to interpret these predictions as applying to world events like the rise of Napoleon or the September 11, 2001, attacks. Though such attempts accrue popular interest, like internet conspiracies or television specials, these "prophecies" are usually broad statements easily connected to numerous events by overenthusiastic followers. Unlike the words of such false prophets, God's apocalyptic depiction of Persian and Greek history given in Daniel 11 is one of astonishing detail and accuracy, proclaiming God's omniscient power over all human wisdom and powers.

Though we fall into darkness because of sin, God's light never ceases to shine.

Nature: In the Mariana Trench, the Pacific Ocean floor plummets nearly seven miles. Imagine submerging in a submarine from the top of the ocean, where the sunlight streaming through the water still colors everything you see a beautiful blue. As you descend, the water grows darker, reaching absolute darkness at the aphotic "midnight" zone—less than a mile below the surface. Several miles below that, the pit of the Mariana Trench is pitch black. The sun's light never changes, yet the amount we perceive depends on our depth. Sometimes sin carries us so far into darkness that we lose sight of God's mercy in our perception of his judgment. However, though we may be too deep to see its effects, God's light of love still shines, and his warmth is never so far away that we cannot rise to meet it once again.

Beware of utilizing faith as a banner for personal goals or ideology.

Church History: Forms of Christian zealotry have appeared at times throughout church history for achieving military or political aims rather than serving God and his true kingdom. For example, our faith was used to unify state and church under the Roman/Byzantine emperor Constantine the Great, who ruled AD 306–37. Tragically, and more violently, the papacy used Crusaders in the eleventh to thirteenth century to conduct holy wars in Palestine for wealth and power. Even today, the temptation to use faith as an evangelical banner for national idealism persists. In contrast, our commitment to God's kingdom—first and foremost—must take priority over all allegiances to the kingdoms of this world. The pulpit should not become a platform for political persuasions or inappropriate patriotism for any transient kingdom that will one day pass away in favor of God's eternal rule.

Naming the Unnamed Kings in Daniel 11:2–28

Because Daniel's otherwise detailed vision does not include names of these kings or events, an interpretive paraphrase of the NIV text is provided here, with some occasional ellipses for the sake of brevity.[1]

Persia to Greece (11:2–4)

[2]Now then, I tell you the truth: After Cyrus the Great (539–530 BC), three more kings will arise in Persia: Cambyses II (530–522 BC), Gaumata (522 BC), and Darius I (522–486). Then a fourth will arise, Xerxes I (486–465 BC), who will be far richer than all the others. When he has gained power by his wealth, he will stir up everyone against the kingdom of Greece. [3]Then a mighty king will arise, Alexander the Great (336–323 BC), who will rule with great power and do as he pleases. [4]After he has arisen, his empire will be . . . uprooted and given to his four generals: Cassander (Greece and Macedon), Lysimachus (Thrace and Asia Minor), Seleucus (Syria and Mesopotamia), and Ptolemy (Egypt and the land surrounding Judea).

Egyptian, Ptolemaic Dominance of Judea (11:5–13)

[5]Ptolemy I of Egypt (323–285 BC), will become strong, but one of his commanders, Seleucus I (312–280 BC), will become even stronger than he and will rule his own kingdom of Syria with great power. [6]After some years, they will become allies. Berenice, the daughter of Ptolemy II (285–246 BC), will go to Antiochus II of Syria (261–246 BC) to make an alliance, but she will not retain her power, and he and his power will not last. In those days she will be betrayed, together with her royal escort and her father, Ptolemy, and Antiochus, who supported her.

[7]Berenice's brother, Ptolemy III (246–221 BC), will arise to take her place. He will attack . . . Seleucus II (246–226 BC) and enter his fortress; he will fight against them and be victorious. [8]He will also seize their gods, their metal images and their valuable articles of silver and gold and carry them off to Egypt. For some years he will leave Seleucus alone. [9]Then Seleucus will invade Ptolemy's realm but will retreat to his own country. [10]His sons Seleucus III (226–223 BC) and Antiochus III (223–187 BC) will prepare for war and assemble a great army, which will sweep on like an irresistible flood and carry the battle as far as the fortress of Ptolemy IV (221–204 BC). [11]Then Ptolemy will march out in a rage and fight against Antiochus, who will raise a large army, but it will be defeated in the battle of Raphia (217 BC). [12]When the army is carried off, Ptolemy will be filled with pride and will slaughter many thousands, yet he will not remain triumphant. [13]For Antiochus will muster another army, larger than the first; and after several years, he will advance with a huge army fully equipped.

Syrian, Seleucid Dominance of Judea (11:14–28)

14In those times many will rise against Ptolemy V (204–181 BC). Those who are violent among the Judeans will rebel in fulfillment of the vision, but without success. **15**Then Antiochus will come and build up siege ramps and will capture the fortified city of Gaza (201 BC). Ptolemy's forces will be powerless to resist; even his best troops will not have the strength to stand against him in the battles of Paneas and Sidon (200, 198 BC). **16**Antiochus will do as he pleases; no one will be able to stand against him. He will establish himself in Judea and will have the power to destroy it. **17**He will determine to come with the might of his entire kingdom and will make an alliance with Ptolemy. And Antiochus will give Ptolemy his daughter Cleopatra in marriage in order to overthrow the kingdom, but his plans will not succeed or help him. **18**Then Antiochus will turn his attention to the coastlands of the Mediterranean and will take many of them, including Thrace (196 BC). But the Roman commander Cornelius Scipio will put an end to his insolence and will turn his insolence back on him in the battles of Thermopylae and Magnesia (191–190 BC).

19After this, he will turn back toward the fortresses of his own country, Syria, but will stumble and fall, to be seen no more. **20**His successor, Seleucus IV (187–175 BC), will send out his tax collector Heliodorus to Jerusalem to maintain the royal splendor. In a few years, however, Seleucus will be destroyed, yet not in anger or in battle.

21Seleucus will be succeeded by Antiochus IV Epiphanes (175–164 BC), a contemptible person, who had not been given the honor of royalty. He will invade Seleucus's kingdom when its people feel secure, and he will seize it through intrigue. **22**Then an overwhelming army will be swept away before him; both it and a prince of a covenant, Ptolemy VI (181–146 BC), will be destroyed. **23**After coming to an agreement with him, Antiochus will act deceitfully, and with only a few people he will rise to power. **24**When the richest provinces feel secure, he will invade them . . . but only for a time.

25With a large army Antiochus will stir up his strength and courage against Egypt. Ptolemy will wage war with a large and very powerful army, but he will not be able to stand because of the plots devised against him. **26**Ptolemy's advisors Eulaeus and Lenaeus will try to destroy him; his army will be swept away, and many will fall in battle. **27**Antiochus and Ptolemy, with their hearts bent on evil, will sit at the same table and lie to each other, but to no avail, because an end will still come at the appointed time. **28**Antiochus Epiphanes will return to Syria with great wealth, but his heart will be set against Judea.

Until the Roman conquest, the rivalry for power in the Hellenistic world between the Ptolemaic and the Seleucid kingdoms led to almost constant warfare. The land of Israel became caught in the middle of many of these conflicts and changes in leadership. This sculpted head, found at the Villa of the Papyri in Herculaneum, portrays Ptolemy III.

A Contemptible Person

Big Idea *Although severe times of persecution may come for God's people, he refines and purifies the faithful.*

Understanding the Text

The Text in Context

See the unit on 10:1–11:1 for a discussion of the larger context, structure, and comparisons of chapters 10–12, including its fourfold division. Against this backdrop, 11:21–39 (the extended unit's third section) continues to chronicle the Ptolemaic and Seleucid wars, with a climactic emphasis on Jewish persecution by Antiochus Epiphanes. It divides into two parts: Antiochus's first Egyptian campaign and his oppression of Judea (11:21–28) and his second Egyptian campaign, including his severe persecution of Judea (11:29–39).

Historical and Cultural Background

Antiochus IV Epiphanes (175–164 BC) stole the throne after the assassination of his brother Seleucus IV (see comments on 11:3–4, 21). Among his goals was the forced conversion of the Jews in and around Jerusalem. Those who opposed his Hellenizing efforts faced death. Coins from this era bear the arrogant title "Theos Epiphanes" ("God Manifest"), which his critics pronounced "Epimanes" ("madman"; Polybius, *Hist.* 26.1.1). Key events in his rule include the murder of the Jewish high priest Onias III (171 BC), two wars with the Ptolemies (169–168 BC), the persecution of Judea, and his desecration of Jerusalem's temple. The last sparked the Maccabean Revolts (167–164 BC) and reconsecration of the temple, celebrated in the Jewish holiday of Hanukkah. Antiochus died in Persia in December 164 BC. The Jewish resistance led to a revived Kingdom of Judah under the Hasmonean Dynasty, beginning in 104 BC (see 1 and 2 Maccabees), which lasted until its conquest by Rome in 64 BC.[1]

Interpretive Insights

11:21 *a contemptible person.* Antiochus IV was returning from captivity in Rome in 175 BC when his brother Seleucus IV was assassinated (see 11:18–20). Immediately, Heliodorus proclaimed himself regent on behalf of Seleucus's eldest son, Demetrius, who was imprisoned in Rome. The people felt "secure" with this regency when Antiochus seized the throne "through intrigue" (aided by Eumenes II of Pergamum). He made Seleucus's infant son (also named Antiochus) coregent, until the child was murdered in 170 BC.[2]

11:22–24 *an overwhelming army will be swept away.* On the one hand, this may be a chronologically displaced allusion to the Jerusalem priesthood ("prince of the covenant") and Antiochus's agreement to Judea's internal rule. Here, the "army" that is "swept away" is the Syrian force Antiochus originally overcame (11:21). His acting "deceitfully" relates to the anti-Hellenistic Jewish high priest Onias III, whom the king deposed. Antiochus was induced by a large bribe to replace Onias with pro-Hellenistic priest Jason (whom he also deposed), then again with an even larger bribe to replace Jason with Menelaus (172 BC). Antiochus's overthrowing "the richest provinces" and distributing "wealth" generally describes his rule (see Polybius, *Hist.* 26.1; Josephus, *Ant.* 12.7.2).[3] On the other hand, these verses may be in chronological sequence between Antiochus's usurping the Seleucid throne (11:21) and his first Egyptian campaign (11:25–29). Here, Ptolemy VI is the "prince of a covenant" (there is no definite article in the Masoretic Text) in his deceitful "agreement" with Antiochus. The scenario, therefore, previews the events of 11:25–28.[4] Both interpretations have merit, although neither is obvious. In both, this contemptible person's successes last "only for a time."

11:25–26 *he will stir up his strength . . . against the king of the South.* At this

Key Themes of Daniel 11:21–39

- A contemptible person arises in the kingdom of the North to dominate the remainder of the Greek civil war.
- This anti-God ruler persecutes the Jews in Jerusalem, killing many of them and desecrating the temple before his death.
- Wise Jews who know their God remain faithful even at the cost of their lives.

point, Antiochus's first Egyptian campaign (169 BC) is clearly intended. Ptolemy VI, son of Antiochus's sister Cleopatra (11:17), provoked the war. The young Ptolemy, urged by his advisors after his mother's death (Polybius, *Hist.* 28.20–21), made plans to reconquer Syria and Samaria/Judea. Antiochus learned of this and struck first "with a large army" at Pelusium on Egypt's border, where Ptolemy was taken captive. Antiochus failed, however, to control Alexandria, where Ptolemy's younger brother Ptolemy VII was crowned. The "plots devised against" Ptolemy VI most likely refer to his advisors Eulaeus and Lenaeus, who ate "from the king's provisions" and foolishly advised him to attack Antiochus.[5]

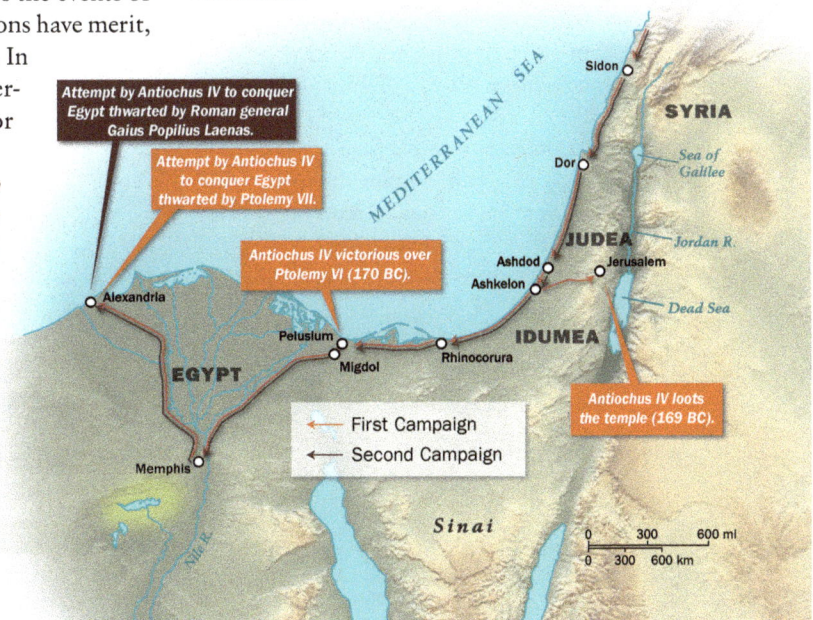

Attempt by Antiochus IV to conquer Egypt thwarted by Roman general Gaius Popilius Laenas.

Attempt by Antiochus IV to conquer Egypt thwarted by Ptolemy VII.

Antiochus IV victorious over Ptolemy VI (170 BC).

Antiochus IV loots the temple (169 BC).

First Campaign
Second Campaign

Attempts by Antiochus IV to conquer Egypt were thwarted first by Ptolemy VII and later by the Roman general Gaius Popilius Laenas. This map shows the military campaigns of Antiochus IV into Egypt.

11:27–28 *The two kings . . . lie to each other.* Antiochus agreed to set up his nephew and prisoner Ptolemy VI in Memphis as king against Ptolemy VII (both partners in the agreement had their own agenda). Their schemes unraveled when Cleopatra II (sister of the two Ptolemies) helped her brothers reconcile, so that they ruled Egypt together from 169 to 164 BC. The "appointed time" recalls similar phrases in the chiastically paralleled vision of chapter 8 (cf. 11:17–19) and anticipates the historical climax fast approaching in 11:29, 35; and 12:7. On his way home from his defeat in the South—with his heart "set against the holy covenant"—Antiochus slaughtered many Jews in Jerusalem, desecrated and sacked the temple, and carried off its wealth (1 Macc. 1:20–24).

11:29–30a *At the appointed time he will invade the South again.* Antiochus's second Egyptian campaign came in 168 BC. This time, "ships of the western coastlands" intervene on behalf of the Ptolemies. More specifically, the Roman general Gaius Popilius Laenas personally ordered Antiochus to abandon his hopes of controlling Egypt and to withdraw—which Antiochus did at once (Polybius, *Hist.* 29.27).

11:30b–32a *vent his fury against the holy covenant.* Again thwarted in the South, Antiochus redirected his wrath toward Judea (167 BC). His tactics were fourfold. First, he weakened Jewish unity by deceitfully showing "favor" to those willing to "forsake the holy covenant" and Hellenize. Foremost among these persons was Menelaus, the pro-Hellenist high priest appointed by Antiochus. Second, he forbade observance of the Mosaic law, including circumcision, reading of Torah, sacrificing to Yahweh, and celebrating holy days—all on penalty of death. Third, he desecrated "the temple fortress" by offering unclean sacrifices to pagan gods and erecting an idol of Olympian Zeus on the altar: "the abomination that causes desolation" (cf. the parallel reference in 9:27).[6] Fourth, while doing these things, his army plundered Jerusalem, destroying its walls and houses.[7]

11:32b–35 *the people who know their God will firmly resist him.* Amid Antiochus's corrupting persecution, "wise" and faithful servants of Yahweh appeared, who honored

Rather than abandon their faith and religious practice to obey the commands of Antiochus IV, many Jews chose torture and death. This illumination from a manuscript (Royal 15 D I) of the second edition of the Bible Historiale by Guyart des Moulins (ca. 1291–95) shows persecutions by Antiochus IV Epiphanes like those recorded in 2 Maccabees 7.

God's covenant and instructed others to do the same (cf. 12:3).[8] Many chose death or enslavement over surrendering their faith and practice (1 Macc. 1–2; 2 Macc. 6; see also the comments on 7:25–26 and 8:9–14). The "little help" they receive alludes to the Maccabean Revolts, which were sparked by Jerusalem's persecution (167 BC). The violent methods of the priest Mattathias and his sons (notably, Judas Maccabeus) led many Jewish zealots who were "not sincere" in their beliefs to join the rebellion. The purpose of the sufferings of the "wise" is spiritual purification. Moreover, these hardships last only "for a time," that is, until "the time of the end," which comes "at the appointed time." These phrases intentionally allude to the approximately three and a half years of Jewish persecution presented throughout Daniel (7:25; 8:13–14; 9:26–27; 12:7, 11–12).

11:36–39 *The king will do as he pleases.* This description is also attributed to the kings of Media and Persia (8:4, 20), to Alexander the Great (11:3), and to Antiochus III (11:16). Although some commentators see here a sudden change of subject to "antichrist" in the eschatological future,[9] such speculation is not warranted by the grammar or wording of the text. More likely, "the king" in 11:36 is the same as "the king of the North" in 11:28: Antiochus IV. Five reasons suggest that these verses constitute a summary of his character and policies. First, coins bearing his chosen title "Theos Epiphanes" ("God Manifest") evidence his self-exaltation "above every god" and, specifically, "the God of gods" (cf. 7:25; 8:25). Second, he was "successful" throughout the "determined" time of his "wrath" on Judea. Third, in favor of Olympian Zeus,

References to the "Antichrist" in the Bible

To use the term "antichrist" prior to the New Testament era is anachronistic, although Antiochus IV is clearly an "anti-God" figure in Daniel (7:25; 8:25; 11:36). The technical term first appears in the New Testament in two of John's short letters (AD 85–95), where it describes an ultimate "antichrist" who follows "many antichrists" already having existed by John's time (1 John 2:18). In a broader sense, "whoever denies that Jesus is the Christ" is an "antichrist" (2:22), because that person has "the spirit of the antichrist" (4:3; cf. 2 John 7). Earlier, Paul alludes to the ultimate antichrist as "the man of lawlessness" who is part of the "rebellion" in the "day of the Lord" (2 Thess. 2:1–4). This passage appears to borrow anti-God imagery from the book of Daniel.

he marginalized the traditional Greek god Apollo, as well as the Ptolemaic deity Tammuz-Adonis ("one desired by women"; cf. Ezek. 8:14). Fourth, the "god of fortresses" could refer to Jupiter Capitolinus (a citadel god).[10] Fifth, his liberal distribution of wealth to those who followed him is well attested (see the comments on 11:22–24).

Theological Insights

Three characteristics of the person and work of God are evident in 11:21–39. First, the sovereign Lord of history foresees and controls the events of mere mortals, allotting to each its "appointed time." Second, in the midst of our suffering, God gives to those who know and obey him the will and strength to resist evil. Third, even though arrogant people may exalt their own false gods, or even themselves, the one true God rules supremely as the "God of gods."

Teaching the Text

1. *God's foreknowledge and foreordination.* As the Lord of history, God both foresees

Antiochus IV exalted himself above all gods as evidenced by the coins he authorized, like the one shown here, which was struck with the words, in Greek, "ΒΑΣΙΛΕΩΣ ΑΝΤΙΟΧΟΥ ΘΕΟΥ ΕΠΙΦΑΝΟΥΣ," translated, "King Antiochus, God manifest."

and oversees all human events, allotting to each its appointed time. This important theme pointedly marks the opening verses of Daniel (1:1–2) and sustains its theology through this last climactic vision. It cannot be overemphasized when teaching the book of Daniel. God's sovereignty is evident in the "seventy years" of exile, as well as in the "seventy 'sevens'" that this passage chronicles. Paint the big picture for your listeners of how God foresees and oversees the events in their lives and in the world around them, just as he does in Daniel. Show them how this reveals God's character as the all-knowing and all-powerful God who holds them accountable for their sin and yet cares deeply about their suffering.

2. *God's sanctification of the wise and faithful.* In the midst of our suffering, God gives to those who know and obey him the will and strength to resist evil and grow spiritually. An overemphasis on God's foreknowledge can make some of your listeners think that their behavior makes little difference in the outcome of events. Assure them that because God cares about our suffering—even when our corporate punishment is deserved—he will give us the courage and endurance to persevere until "the appointed time." But balance this with the call to know and obey God. This is a

good place to turn to Deuteronomy 7:9, as Daniel does in his prayer: "Lord, the great and awesome God, who keeps his covenant of love with those who love him and keep his commandments . . ." (Dan. 9:4). Present a balanced theology of God's sovereignty and human responsibility, as well as faith and obedience.

3. *The supremacy of the one true God.* Even though arrogant people may exalt their own false gods, or even themselves, the one true God rules supremely as the God of gods. It is a sad reality, but we live in a relativistic world, in which belief in false gods continues to challenge biblical faith. There are still people who exalt themselves above all gods, even the God of gods. Yet knowing that the one true God is still above all gods—as well as persons who make such blasphemous boasts—can bring an inner peace in our assurance that worshiping him alone is worth the risk, suffering, or sacrifice.

What not to teach. When preaching or teaching this text in a church context, do not spend too much time discussing where in this text the historical description of the career of Antiochus ends and where the ultimate "end times" begin. Keep your focus on what God is doing with evil, anti-God rulers.

Illustrating the Text

God knows the future and appoints its times, yet we are responsible for our choices.

Quote: **J. I. Packer.** Imagine seeing these words overhead when entering heaven: "Let the one who is thirsty come; and let the one who wishes take the free gift of the water of life" (Rev. 22:17). Then, after entering, you look back and read, "You did not choose me, but I chose you and appointed you" (John 15:16a). Attempts to understand the theological paradox of divine sovereignty and human responsibility have challenged theologians throughout history. As J. I. Packer observes:

> The antinomy . . . is only one of a number that the Bible contains. We may be sure that they all find their reconciliation in the mind and counsel of God, and we may hope that in heaven we shall understand them ourselves. But meanwhile, our wisdom is to maintain with equal emphasis both of the apparently conflicting truths in each case, to hold them together in the relation in which the Bible itself sets them, and to recognize that here is a mystery which we cannot expect to solve in this world.[11]

God allows suffering, in part, so we can grow in strength and godliness.

Sports: The biological process of physical training is a form of suffering the body uses to a positive effect. The actual fibers of the muscle's anatomical structure do not grow by remaining stationary. Rather, they must be torn before they can be rebuilt larger, causing the pain we feel in training. A good coach knows how far to push her athletes to achieve their best, challenging them to endure pain so that they can be stronger. Though the players do not always enjoy this routine, it is because of her extra push that they are able to succeed at game time. God grants us challenges so that we might learn perseverance. The suffering and the consequences of our sin are never in vain but serve to make us stronger for the future (Rom. 5:3–5).

The temptation to idolatrous pagan worship continues even today.

Culture: A recent rise in neopaganism has capitalized on modern interests in "spirituality" through practices such as meditation, magic, and ritual services. New religious forms, such as Neo-Druidism and Neo-Wicca, draw significantly on past traditions and ancient mythology to form occult practices that often focus on the worship of gods and goddesses and the community celebration of pagan festivals. These interests are in many ways an attempt to synthesize the traditions and history of the past with the modern Western interest in spirituality and self-realization. This kind of occult paganism is growing in force and captivating many looking for "spiritual" experiences and a connection with cultural and ethnic traditions. Yet it represents the same temptation and danger as the paganism of the past: idolatry and the exchanging of the immortal God for divinities and spiritual rituals contrived by mere mortals (Ps. 115:4; Rom. 1:22–23).

Resurrection and Accountability

Big Idea *The wise should understand that the struggle of human history ends with resurrection to everlasting life for the righteous and to everlasting punishment for the wicked.*

Understanding the Text

The Text in Context

See the unit on 10:1–11:1 for a discussion of the larger context, structure, and comparisons of chapters 10–12, including its fourfold division. Against this backdrop, 11:40–12:13 completes the last section of Daniel's final appearance vision (chaps. 10–12), the book's two Hebrew sections (chaps. 1 and 8–12), the book's four apocalyptic visions (chaps. 7–12), and, of course, the book of Daniel as a whole. Daniel 11:40–12:13 divides easily into two sections: 11:40–12:4 completes the vision proper (contained in 11:2–12:4) and 12:5–13 concludes this larger vision

in general, paralleling its introduction (10:1–11:1).

Historical and Cultural Background

The "book" in 12:1 is comparable to the "book of names" of those destined for death that Enkidu sees in his dream of the netherworld, contained in the Gilgamesh Epic from the second millennium BC.[1] In this Mesopotamian poem, when someone's sins are sufficient to warrant divine

The idea of resurrection was generally not part of the worldview of the ancient Near East. One of the closest suggestions of resurrection is found in this painting from the coffin of Nespawershepi from Thebes (984 BC). It shows new seedlings rising from the body of the mummified Osiris as rain is sent from Nut, the sky goddess. Osiris was the god of the underworld, but he was also the god of fertility and new life.

judgment, that person's name is blotted out of the book, leading to his or her death. Those who remain can expect "continued" life, although "eternal" life is not specified.[2]

The fundamental aspect of afterlife in the ancient Near East was a continuing existence in a grave-like netherworld with no differentiation between the righteous and the wicked. In Canaan and Mesopotamia, the gods governed this realm. The Egyptian Book of the Dead allows a select few to move beyond judgment, though those who fail to do so are devoured. There was no "resurrection" out of this realm, although there could be a temporary "awakening" of one's spirit. Fertility gods "awoke" in the spring after their annual wintery death into the netherworld. The rise of Zoroastrianism (fifth century BC) included a universal, material, and individual idea of resurrection out of this netherworld into a permanent immortality that distinguished the righteous and the wicked.[3]

Interpretive Insights

11:40–45 *At the time of the end the king of the South . . . the king of the North.* These phrases, as well as the assertion that "the king" dies without anyone to "help him" (cf. 8:19, 25), suggest continuity with 11:21–39. Yet the events described in 11:40–45 do not fit into what is known to date of the last year and a half of Antiochus's life (165–164 BC), which includes a failed campaign in Persia and his death there (cf. 1 Macc. 6:1–17; 2 Macc. 1:11–17; 9:1–29; Polybius, *Hist.* 31.9).[4] There is no record of him invading Egypt or Judea, with Edom, Moab, and Ammon "spared" in such events. Rather, these verses seem to be an apocalyptic transition—expressed

Key Themes of Daniel 11:40–12:13

- An unparalleled time of suffering comes for God's people at the end of time.

- All who have ever lived face a final resurrection: some to everlasting life and some to everlasting shame and contempt.

- Spiritually wise persons, like Daniel, understand this essential message and can rest assured of an ultimate divine deliverance.

Sheol in the Old Testament

The word Sheol (*she'ol*) is used most frequently in the Hebrew Bible to describe the place of the dead (e.g., Gen. 37:35). Its semantic range includes the "grave, underworld, and state of death." It exists below the earth (Ezek. 31:16–17) and is a place of dust (Job 17:16), darkness (Job 10:21), silence (Ps. 94:17), and forgetfulness (Ps. 88:12). Aspects of earthly life describe it (Isa. 14:9), but it remains a place of despair absent of wisdom (Eccles. 9:10) and from which one cannot worship God (Isa. 38:18). Sometimes it is a place of punishment, especially when one dies prematurely (Num. 16:30–33). Yet one may die a natural death and enter Sheol in peace (Job 21:13). Yahweh is sovereign over Sheol (Ps. 139:8). He can deliver a person from its grips (Ps. 86:13) and even raise one up from there (Ps. 49:15)—although the existence to which one is raised remains unclear.[a] Sheol is not associated with sustained torment after death, and no alternatives are presented to its existence. Generally, those spared from it remain alive rather than going to another place.[b]

[a] *NBD*, 1092.
[b] *IVPBBCOT*, 603; see Collins, *Daniel*, 394–98.

in Antiochene rhetoric—to eschatological kings at the ultimate "time of the end," confirmed by a final resurrection in 12:2. Although some see this shift in historical focus beginning in 11:36 (NIV),[5] the clearer transition seems to occur here.[6]

12:1 *At that time Michael . . . will arise.* The phrase "at that time" concerns the time of Judea's suffering under Antiochus IV in 8:17 and anticipates an ultimate "time of the end" described hyperbolically in Antiochene terms (cf. 11:35, 40; 12:4, 9, 13). The reappearance of "Michael" (cf. 10:13, 21) unifies the larger vision and reminds the reader that earthly struggles have heavenly counterparts. The "time of distress" (*'et tsarah*; cf. Jer. 30:7) stands parallel to the "latter wrath" (*'aharit hazza'am*) in 8:19. A motif describing Antiochus's persecutions is reapplied to suffering unparalleled since the "beginning of nations."

But at that time your people . . . will be delivered. These are God's Old Testament people, by this time the Jewish remnant, as evidenced by Daniel's prayer (cf. 9:15–16, 19–24) and by the broader context of this vision (10:14; 11:14). The deliverance of God's people from a time of suffering is foreseen in 7:25–27 and 8:9–14, 24–26. The "book" containing the names of the saints refers to "the book" God writes (Exod. 32:31–34)—implicitly, a book of life—rather than the "Book of Truth" (10:21), which contains this vision proper.

12:2–3 *Multitudes who sleep in the dust of the earth will awake.* This metaphor connotes those who have died, usually understood in the Old Testament world as being in "Sheol." Only a few other passages in the Hebrew Bible allude to a hope of the righteous being raised up or awakened from death (1 Sam. 2:6; Isa. 26:19).[7] The distinction between "everlasting life" and "everlasting contempt" is unparalleled in Scripture until the New Testament (cf. Matt. 25:46; John 5:29; Acts 24:15). The reward for "those who are wise" and "lead many to righteousness" brings the light of "sun" and "stars" (cf. 8:10) to an otherwise dark vision—much like the appearance of the Ancient of Days does in 7:9–10.

12:4 *seal . . . the scroll until the time of the end.* The messenger's charge to Daniel parallels that in 8:26 and also signals the end of the vision proper (11:2–12:4). No significant information is added in the brief conclusion that follows (12:5–13). The reference to those who "go here and there to increase knowledge" speaks to a future desire to understand this vision. Such an understanding grows as the vision's fulfillment emerges throughout Persian and Greek history.[8]

12:5–7 *I, Daniel, looked . . . "How long will it be . . . ?"* This resumptive phrase introduces and concludes sections of previous visions (cf. 7:15, 28; 8:1, 15, 27; 9:2). Here, it returns the reader to the earlier conversation with Gabriel in this vision's introduction (10:2, 7). Daniel's inquiry elicits a response that appears identical (in English translations) to that which he receives in 7:25: "a *time, times* and half a *time*" (Aramaic *'iddan*). However, the term used here connotes "appointed times" (*mo'ed*). This is typical of the intensified rhetoric in this vision as Antiochene persecutions are reapplied to the eschatological future. The breaking of "the power of the holy people" alludes to Antiochus temporarily "defeating" and "destroy[ing]" the Jews (7:21; 8:4). "Finally broken" is better rendered "completely broken,"[9] using the same Hebrew word, *kalah* ("to be complete, finished"), that appears in 9:24, meaning, "finish [or "complete"] transgression."[10]

12:8–10 *I did not understand . . . "what will the outcome of all this be?"* Daniel's request changes from focusing on the "times" to understanding the "outcome." In response, Gabriel again contrasts good and evil at "the time of the end" (cf. 12:2):

the righteous are purified and "refined," while the wicked are not; and the "wise" understand, while the wicked do not. This clarification redirects Daniel's desire for more information toward understanding the larger purpose of the vision.[11]

12:11–12 *daily sacrifice is abolished . . . abomination that causes desolation.* These clauses draw on the rhetoric of Antiochus's persecution described earlier (8:13; 9:26–27; 11:31). Although Jesus does not clarify the context in Daniel when he speaks of the "abomination that causes desolation" (Matt. 24:15), he is most likely referring to this last section of Daniel's last vision, which reaches past Jesus's earthly ministry. The concluding "1,290" and "1,335" days approximate Daniel's familiar three and a half years (7:25; 8:13–14; 9:26–27), the latter describing those "blessed" to survive the intense period of suffering. No symbolic significance attaches to these numbers.

12:13 *go your way . . . rest . . . receive your allotted inheritance.* This final, future-time reference to "the end of the days" retains the apocalyptic tone of the last half of the book of Daniel (chaps. 7–12). Yet, at the same time, the personal encouragement to the sage, prophet, and seer—now in his mideighties—recalls God's faithful servants in the book's narratives (chaps. 1–6). Finally, these closing words place Daniel among the multitudes who will "rise" in "the end" to receive God's gracious "inheritance" of everlasting life (cf. 12:2).[12]

Theological Insights

Daniel 11:40–12:13 puts into perspective three realities about God's dealings with humanity. First, God delivers his faithful people from times of distress and sacrifice unto everlasting life. Second, God delivers those who stubbornly remain in rebellion against him to everlasting punishment. Third, God gives sufficient wisdom to his people so that they can understand the essential message of his visions regarding the future.

Teaching the Text

1. *Everlasting life.* God delivers faithful people from times of suffering and sacrifice for his sake, and he redeems them unto everlasting life. In Daniel 7, the appearance of the Ancient of Days brings the light and hope of God's kingdom. Here, even more so, the announcement of the ultimate resurrection of the righteous to "everlasting life" (unparalleled in the OT)

> Daniel is told to "roll up and seal the words of the scroll" (12:4). This reconstruction shows how a papyrus scroll would be sealed with several bullae, soft clay balls that would be positioned over the knot, flattened with a stamp seal, and allowed to harden.

brings light and hope into the darkness of human suffering on a personal level. Invite your listeners to join the community of the "wise" among God's people who "lead many to righteousness." Although he should not be regarded as an unattainable saint, Daniel joins the "multitudes" of those who remain faithful to the end. Call God's people to a lifetime of faithfulness with the assurance of their final "inheritance."

2. *Everlasting shame and contempt.* God delivers those who remain in rebellion against him to everlasting punishment. Speak to the difficult negative issue of "shame and everlasting contempt." Although often unpopular, addressing the doctrine of hell is a necessary component of teaching the text. The Old Testament speaks often of temporal judgment, but this pericope announces one that lasts forever. Use images from the book of Daniel of those who live life apart from God, or those who arrogantly oppose God and persecute his people. Call your congregation or class to choose the path of wisdom, to recognize and submit to God's sovereignty, and to experience his righteousness through the Son of Man.

3. *Be content with the message.* God gives sufficient wisdom to understand the essential message of his visions—but not all the details. Some in your congregation may be disappointed that, having completed a study of Daniel, they have not yet experienced a crash course on systematic eschatology. Firmly exhort them to begin with the Bible in its literary, historical, and cultural context and to follow where it leads. Show them it is possible to understand the essential message of apocalyptic texts and to draw from these enduring principles for godly living. Encourage them to embrace texts like these rather than to avoid them. Help them to affirm, in a practical way, that Daniel's visions are part of God's all-sufficient Word.

What not to teach. Throughout church history the theological concepts in this pericope have contributed to a broader theology of "antichrist." Since they do not find direct fulfillment in Antiochus IV, this is legitimate. What is not legitimate, however, is to detach this passage from its literary, historical, and theological contexts in order to use it to construct detailed predictions of end-time events.

Illustrating the Text

The good news: in the end, believers will arise to everlasting life.

Personal Testimony: During the last two years, in which I have been writing this commentary, four fellow believers who were dear to me have died: three remarkable women who ministered faithfully in our adult fellowship at church, and a former student, pastor, and chaplain. Physical death challenges us to practice our belief in eternal life. The apostle Paul encourages his readers with these words: "Brothers and sisters, we do not want you to be uninformed about those who sleep in death, so that you do not grieve like the rest of mankind, who have no hope. For we believe that Jesus died and rose again" (1 Thess. 4:13–14). Through the pain, suffering, and grieving of this life, we can still believe, and through that belief we can be a witness to the world around us of the unimaginable joy of resurrection to eternal life.

The bad news: in the end, the wicked will face shame and everlasting contempt.

Theological Book: Rob Bell's controversial bestseller *Love Wins* appeared in June 2011, in part earning him a place on *Time* magazine's list of the "100 Most Influential People in the World." Although he did not explicitly acknowledge the title of "universalist," the book's essential message came across to many evangelical leaders as just that—while others felt there was room for some disagreement on this issue. The clarity of the statement in Daniel 12:2, along with other passages in the New Testament, makes the historic, orthodox doctrine of "hell" one of the "hard sayings" in Scripture. Nevertheless, we must not shrink back from this truth, however dreadful it feels. Rather, we must affirm the full inspiration and authority of God's Word, while communicating its message with love, humility, and respect.

We can be content with understanding the essential message of Daniel.

Personal Testimony: Edward M. Curtis has been a good friend and colleague of mine at Biola University since 1978, specializing in Old Testament wisdom literature and writing *Discovering the Way of Wisdom* (2004). I have frequently sought his advice in applying biblical wisdom in both Christian ministry and personal life. One of my many favorite pithy sayings of Ed's is this one: "If we just did what the text clearly says, we would have more on our plates than we could say grace over." Write this in the margin of your Bible somewhere in the apocalyptic section of Daniel. In the end, God comforts the faithful Judean sage and prophet—now in his eighties—with these words: "As for you, go your way till the end. You will rest, and then at the end of the days you will rise to receive your allotted inheritance" (Dan. 12:13).

God will deliver "some to everlasting life, others to shame and everlasting contempt" (12:2). Shown here is a fourteenth-century AD fresco depicting the last judgment.

Notes

Introduction to Daniel

1. Yamauchi, "Daniel and Contacts."

2. Modern versions generally follow the Septuagint arrangement (Greek LXX translation from third–first century BC), which places Daniel with the so-called Major Prophets: Isaiah, Jeremiah, and Ezekiel.

3. Other arguments are discussed in most scholarly commentaries: e.g., Miller, *Daniel*, 22–43; Lucas, *Daniel*, 306–15; and Collins, *Daniel*, 24–38. See also Hasel's articles, "Book of Daniel: Evidences Relating to Persons and Chronology," and "Book of Daniel and Matters of Language."

4. Gooding, "Literary Structure of the Book of Daniel."

5. There is a general consensus that Belshazzar began his co-regency under Nabonidus in 553 BC. For the minority view that this event took place in 550 BC, see Hasel, "First and Third Years," and Shea, "Nabonidus, Belshazzar."

6. See Patterson, "Key Role of Daniel 7."

7. For more on Daniel's twofold literary structure, see Lucas, *Daniel*, 22–36.

8. See Yamauchi, "Hermeneutical Issues."

9. For an interesting introduction to the theology of the book of Daniel as organized around the themes of power, education, and religion, see Goldingay, "Daniel in the Context of Old Testament Theology."

Daniel 1:1–7

1. *ZIBBCOT*, 519–23.

2. *IVPBBCOT*, 730.

3. *ZIBBCOT*, 526–27; *ANEHST*, 386–88, 407–25.

4. See Mercer, "Daniel 1:1," 181–82; Millard, "Daniel 1–6 and History."

5. On the temple as an organizing theme in the book of Daniel, see Goswell, "Temple Theme."

6. See Miller, *Daniel*, 62–64.

7. Collins, *Daniel*, 139n109, 142.

8. See Arnold, "Wordplay and Characterization in Daniel 1."

9. On intentional changes to the Babylonian names with their theological and archaeological ramifications, see Shea, "Bel(te)shazzar Meets Belshazzar," 80–81.

10. Excerpts from "O Father, You Are Sovereign" by Margaret Clarkson © 1982 Hope Publishing Company, Carol Stream, IL 60188. All rights reserved. Used by permission.

11. http://www.scholastic.com/ispy/.

Daniel 1:8–16

1. *IVPBBCOT*, 730–31.

2. Oppenheim, *Ancient Mesopotamia*, 189–91.

3. *ZIBBCOT*, 528–30.

4. Arnold, "Wordplay and Characterization in Daniel 1," 238–41.

5. BDB, 524.

6. See Miller, *Daniel*, 66–68; Steinmann, *Daniel*, 99–100.

7. See Steinmann, *Daniel*, 100–102.

8. Walther Eichrodt, *Theology of the Old Testament* (Philadelphia: Westminster, 1967), 2:164.

Daniel 1:17–21

1. See Oppenheim, *Ancient Mesopotamia*, 221–22.

2. *IVPBBCOT*, 731–32.

3. *ZIBBCOT*, 530–31.

4. See Steinmann, *Daniel*, 100–102.

5. See Miller, *Daniel*, 71.

6. See Stefanovic, "Daniel." He sees a reference back to 1:12: the Judeans are tested for "ten days" and are proven to be "ten times better."

7. Cf. Joseph and Moses in Egypt (Gen. 41:8; Exod. 7–9).

8. On Daniel as portrayed as a "mantic sage" quite similar to the Mesopotamian magicians and enchanters, see Lawson, "'God Who Reveals Secrets,'" 75–76.

9. See Collins, *Daniel*, 45.

10. Jesse Carey, "2012: The Year of the Outspoken Christian Athlete," *Relevant Magazine*, December 26, 2012, http://

www.relevantmagazine.com/culture/2012-year-outspoken
-christian-athlete.

11. "British Empire," Wikipedia, http://en.wikipedia
.org/wiki/British_Empire.

Daniel 2:1–16

1. *ZIBBCOT*, 531–32.

2. *IVPBBCOT*, 732–33.

3. Miller, *Daniel*, 76–77; Steinmann, *Daniel*, 111–12. On
the hermeneutical challenges of harmonization, see Dillard,
"Harmonization."

4. Feinberg, *Daniel*, 30.

5. See Miller, *Daniel*, 80.

6. Oppenheim, *Interpretation of Dreams*, 219.

7. See Stefanovic, "Daniel," 139–42, 146; see also Collins, "Court-Tales."

8. On Daniel's wisdom as set against the power of kings
and the sociological function of these dream accounts for the
book's diasporic audience, see Smith-Christopher, "Prayers
and Dreams," 1:274–89.

Daniel 2:17–30

1. Prinsloo, "Two Poems," 93–94, 100, 107–8.

2. *IVPBBCOT*, 733; Cowley, *Aramaic Papyri*, nos. 30:2,
28; 31:23; 32:4; 38:3, 5; 40:1; see also Collins, *Daniel*, 159.

3. Lucas, *Daniel*, 72.

4. Collins, "Court-Tales," 220–24, 229–34.

5. BDB, 1085.

6. On the impact of God's power and wisdom above
that of kings for Daniel's audience, see Smith-Christopher,
"Prayers and Dreams," 1:286–89.

7. Collins, "Court-Tales," 220–24.

8. See Smith-Christopher, "Prayers and Dreams,"
1:286–89.

9. Westminster Shorter Catechism, Q & A 1.

Daniel 2:31–49

1. See Collins, *Daniel*, 162–65.

2. *ZIBBCOT*, 533.

3. *ZIBBCOT*, 534–36. See the excursus on the four kingdoms in Collins, *Daniel*, 166–70. On Babylonian dynastic
prophecy as the primary background for identifying the
four kingdoms, see Hasel, "Four World Empires," 17–23.

4. Augustine, *Homilies on 1 John* 1.12, and Gregory of
Nyssa, *On the Baptism of Christ*; cited in Stevenson and
Glerup, *Ezekiel, Daniel*, 170–71.

5. Montgomery, *Daniel*, 171.

6. See Lucas, *Daniel*, 74–77.

7. See Smith-Christopher, "Prayers and Dreams,"
1:266–89.

8. See Lawson, "'God Who Reveals Secrets.'"

Additional Insights

1. Gurney (*God in Control*, 1–94) pioneered an evangelical Greek view on the four kingdoms.

2. Feinberg, *Daniel*, 30.

3. See Steinmann (Amillennial), *Daniel*, ad loc., esp.
144–57; see also Miller (Dispensational), *Daniel*, ad loc. For

a historical overview of Roman interpretations, see Pfandl,
"Interpretations of the Kingdom."

4. Greek views are not divided over systematic eschatology. See Gurney, "Four Kingdoms"; Lucas, *Daniel*, 88–91;
Walton, "Four Kingdoms."

Daniel 3:1–12

1. Adapted from Lucas, *Daniel*, 86.

2. *IVPBBCOT*, 735; see also *ANEHST*, 350–56.

3. *ZIBBCOT*, 536–38.

4. Miller, *Daniel*, 109–11.

5. Steinmann, *Daniel*, 174–75.

6. On lists as satire, see Avalos, "Comedic Function."

7. Yamauchi, "Daniel and Contacts."

8. Alexander, "New Light."

9. Fewell, *Circle of Sovereignty*, 66.

10. See *HALOT*, 1903.

11. Fifty-Fourth Annual National Prayer Breakfast,
Washington, DC, 2006, quoted in Greg Garrett, *We Get to
Carry Each Other: The Gospel according to U2* (Louisville:
Westminster John Knox, 2009), 87.

Daniel 3:13–23

1. *IVPBBCOT*, 735. See also Yamauchi, "Daniel and
Contacts"; on lists as satire, see Avalos, "Comedic Function."

2. See *ANETP*, 158; cf. Herodotus, *Hist.* 1.86.

3. On further literary and cultural backgrounds to
this form of punishment, see Beaulieu, "Babylonian Background"; see also Collins, *Daniel*, 184–86.

4. *ZIBBCOT*, 538.

5. Cf. Steinmann, *Daniel*, 186–87.

6. See esp. Lucas, "A Statue, a Fiery Furnace," 291–93;
also Coxon, "Daniel III 17."

7. So also Miller, *Daniel*, 119. Contra Montgomery,
Daniel, 206; Steinmann, *Daniel*, 186–87. See also Goldingay, *Daniel*, 66, 73–74.

8. "Mandela at 90," CNN report by Robyn Curnow, July
18, 2008, http://edition.cnn.com/2008/WORLD/africa/07/18
/mandela.birthday/.

Daniel 3:24–30

1. *ANETP*, 107–33.

2. Collins, *Daniel*, 190–91.

3. *IVPBBCOT*, 736; *ZIBBCOT*, 538.

4. Steinmann, *Daniel*, 192–93.

5. In defense of this reading, see Miller, *Daniel*, 122–24;
Steinmann, *Daniel*, 193–96.

6. See Lucas, *Daniel*, 93.

7. Slotki, *Daniel*, 27.

8. Collins, *Daniel*, 191, notes helpful Mesopotamian
parallels even though he rejects the historicity of this decree
by Nebuchadnezzar.

9. *HALOT*, 1964.

Daniel 4:1–18

1. On chiastic structure in chapters 2–7 and within chapter 4, see Shea, "Further Literary Structures in Daniel 2–7:
An Analysis of Daniel 4."

2. *IVPBBCOT*, 736; *ZIBBCOT*, 538–39.

3. *IVPBBCOT*, 736. On the symbolism of trees in the Old Testament, see Coxon, "Great Tree of Daniel 4," 94–96.

4. *ZIBBCOT*, 539.

5. Contra Charles, *Daniel*, 79–82; see the discussion in Steinmann, *Daniel*, 207–8.

6. On the use of the first person as a literary/narrative device, see Meadowcroft, "Point of View in Storytelling," 30–34.

7. On the Hebrew author's treatment of references to Babylonian deities within names, see Shea, "Bel(te)shazzar Meets Belshazzar," 80–81.

8. *HALOT*, 1946.

9. See Montgomery, *Daniel*, 233; Miller, *Daniel*, 133.

10. See discussion in Steinmann, *Daniel*, 235.

11. So also Steinmann, *Daniel*, 236–37. Contra Miller, *Daniel*, 134–35; Collins, *Daniel*, 228.

12. Francis A. Schaeffer, *The Francis A. Schaeffer Trilogy: The Three Essential Books in One Volume* (Westchester, IL: Crossway, 1990), 140–41.

Daniel 4:19-27

1. See Meadowcroft, "Point of View in Storytelling," 30–34.

2. See the discussion in Collins, *Daniel*, 226–27.

3. *IVPBBCOT*, 736.

4. So also Steinmann, *Daniel*, 242. Miller (*Daniel*, 136) prefers the first option. Collins (*Daniel*, 228–29) acknowledges the options and seems to prefer the second as primary.

5. See Steinmann, *Daniel*, 245–47.

6. So also Steinmann, *Daniel*, 236, 245. Miller (*Daniel*, 137–38) prefers to see a specific reference to seven years. Cf. Collins, *Daniel*, 228.

7. See Steinmann, *Daniel*, 245.

8. *HALOT*, 1959.

9. See Miller, *Daniel*, 138–39, esp. nn. 38–39.

10. See esp. Steinmann, *Daniel*, 245–47.

11. Martin Luther King Jr., "Beyond Vietnam" (Clergy and Laymen Concerned about Vietnam Meeting, Riverside Church, New York, NY, April 4, 1967).

Daniel 4:28-37

1. *NBD*, 112; Miller, *Daniel*, 140–41.

2. *ANETP*, 39–71, 379–83.

3. *ZIBBCOT*, 540–41. See Coxon, "Another Look"; on Gilgamesh, see Garrison, "Nebuchadnezzar's Dream"; on Ahiqar, see Montgomery, *Daniel*, 244; Collins, *Daniel*, 230–31.

4. See Steinmann, *Daniel*, 250.

5. Miller, *Daniel*, 139–41.

6. On the Mesopotamian backgrounds and possible literary significance of Nebuchadnezzar's illness, see Hays, "Chirps from the Dust."

7. This leads some commentators to dismiss the historicity of Nebuchadnezzar's affliction. See Collins, *Daniel*, 228–33.

8. Steinmann, *Daniel*, 252–53. Contra Miller, *Daniel*, 144. Lucas (*Daniel*, 114–18) calls Nebuchadnezzar "half-converted."

9. *HALOT*, 1875.

10. Miller, *Daniel*, 143.

11. C. S. Lewis, *Mere Christianity* (New York: Macmillan, 1952), 123–24.

12. Charles Haddon Spurgeon, "Two Essential Things," in *Metropolitan Tabernacle Pulpit: Sermons, Parts 405–416* (London: Passmore & Alabaster, 1889), 127.

Daniel 5:1-9

1. Lucas, *Daniel*, 123–25. See also the discussion in Shea, "Further Literary Structures in Daniel 2–7: An Analysis of Daniel 5."

2. *ANEHST*, 418–20. See Shea, "Nabonidus, Belshazzar"; cf. Grabbe, " Belshazzar of Daniel"; see also Miller, *Daniel*, 147–48nn1–10.

3. Koldewey and Johns, *Excavations at Babylon*, 104; Miller, *Daniel*, 155.

4. *ZIBBCOT*, 542.

5. Shea, "Bel(te)shazzar Meets Belshazzar," 80–81.

6. Goldingay, *Daniel*, 106–7.

7. *HALOT*, 1885.

8. Montgomery, *Daniel*, 251; on the author's subtle literary technique (metaphonic paronomasia) to emphasize sacrilege above drunkenness, see Arnold, "Wordplay and Narrative Techniques," 479–82; on drunkenness as the primary referent, see Wood, *Daniel*, 132–33.

9. For this reading, see Steinmann, *Daniel*, 260–65, 276–77.

10. So also Miller, *Daniel*, 160–61.

11. Miller, *Daniel*, 152–54.

12. Steinmann, *Daniel*, 275.

13. Slotki, *Daniel*, 45–46; see also Wolters, "Riddle of the Scales."

14. Erik Thoennes, *Godly Jealousy: A Theology of Intolerant Love* (Fearn, Scotland: Mentor, 2005), 258.

Daniel 5:10-17

1. *IVPBBCOT*, 738. So Miller, *Daniel*, 159–60; contra Steinmann, *Daniel*, 260–63.

2. *NBD*, 110–12.

3. Miller, *Daniel*, 159–60.

4. On irony as a unifying literary device in the book, see Woodard, "Literary Strategies and Authorship," 50–53.

5. See Deventer, "Another Wise Queen (Mother)."

6. See Lucas, *Daniel*, 130–31; Steinmann, *Daniel*, 277.

7. Steinmann, *Daniel*, 281–82.

8. See Shea, "Nabonidus, Belshazzar."

9. R. A. Torrey, *The Person and Work of the Holy Spirit* (New York: Revell, 1910), 3–4.

Daniel 5:18-31

1. Longman, *Daniel*, 142; Wolters, "Riddle of the Scales," 155.

2. *IVPBBCOT*, 738.

3. See Lucas, *Daniel*, 126–27; Miller, *Daniel*, 166–69.

4. *ZIBBCOT*, 544.

5. See Woodard, "Literary Strategies and Authorship," 52–53.

6. On the text as cuneiform numbers adding up to three and a half and Daniel's translation into Aramaic, see Brewer, "*MENE MENE TEQEL UPARSIN*."

7. On Daniel as offering a mantic interpretation of this sacred text and the overlap between Jewish and Mesopotamian scribal tradition, see Broida, "Textualizing Divination."

8. On further wordplay, particularly in the vocalization of this text, see Wolters, "Riddle of the Scales."

9. See Zimmermann, "Writing on the Wall."

10. Archer ("Daniel," 76) accepts the MT chapter division.

11. Goldingay, *Daniel*, 112.

12. George Santayana, *Reason and Common Sense*, vol. 1 of *The Life of Reason* (Amherst, NY: Prometheus, 1905), 284.

13. Thomas Jefferson, "Counsel to a Namesake," Monticello, February 21, 1825; see http://www.let.rug.nl/usa/presidents/thomas-jefferson/letters-of-thomas-jefferson/jefl281.php.

Additional Insights

1. See Charles, *Daniel*, 138–46; Sparks, "On the Origin of 'Darius the Mede.'"

2. See Shea, "An Unrecognized Vassal King (Part 1)," in a series of articles from 1971 to 1972 (see the bibliography). Shea updates his position to identify Darius as Cyrus in his 1991 article "Darius the Mede in His Persian-Babylonian Setting." See also Dillard and Longman, *Introduction*, 334–37.

3. See Wiseman, "Last Days of Babylon"; Wiseman, "Some Historical Problems"; Steinmann, *Daniel*, 290–96; Miller, *Daniel*, 171–77; Shea, "Darius the Mede in His Persian-Babylonian Setting"; as well as the extended treatments of Whitcomb, *Darius the Mede*, and Rowley, *Darius the Mede*.

4. Steinmann, *Daniel*, 290–96; Colless, "Cyrus the Persian as Darius the Mede."

Daniel 6:1–9

1. Goldingay, *Daniel*, 124; Lucas, *Daniel*, 146.

2. Arnold, "Wordplay and Narrative Techniques"; for an interesting analysis of the literary structure of this passage in terms of plot and possible correspondence to apocalyptic storytelling, see Boogaart, "Daniel 6."

3. Hartman and Di Lella, *Daniel*, 197–98; Collins, *Daniel*, 264; Cook, *Persian Empire*, 77–85.

4. See Young, *Daniel*, 134, for an argument to the contrary.

5. Walton, "Decree of Darius," 285–86.

6. Montgomery, *Daniel*, 270; Steinmann, *Daniel*, 316.

7. *ANETP*, 155–78; *IVPBBCOT*, 738–39.

8. See Steinmann, *Daniel*, 301–4, 313–14.

9. *HALOT*, 1979.

10. Walton, "Decree of Darius," 285.

11. Steinmann, *Daniel*, 301–4.

12. *ZIBBCOT*, 546.

13. Steinmann, *Daniel*, 316.

14. Cited in Heiko A. Oberman, *Luther: Man between God and the Devil*, trans. Eileen Walliser-Schwarzbart (New Haven: Yale University Press, 1989), 203.

Daniel 6:10–18

1. See the discussion in Collins, *Daniel*, 268–69.

2. Lacocque, *Daniel*, 118; Cook, *Persian Empire*, 142.

3. See, e.g., *ANETP*, 372; *IVPBBCOT*, 739. On further Mesopotamian backgrounds to Daniel 6, see Toorn, "Scholars at the Oriental Court," 1:42–53.

4. *IVPBBCOT*, 739.

5. Goldingay, *Daniel*, 128–29.

6. Collins, *Daniel*, 268–69.

7. Goldingay, *Daniel*, 132.

8. Although Peterson plays off the prophet Jeremiah in his classic devotional on the Psalms of Ascent (*A Long Obedience in the Same Direction*), he could just as well have used the elderly Daniel in this text as his example.

9. See Lucas, *Daniel*, 145–47.

10. William Wirt, *Sketches of the Life and Character of Patrick Henry* (Philadelphia: Webster, 1817), 123.

Daniel 6:19–28

1. Lucas, *Daniel*, 145–47. On possible literary links between chapter 6 and the following apocalyptic sections, see Boogaart, "Daniel 6."

2. See Miller, *Daniel*, 186–88.

3. *IVPBBCOT*, 739–40.

4. Steinmann (*Daniel*, 320) notes that the divine title, "the living God," is uttered by a gentile only in this chapter.

5. See also Prinsloo's comparison of 2:20–23 with 6:27–28 in "Two Poems."

6. This may account for the ambiguity of the chapter division regarding 4:1–3 (MT 3:31–33).

7. On both the structure and function of the poem, see Prinsloo, "Two Poems," 103–6.

8. See *ZIBBCOT*, 547; Miller, *Daniel*, 189–90.

9. Walton and Walton, *Bible Story Handbook*, 253.

10. Oswald Chambers, *My Utmost for His Highest*, rev. ed. (Grand Rapids: Discovery House, 1992), Jan. 6.

Daniel 7:1–14

1. See Oppenheim, *Interpretation of Dreams*, 186–205; Lucas, *Daniel*, 31–35.

2. See Patterson, "Key Role of Daniel 7."

3. On Daniel 2 and 7 as primary backgrounds for the concept of the kingdom of God, see Wenham, "Kingdom of God and Daniel."

4. On the co-regency of Belshazzar and Nabonidus as a possible background to understanding the co-regency of the son of man and the Ancient of Days, see Shea, "Neo-Babylonian Historical Setting."

5. *ZIBBCOT*, 547–51. See Walton, "*Anzu* Myth," 1:78–82, 86; Kee, "Heavenly Council and Its Type-Scene," 259–70.

6. See Steinmann, *Daniel*, 332–35; Walton, "*Anzu* Myth," 1:85–88; Lucas, "Source of Daniel's Animal Imagery." On Daniel 7:9–10 as directly dependent on other apocalyptic texts, but with a unique theological focus, see Kvanvig, "Throne Visions and Monsters."

7. It is commonly accepted that Belshazzar began his co-regency under Nabonidus in 553 BC. For an alternate view, see Hasel, "First and Third Years"; Shea, "Nabonidus, Belshazzar."

8. Longmann, *Daniel,* 180–81.

9. See Walton, "Four Kingdoms." Also see the discussion in Steinmann, *Daniel*, 327–35.

10. See Beasley-Murray, "Interpretation of Daniel 7."

11. See Lucas, *Daniel*, 163–67, 183–85.

12. Cited in Goldwurm, *Daniel*, 206–7. In contrast, later Jewish interpreters see here the angel Michael or corporate Israel (*Jewish Study Bible*, 1656–57, notes at 7:13–14). For an evangelical who explores a nonmessianic reading of this text, see Walton, "*Anzu* Myth," 1:78–85.

13. See Beasley-Murray, "Interpretation of Daniel 7," 58; Shepherd, "Daniel 7:13."

14. See Walton, "Four Kingdoms," 35.

15. John Milton, *Paradise Lost*, ed. Leland Ryken (Wheaton: Crossway, 2013), 1.44–49; 12.460–62.

Daniel 7:15-28

1. *ZIBBCOT*, 551–53. See Habel, "Introducing the Apocalyptic Visions."

2. *ANETP*, 28–36, 92–99; *ZIBBCOT*, 553.

3. *IVPBBCOT*, 741–42.

4. Steinmann, *Daniel*, 364–65.

5. See Steinmann's (*Daniel*, 366–70) particularly strong defense of the traditional position. For the angelic position with room for identification with the Jewish people, see the in-depth excursus in Collins, *Daniel*, 312–18.

6. See Hasel, "Saints of the Most High"; Poythress, "Holy Ones of the Most High." Poythress identifies this group as "eschatological faithful Israel." See also Beasley-Murray, "Interpretation of Daniel 7."

7. See Collins, *Daniel*, 311–12; Lucas, *Daniel*, 187–91; contra Steinmann, *Daniel*, 371–72, 376–84, 389–91.

8. Pierce, "Covenant Conditionality."

9. Since Daniel uses rounded numbers like the "seventy years" of exile from 605–539 BC, it is not necessary to understand the number "ten" here literally. However, if one counts Alexander the Great as the first and Seleucus I through Seleucus IV as 2–8, then the latter's legitimate heirs Demetrius and Antiochus would be 9 and 10. This would make Seleucus IV and his two sons the "three kings" Antiochus IV "uproots" in 7:24. See Collins, *Daniel*, 320–21; Lucas, *Daniel*, 193–94; contra Miller, *Daniel*, 212–26. For an alternate identification within an evangelical, Greek interpretation, see Walton, "Four Kingdoms," 32–34.

10. See Miller, *Daniel*, 214–16.

11. Steinmann, *Daniel*, 384. On the development of the Danielic kingdom of God concept through Second Temple and New Testament eras, see Evans, "Daniel in the New Testament," 2:490–519.

12. Julia Ward Howe, "Mine Eyes Have Seen the Glory," in *The Covenant Hymnal* (Chicago: Covenant Press, 1973), no. 592.

Daniel 8:1-14

1. See Steinmann, *Daniel*, 389–90; Lucas, *Daniel*, 208–10.

2. See alternate dating in Collins, *Daniel*, 343; Steinmann, *Daniel*, 390–91; Hasel, "First and Third Years."

3. *ZIBBCOT*, 552–53.

4. *IVPBBCOT*, 743.

5. See Collins, *Daniel*, 330.

6. BDB, 838.

7. See Collins, *Daniel*, 333. On Antiochus's fight against God and his people, and on the "prince" as a reference to the preincarnate Christ, see Steinmann, *Daniel*, 401–3.

8. BDB, 1020.

9. On the temple as a prominent, unifying theme in Daniel, see Goswell, "Temple Theme." On Antiochus's actions in relation to the "abomination of desolation," see Lust, "Cult and Sacrifice in Daniel."

10. BDB, 833.

11. For a discussion of alternate readings of this difficult verse, see Lucas, *Daniel*, 216–17.

12. See Miller, *Daniel*, 228–30, who favors the latter view.

13. "I Still Believe" (Great Design). Words and Music by Michael Been and James Goodwin. Copyright © 1986 Tileface Music, Neeb Music, Almo Music Corp. and Tarka Music. All Rights on behalf of Tileface Music Administered by Music & Media International. All Rights on behalf of Neeb Music Administered by BMG Rights Management (US) LLC. All Rights Reserved Used by Permission. *Reprinted by Permission of Hal Leonard Corporation.*

Daniel 8:15-27

1. See *IVPBBCOT*, 743–44.

2. *IVPBBCOT*, 751. See Steinmann, *Daniel*, 417; Lucas, *Daniel*, 221.

3. Miller, *Daniel*, 231; Steinmann, *Daniel*, 412–13.

4. Collins, *Daniel*, 336.

5. See *ZIBBCOT*, 555–56.

6. BDB, 276.

7. See Miller, *Daniel*, 233; Lucas, *Daniel*, 219–20. See also the excursus on dispensational readings of Daniel 8 in Steinmann, *Daniel*, 418–21.

8. Steinmann, *Daniel*, 414.

9. See Goldingay, *Daniel*, 217.

10. BDB, 738, 815.

11. On Daniel's use of irony, see Woodard, "Literary Strategies and Authorship."

12. BDB, 783.

13. See Collins, *Daniel*, 333; Steinmann, *Daniel*, 416–17.

14. See Miller, *Daniel*, 236.

15. Pliny, *Letters* 10.96–97.

Daniel 9:1-6

1. See Lucas, *Daniel*, 31–35.

2. BDB, 909.

3. *ZIBBCOT*, 556. See Wiseman, "Some Historical Problems," 15; Shea, "Darius the Mede in His Persian-Babylonian Setting," 235–37, 252–53.

4. *IVPBBCOT*, 744.

5. See, e.g., *ANETP*, 205–25.

6. See Steinmann, *Daniel*, 434–37; Collins, *Daniel*, 348–50; Miller, *Daniel*, 244–45.

7. BDB, 573.

8. Miller, *Daniel*, 240.

9. BDB, 706.

10. Brownlee, "Ineffable Name."

11. On irony, see Woodard, "Literary Strategies and Authorship."

12. BDB, 58.

13. BDB, 247, 12.

14. See Pierce, "Covenant Conditionality," 33–35.

15. See Steinmann, *Daniel*, 436–37.

Daniel 9:7–19

1. See Steinmann, *Daniel*, 436–37.

2. Moabite Stone: *ANEHST*, 311–16; Black Obelisk of Shalmaneser III: *ANETP*, 258; Taylor and Sennacherib prisms: *ANETP*, 269–71; Awel-Marduk's rations lists: *ANEHST*, 286–87.

3. Moabite Stone: *ANEHST*, 312–13; inscriptions from Khirbet el-Qom (Judea) and Kuntillet Ajrud: *ANETP*, 287–93; Arad Ostraca: *ANETP*, 291; Lachish letters: *ANETP*, 292–93.

4. See Lucas, *Daniel*, 238.

5. Lucas, *Daniel*, 238.

6. Trible, *God and the Rhetoric of Sexuality*, 31–59.

7. See Lucas, *Daniel*, 238–39.

8. See Goswell, "Temple Theme," who understands the temple as a central theme in the book.

9. Lacocque, *Daniel*, 184n31; Collins, *Daniel*, 350.

10. Pierce, "Covenant Conditionality," 27–32.

11. BDB, 773.

12. See Steinmann, *Daniel*, 426, 440.

13. So Miller, *Daniel*, 248.

14. For opposing views on God "relenting" or "changing his mind," see Pinnock et al., *Openness of God*; and Ware, *God's Lesser Glory*.

15. See Steinmann, *Daniel*, 426, 441–42.

16. See Miller, *Daniel*, 249.

17. Contra Ferguson, *Daniel*, 176–81.

18. Dietrich Bonhoeffer, *The Cost of Discipleship* (New York: Touchstone, 1995), 44–45.

19. *The Nature and Scope of Sexual Abuse of Minors by Catholic Priests and Deacons in the United States 1950–2002*, research study conducted by the John Jay College of Criminal Justice for the United States Conference of Catholic Bishops (Washington, DC, 2004).

Daniel 9:20–27

1. Sumerian royal inscriptions: see, e.g., *ANETP*, 180–82; Amarna letters: *ANETP*, 429–43.

2. *ANEHST*, 354–55. McComiskey, "Seventy 'Weeks' of Daniel," 37–40.

3. *ZIBBCOT*, 558.

4. See Lucas, *Daniel*, 232–34.

5. BDB, 619.

6. BDB, 419.

7. See Steinmann, *Daniel*, 450–51; Collins, *Daniel*, 352.

8. Counting back 490 years from 605 BC (to 1095 BC) takes one literally just before the beginning of the United Kingdom (1050 BC). Specific dates are from Hill and Walton, *Survey of the Old Testament*, 189.

9. The view expressed in this commentary differs on this point from my earlier article: Pierce, "Spiritual Failure."

10. See *IVPBBCOT*, 744–45.

11. See Collins, *Daniel*, 354–55; McComiskey, "Seventy 'Weeks' of Daniel," 26; contra Steinmann, *Daniel*, 468–72.

12. See Fuller and Choi, *Invitation to Biblical Hebrew*, 26–27; Greenberg, *Introduction to Hebrew*, 134; Tov, *Textual Criticism*, 67–71.

13. See Lucas, *Daniel*, 242–44.

14. See Redditt, "Daniel 9." For a reading arguing for Jesus as "the Anointed One" in this text, see Miller, *Daniel*, 262–66.

15. See discussion in Lucas, *Daniel*, 242–54.

16. BDB, 1007.

17. Collins, *Daniel*, 357.

18. In Matthew 24:15, Jesus uses this image typologically (indicated by Matthew's comment, "let the reader understand") to refer to similar events after his earthly ministry (cf. Mark 13:14). See Lucas, *Daniel*, 244–45; Evans, "Daniel in the New Testament," 2:519–23; Lust, "Cult and Sacrifice in Daniel."

19. Liz Thomas, "We Must Not Forgive Too Easily, Says Archbishop of Canterbury," *Daily Mail*, April 12, 2011, http://www.dailymail.co.uk/news/article-1375952/We-forgive-easily-says-Archbishop-Canterbury.html.

Additional Insights

1. This brief overview is focused on Christian readings of this text. For early Jewish interpretations, see Grabbe, "Seventy-Weeks Prophecy," 595–611; Goldwurm, *Daniel*, 259–67. Modern Jewish scholars generally follow an Antiochene view (cf. NJPS footnote at 9:24–27).

2. Knowles, "Interpretation of the Seventy Weeks"; Young, *Daniel*, 191.

3. Steinmann, *Daniel*, 453–56, esp. fig. 12.

4. Young (*Daniel*, 192–221) is representative of a covenant-theology position and summarizes the variations within this camp.

5. Wilkinson, *For Zion's Sake*, 95–134.

6. Feinberg ("Exegetical and Theological Study," 189–220) writes from a dispensational perspective but summarizes the range of views. For other dispensational commentaries, see Walvoord, *Daniel*, 216–37; Wood, *Daniel*, 247–63; Miller, *Daniel*, 252–73.

7. E.g., McComiskey, "Seventy 'Weeks' of Daniel."

8. Lucas, *Daniel*, 247.

9. This differs from my earlier view (1989), where I used a strictly literal hermeneutic to contend for an Antiochene view: Pierce, "Spiritual Failure." I believe this is still a viable option yet most likely not the intent of the author.

10. Lucas is a good example of an evangelical commentary that takes a consistent Antiochene view throughout (*Daniel*, ad loc.; see esp. 240–54). For a nonevangelical discussion of this passage, see Collins, *Daniel*, 352–60.

Daniel 10:1–11:1

1. *IVPBBCOT*, 746; Collins, *Daniel*, 372.

2. See *ANETP*, 365–74.

3. *IVPBBCOT*, 743, 746; *ZIBBCOT*, 555–56, 560.

4. *ANETP*, 28–36, 92–99. On Daniel's use of *Enuma Elish*, see Lucas, "Source of Daniel's Animal Imagery," 162–65; for his use of the Anzu Myth, see Walton, "*Anzu* Myth."

5. *IVPBBCOT*, 742, 746.

6. Collins, *Daniel*, 372–73.

7. See Steinmann, *Daniel*, 498–501.

8. Young, *Daniel*, 225; Miller, *Daniel*, 281–82.

9. Keil and Delitzsch, *Ezekiel, Daniel*, 409–15; Towner, *Daniel*, 149–50.

10. On Daniel's unique cosmology and the identification of the princes as allowing for both terrestrial and heavenly identification, see Meadowcroft, "Who Are the Princes of Persia and Greece?" On viewing these as humans, see Shea, "Wrestling with the Prince of Persia."

11. See Lucas, *Daniel*, 264–66, 277–78.

12. Charles Wesley, "Come, Ye Weary Sinners Come," in *Hymns for Divine Worship: Complied for the Use of the Methodist New Connexion* (London: John Hudston, 1879), no. 395.

Daniel 11:2–20

1. *ZIBBCOT*, 568–69.

2. See Steinmann, *Daniel*, 518–20.

3. Yamauchi, *Persia and the Bible*, 138–43.

4. *IVPBBCOT*, 746–47; see Lucas, *Daniel*, 279–80.

5. Collins, *Daniel*, 378; Steinmann, *Daniel*, 520–22.

6. See Steinmann, *Daniel*, 521, fig. 15.

7. See Collins, *Daniel*, 378.

8. So also Lucas, *Daniel*, 280; Steinmann, *Daniel*, 522.

9. See discussion in Collins, *Daniel*, 378–79.

10. For other theories, see Collins, *Daniel*, 379–80.

11. On 11:13–19, see Steinmann, *Daniel*, 523–25.

12. Collins, *Daniel*, 381; Niskanen, "Daniel's Portrait of Antiochus IV."

Additional Insights

1. See the helpful discussion and diagram (fig. 15) in Steinmann, *Daniel*, 518–25.

Daniel 11:21–39

1. See *ZIBBCOT*, 564–67; *IVPBBCOT*, 749–50.

2. See Collins, *Daniel*, 382. On Antiochus as a "scorned" rather than "contemptible" person and the historical accuracy of Daniel's account in chapter 11, see Scolnic, "Antiochus IV as the Scorned Prince."

3. Steinmann, *Daniel*, 525–27; Longman, *Daniel*, 278.

4. Miller, *Daniel*, 299.

5. Hartman and Di Lella, *Daniel*, 296.

6. See Lust, "Cult and Sacrifice in Daniel."

7. See Steinmann, *Daniel*, 528–31.

8. Lucas, *Daniel*, 287–89.

9. Archer, "Daniel," 143; Young, *Daniel*, 270; Steinmann, "Is the Antichrist in Daniel 11?" On the New Testament's use of Daniel's "abomination of desolation," see Evans, "Daniel in the New Testament," 2:519–23.

10. Montgomery, *Daniel*, 461. On the exclusion of Antiochus as the king of 11:37–38 on religious grounds, see Mercer, "Benefactions of Antiochus IV."

11. J. I. Packer, *Evangelism and the Sovereignty of God* (Downers Grove, IL: InterVarsity, 2008), 32.

Daniel 11:40–12:13

1. *ANETP*, 39–72.

2. *IVPBBCOT*, 750–51.

3. *IVPBBCOT*, 751; see also M. S. Moore, "Resurrection and Immortality."

4. On 11:40–12:3 as rooted in OT hope and Daniel's historical circumstances, yet ultimately indicative of a misapprehension of the "signs of the times," see Woude, "Prophetic Prediction."

5. Longman, *Daniel*, 280–83. On 11:36–45 as referring to the events of 67–70 AD with 12:1–3 pertaining to messianic enthronement, see Parry, "Desolation of the Temple and Messianic Enthronement."

6. Goldingay, *Daniel*, 305. See also Niskanen, "Daniel's Portrait of Antiochus IV."

7. On the development of the concept of the resurrection in Judaism—particularly as reflected in Qumran texts and Daniel—see Hobbins, "Resurrection in the Daniel Tradition," 2:395–418.

8. Steinmann, *Daniel*, 563.

9. Miller, *Daniel*, 323.

10. BDB, 477.

11. See Lucas, *Daniel*, 297–98.

12. Steinmann, *Daniel*, 577; cf. Wong, "Faithful to the End."

Bibliography

Recommended Resources

Archer, Gleason L., Jr. "Daniel." In *Daniel–Minor Prophets*, vol. 7 of *The Expositor's Bible Commentary*, edited by Frank E. Gaebelein, 1–157. Grand Rapids: Zondervan, 1985.

Baldwin, Joyce G. *Daniel: An Introduction and Commentary*. Edited by D. J. Wiseman. Downers Grove, IL: InterVarsity, 1978.

Collins, John J. *Daniel: A Commentary on the Book of Daniel*. Edited by Frank M. Cross. Minneapolis: Fortress, 1993.

Goldingay, John E. *Daniel*. Word Biblical Commentary 30. Nashville: Nelson, 1989.

Hartman, Louis F., and Alexander A. Di Lella. *The Book of Daniel*. Anchor Bible 23. New Haven: Yale University Press, 1978.

Longman, Tremper, III. *Daniel*. NIV Application Commentary. Grand Rapids: Zondervan, 1999.

Lucas, Ernest C. *Daniel*. Apollos Old Testament Commentary 20. Downers Grove, IL: InterVarsity, 2002.

Miller, Stephen R. *Daniel*. New American Commentary 18. Nashville: Broadman & Holman, 1994.

Steinmann, Andrew E. *Daniel*. Concordia Commentary. Saint Louis: Concordia, 2008.

Wood, Leon J. *A Commentary on Daniel*. Grand Rapids: Zondervan, 1973.

Young, Edward J. *The Prophecy of Daniel*. Grand Rapids: Eerdmans, 1949.

Additional Works Cited

Alexander, John B. "New Light on the Fiery Furnace." *Journal of Biblical Literature* 69 (1950): 375–76.

Andreasen, Niels-Erik A. "The Role of the Queen Mother in Israelite Society." *Catholic Biblical Quarterly* 45 (1983): 179–93.

Arnold, Bill T. "Wordplay and Characterization in Daniel 1." In *Puns and Pundits: Word Play in the Hebrew Bible and Ancient Near Eastern Literature*, edited by Scott B. Noegel, 231–48. Bethesda: CDL, 2000.

———. "Wordplay and Narrative Techniques in Daniel 5 and 6." *Journal of Biblical Literature* 112 (1993): 479–85.

Avalos, Hector I. "The Comedic Function of the Enumerations of Officials and Instruments in Daniel 3." *Catholic Biblical Quarterly* 53 (1991): 580–89.

Beale, Gregory K. "The Influence of Daniel upon the Structure and Theology of John's Apocalypse." *Journal of the Evangelical Theological Society* 27 (1984): 413–23.

Beasley-Murray, George R. "The Interpretation of Daniel 7." *Catholic Biblical Quarterly* 45 (1983): 44–58.

Beaulieu, Paul-Alain. "The Babylonian Background of the Motif of the Fiery Furnace in Daniel 3." *Journal of Biblical Literature* 128 (2009): 273–90.

Berg, Sandra Beth. *The Book of Esther: Motifs, Themes, and Structure*. Missoula, MT: Scholars Press, 1979.

Boogaart, Thomas A. "Daniel 6: A Tale of Two Empires." *Reformed Review* 39 (1986): 106–12.

Brewer, David Instone. "*MENE MENE TEQEL UPARSIN*: Daniel 5:25 in Cuneiform." *Tyndale Bulletin* 42 (1991): 310–16.

Broida, Marian. "Textualizing Divination: The Writing on the Wall in Daniel 5:25." *Vetus Testamentum* 62 (2012): 1–13.

Brownlee, William H. "The Ineffable Name of God." *Bulletin of the American Schools of Oriental Research* 226 (1977): 39–46.

Charles, R. H. *A Critical and Exegetical Commentary on the Book of Daniel*. 1929. Reprint, Eugene, OR: Wipf & Stock, 2006.

Chavalas, Mark W., ed. *The Ancient Near East: Historical Sources in Translation*. Malden, MA: Blackwell, 2006.

Colless, Brian E. "Cyrus the Persian as Darius the Mede in the Book of Daniel." *Journal for the Study of the Old Testament* 56 (1992): 113–26.

Collins, John J. "The Court-Tales in Daniel and the Development of Apocalyptic." *Journal of Biblical Literature* 94 (1975): 218–34.

———. "The Son of Man in First-Century Judaism." *New Testament Studies* 38 (1992): 448–66.

Cook, J. M. *The Persian Empire*. New York: Schocken, 1983.

Cowley, A. E. *Aramaic Papyri of the Fifth Century B.C.* Oxford: Clarendon, 1923.

Coxon, Peter W. "Another Look at Nebuchadnezzar's Madness." In *The Book of Daniel in Light of New Findings*, edited by A. S. van der Woude, 211–22. Louvain: Leuven University Press, 1993.

———. "Daniel III 17: A Linguistic and Theological Problem." *Vetus Testamentum* 26 (1976): 400–409.

———. "The Great Tree of Daniel 4." In *A Word in Season: Essays in Honour of William McKane*, edited by James D. Martin and Philip R. Davies, 99–111. Supplements to Journal for the Study of the Old Testament 42. Sheffield: Sheffield Academic Press, 1986.

Deventer, H. J. M. van. "Another Wise Queen (Mother): Women's Wisdom in Daniel 5.10–12?" In *A Feminist Companion to Prophets and Daniel*, edited by Athalya Brenner, 247–61. London: Sheffield Academic Press, 2001.

Dillard, Raymond B. "Harmonization: A Help and a Hindrance." In *Inerrancy and Hermeneutic: A Tradition, a Challenge, a Debate*, edited by Harvie M. Conn, 151–64. Grand Rapids: Baker, 1985.

Dillard, Raymond B., and Tremper Longman III. *An Introduction to the Old Testament*. Grand Rapids: Zondervan, 1994.

Dunn, James D. G. "'Son of God' as 'Son of Man' in the Dead Sea Scrolls? A Response to John Collins on 4Q246." In *The Scrolls and the Scriptures: Qumran Fifty Years After*, edited by Stanley E. Porter and Craig A. Evans, 198–210. Sheffield: Sheffield Academic Press, 1997.

Dunne, John Anthony. *Esther and Her Elusive God: How a Secular Story Functions as Scripture*. Eugene, OR: Wipf & Stock, 2014.

Evans, Craig A. "Daniel in the New Testament: Visions of God's Kingdom." In *The Book of Daniel: Composition and Reception*, edited by John J. Collins and Peter W. Flint, 2:490–527. Supplements to Vetus Testamentum 83. Leiden: Brill, 2001.

Feinberg, Charles Lee. *Daniel: The Man and His Visions*. Chappaqua: Christian Herald Books, 1981.

Feinberg, Paul D. "An Exegetical and Theological Study of Daniel 9:24–27." In *Tradition and Testament: Essays in Honor of Charles Lee Feinberg*, edited by John S. Feinberg and Paul D. Feinberg, 189–220. Chicago: Moody, 1981.

Ferguson, Sinclair B. *Daniel*. The Preacher's Commentary 21. Nashville: Nelson, 1988.

Fewell, Danna Nolan. *Circle of Sovereignty: Plotting Politics in the Book of Daniel*. Nashville: Abingdon, 1991.

Fuller, Russell T., and Kyoungwon Choi. *Invitation to Biblical Hebrew: A Beginning Grammar*. Invitation to Theological Studies. Grand Rapids: Kregel, 2006.

Garrison, Jason A. "Nebuchadnezzar's Dream: An Inversion of Gilgamesh Imagery." *Bibliotheca Sacra* 169 (2012): 172–87.

Goldingay, John E. "Daniel in the Context of Old Testament Theology." In *The Book of Daniel: Composition and Reception*, edited by John J. Collins and Peter W. Flint, 2:639–60. Supplements to Vetus Testamentum 83. Leiden: Brill, 2001.

Goldwurm, Hersh. *Daniel: A New Translation with a Commentary Anthologized from Talmudic, Midrashic and Rabbinic Sources*. 2nd ed. New York: Mesorah, 1980.

Gooding, David W. "The Literary Structure of the Book of Daniel and Its Implications." *Tyndale Bulletin* 32 (1981): 43–79.

Goswell, Greg. "The Temple Theme in the Book of Daniel." *Journal of the Evangelical Theological Society* 55 (2012): 509–20.

Grabbe, Lester L. "The Belshazzar of Daniel and the Belshazzar of History." *Andrews University Seminary Studies* 26 (1988): 59–66.

———. "'The End of the Desolations of Jerusalem': From Jeremiah's 70 Years to Daniel's 70 Weeks of Years." In *Early Jewish and Christian Exegesis: Studies in Memory of William Hugh Brownlee*, edited by Craig A. Evans and William F. Stinespring, 67–72. Atlanta: Scholars Press, 1987.

———. "The Seventy-Weeks Prophecy (Daniel 9:24–27) in Early Jewish Interpretation." In *The Quest for Context and Meaning: Studies in Biblical Intertextuality in Honor of James A. Sanders*, edited by Craig A. Evans and Shemaryahu Talmon, 595–611. Leiden: Brill, 1997.

Greenberg, Moshe. *Introduction to Hebrew*. Englewood Cliffs: Prentice-Hall College, 1965.

Gurney, Robert J. M. "The Four Kingdoms of Daniel 2 and 7." *Themelios* 2 (1977): 39–45.

———. *God in Control: An Exposition of the Prophecies of the Book of Daniel*. Worthing, West Sussex: Walter, 1980.

Habel, Norman C. "Introducing the Apocalyptic Visions of Daniel 7." *Concordia Theological Monthly* 41 (1970): 10–26.

Hasel, Gerhard F. "The Book of Daniel: Evidences Relating to Persons and Chronology." *Andrews University Seminary Studies* 19 (1981): 37–49.

———. "The Book of Daniel and Matters of Language: Evidences Relating to Names, Words, and the Aramaic Language." *Andrews University Seminary Studies* 19 (1981): 211–25.

———. "The First and Third Years of Belshazzar (Dan 7:1; 8:1)." *Andrews University Seminary Studies* 15 (1977): 153–68.

———. "The Four World Empires of Daniel 2 against Its Near Eastern Environment." *Journal for the Study of the Old Testament* 12 (1979): 17–30.

———. "The Identity of 'The Saints of the Most High' in Daniel 7." *Biblica* 56 (1975): 173–92.

Hays, Christopher B. "Chirps from the Dust: The Affliction of Nebuchadnezzar in Daniel 4:30 in Its Ancient Near Eastern Context." *Journal of Biblical Literature* 126 (2007): 305–25.

Hill, Andrew E., and John H. Walton. *A Survey of the Old Testament*. Grand Rapids: Zondervan, 1991.

Hobbins, John F. "Resurrection in the Daniel Tradition and Other Writings at Qumran." In *The Book of Daniel: Composition and Reception*, edited by John J. Collins and Peter W. Flint, 2:395–420. Supplements to Vetus Testamentum 83. Leiden: Brill, 2001.

The Jewish Study Bible. Edited by Adele Berlin, Marc Zvi Brettler, and Michael Fishbane. Oxford: Oxford University Press, 2004.

Kee, Min Suc. "The Heavenly Council and Its Type-Scene." *Journal for the Study of the Old Testament* 31 (2007): 259–73.

Keil, C. F., and F. Delitzsch. *Ezekiel, Daniel*. Vol. 9 of *Commentary on the Old Testament in Ten Volumes*. Translated by M. G. Easton. Grand Rapids: Eerdmans, 1983.

Khan, Geoffrey. *A Short Introduction to the Tiberian Masoretic Bible and Its Reading Tradition*. Piscataway, NJ: Gorgias, 2012.

Knowles, Louis E. "The Interpretation of the Seventy Weeks of Daniel in the Early Fathers." *Westminster Theological Journal* 7 (1945): 136–60.

Koldewey, Robert, and Agnes Sophia Griffith Johns. *The Excavations at Babylon*. London: Macmillan, 1914.

Kvanvig, Helge S. "Throne Visions and Monsters: The Encounter between the Danielic and Enochic Traditions." *Zeitschrift für die alttestamentliche Wissenschaft* 117 (2005): 249–72.

Lacocque, André. *The Book of Daniel*. Translated by David Pellauer. Atlanta: John Knox, 1979.

Lawson, Jack N. "'The God Who Reveals Secrets': The Mesopotamian Background to Daniel 2.47." *Journal for the Study of the Old Testament* 74 (1997): 61–76.

Lenzi, Alan. "Secrecy, Textual Legitimation, and Intercultural Polemics in the Book of Daniel." *Catholic Biblical Quarterly* 71 (2009): 330–48.

Lewis, C. S. *The Lion, the Witch and the Wardrobe*. Chronicles of Narnia. United Kingdom: Geoffrey Bles, 1950.

Lucas, Ernest C. "Daniel." In *Zondervan Illustrated Bible Backgrounds Commentary*, edited by John H. Walton, 4:518–71. Grand Rapids: Zondervan, 2009.

———. "The Source of Daniel's Animal Imagery." *Tyndale Bulletin* 41 (1990): 161–85.

———. "A Statue, a Fiery Furnace and a Dismal Swamp: A Reflection on Some Issues in Biblical Hermeneutics." *Evangelical Quarterly* 77 (2005): 291–307.

Lust, Johan. "Cult and Sacrifice in Daniel: The Tamid and the Abomination of Desolation." In *The Book of Daniel: Composition and Reception*, edited by John J. Collins and Peter W. Flint, 2:671–88. Supplements to Vetus Testamentum 83. Leiden: Brill, 2001.

McComiskey, Thomas Edward. "The Seventy 'Weeks' of Daniel against the Background of Ancient Near Eastern Literature." *Westminster Theological Journal* 47 (1985): 18–45.

Meadowcroft, Tim. "Point of View in Storytelling: An Experiment in Narrative Criticism in Daniel 4." *Didaskalia* 8 (1997): 30–42.

———. "Who Are the Princes of Persia and Greece (Daniel 10)? Pointers towards the Danielic Vision of Earth and Heaven." *Journal for the Study of the Old Testament* 29 (2004): 99–113.

Mercer, Mark K. "The Benefactions of Antiochus IV Epiphanes and Dan 11:37–38: An Exegetical Note." *Master's Seminary Journal* 12 (2001): 89–93.

———. "Daniel 1:1 and Jehoiakim's Three Years of Servitude." *Andrews University Seminary Studies* 27 (1989): 179–92.

Millard, Alan R. "Daniel 1–6 and History." *Evangelical Quarterly* 49 (1977): 67–73.

Milton, John. *Paradise Lost*. Edited by Leland Ryken. Wheaton: Crossway, 2013.

Montgomery, James A. *A Critical and Exegetical Commentary on the Book of Daniel*. Edinburgh: T&T Clark, 1927.

Moore, Carey A. *Daniel, Esther, and Jeremiah: The Additions*. Anchor Bible 44. Garden City, NY: Doubleday, 1977.

Moore, Michael S. "Resurrection and Immortality: Two Motifs Navigating Confluent Theological Streams in the Old Testament (Dan 12:1–4)." *Theologische Zeitschrift* 39 (1983): 17–34.

Niskanen, Paul. "Daniel's Portrait of Antiochus IV: Echoes of a Persian King." *Catholic Biblical Quarterly* 66 (2004): 378–86.

Oppenheim, A. Leo. *Ancient Mesopotamia: Portrait of a Dead Civilization*. Edited by Erica Reiner. Rev. ed. Chicago: University of Chicago Press, 1977.

———. *The Interpretation of Dreams in the Ancient Near East: With a Translation of an Assyrian*

Dream-Book. Vol. 46. Philadelphia: American Philosophical Society, 1956.

Parry, Jason Thomas. "Desolation of the Temple and Messianic Enthronement in Daniel 11:36–12:3." *Journal of the Evangelical Theological Society* 54 (2011): 485–526.

Patterson, Richard D. "The Key Role of Daniel 7." *Grace Theological Journal* 12 (1991): 245–61.

Peterson, Eugene H. *A Long Obedience in the Same Direction: Discipleship in an Instant Society.* Downers Grove, IL: InterVarsity, 1980.

Pfandl, Gerhard. "Interpretations of the Kingdom of God in Daniel 2:44." *Andrews University Seminary Studies* 34 (1996): 249–68.

Pierce, Ronald W. "Covenant Conditionality and a Future for Israel." *Journal of the Evangelical Theological Society* 37 (1994): 27–38.

———. "Spiritual Failure, Postponement, and Daniel 9." *Trinity Journal* 10 (1989): 211–22.

Pinnock, Clark, with Richard Rice, John Sanders, William Hasker, and David Basinger. *The Openness of God: A Biblical Challenge to the Traditional Understanding of God.* Downers Grove, IL: InterVarsity, 1994.

Poythress, Vern Sheridan. "The Holy Ones of the Most High in Daniel VII." *Vetus Testamentum* 26 (1976): 208–13.

Prinsloo, G. T. M. "Two Poems in a Sea of Prose: The Content and Context of Daniel 2:20–23 and 6:27–28." *Journal for the Study of the Old Testament* (1993): 93–108.

Pritchard, James B., ed. *The Ancient Near East: An Anthology of Texts and Pictures.* Princeton: Princeton University Press, 2011.

Redditt, Paul L. "Daniel 9: Its Structure and Meaning." *Catholic Biblical Quarterly* 62 (2000): 236–49.

Rowley, H. H. *Darius the Mede and the Four World Empires in the Book of Daniel: A Historical Study of Contemporary Theories.* Cardiff: University of Wales, 1935.

Scolnic, Benjamin. "Antiochus IV as the Scorned Prince in Dan 11:21." *Vetus Testamentum* 62 (2012): 572–81.

Shea, William H. "Bel(te)shazzar Meets Belshazzar." *Andrews University Seminary Studies* 26 (1988): 67–81.

———. "Daniel 3: Extra-Biblical Texts and the Convocation on the Plain of Dura." *Andrews University Seminary Studies* 20 (1982): 29–52.

———. "Darius the Mede: An Update." *Andrews University Seminary Studies* 20 (1982): 229–47.

———. "Darius the Mede in His Persian-Babylonian Setting." *Andrews University Seminary Studies* 29 (1991): 235–57.

———. "Further Literary Structures in Daniel 2–7: An Analysis of Daniel 4." *Andrews University Seminary Studies* 23 (1985): 193–202.

———. "Further Literary Structures in Daniel 2–7: An Analysis of Daniel 5, and the Broader Relationships within Chapters 2–7." *Andrews University Seminary Studies* 23 (1985): 277–95.

———. "Nabonidus, Belshazzar, and the Book of Daniel: An Update." *Andrews University Seminary Studies* 20 (1982): 133–49.

———. "The Neo-Babylonian Historical Setting for Daniel 7." *Andrews University Seminary Studies* 24 (1986): 31–36.

———. "An Unrecognized Vassal King of Babylon in the Early Achaemenid Period (Part 1)." *Andrews University Seminary Studies* 9 (1971): 51–67.

———. "An Unrecognized Vassal King of Babylon in the Early Achaemenid Period (Part 2)." *Andrews University Seminary Studies* 9 (1971): 99–128.

———. "An Unrecognized Vassal King of Babylon in the Early Achaemenid Period (Part 3)." *Andrews University Seminary Studies* 10 (1972): 88–117.

———. "An Unrecognized Vassal King of Babylon in the Early Achaemenid Period (Part 4)." *Andrews University Seminary Studies* 10 (1972): 147–78.

———. "Wrestling with the Prince of Persia: A Study on Daniel 10." *Andrews University Seminary Studies* 21 (1983): 225–50.

Shepherd, Michael B. "Daniel 7:13 and the New Testament Son of Man." *Westminster Theological Journal* 68 (2006): 99–111.

Slotki, Judah J. *Daniel, Ezra, Nehemiah: Hebrew Text and English Translation with Introductions and Commentary.* Soncino Books of the Bible. Edited by A. Cohen. London: Soncino, 1951.

Smith-Christopher, Daniel. "Prayers and Dreams: Power and Diaspora Identities in the Social Setting of the Daniel Tales." In *The Book of Daniel: Composition and Reception,* edited by John J. Collins and Peter W. Flint, 1:66–90. Supplements to Vetus Testamentum 83. Leiden: Brill, 2001.

Sparks, H. F. D. "On the Origin of 'Darius the Mede' at Daniel V. 31." *Journal of Theological Studies* 47 (1946): 41–46.

Stefanovic, Zdravko. "Daniel: A Book of Significant Reversals." *Andrews University Seminary Studies* 30 (1992): 139–50.

Steinmann, Andrew E. "The Chicken and the Egg: A New Proposal for the Relationship between the *Prayer of Nabonidus* and the *Book of Daniel.*" *Revue de Qumran* 20 (2002): 557–70.

———. "Is the Antichrist in Daniel 11?" *Bibliotheca Sacra* 162 (2005): 195–209.

Stevenson, Kenneth, and Michael Glerup. *Ezekiel, Daniel.* Vol. 13 of *Ancient Christian Commentary on Scripture.* Downers Grove, IL: InterVarsity, 2008.

Toorn, Kerel van der. "Scholars at the Oriental Court: The Figure of Daniel against Its Mesopotamian Background." In *The Book of Daniel: Composition and Reception,* edited by John J. Collins and Peter W.

Flint, 1:37–54. Supplements to Vetus Testamentum 83. Leiden: Brill, 2001.

Tov, Emmanuel. *Textual Criticism of the Hebrew Bible.* Minneapolis: Fortress, 1992.

Towner, W. Sibley. *Daniel.* Interpretation: A Bible Commentary for Teaching and Preaching. Atlanta: John Knox, 1984.

Trible, Phyllis. *God and the Rhetoric of Sexuality.* Overtures to Biblical Theology. Philadelphia: Fortress, 1978.

Walton, John H. "The *Anzu* Myth as Relevant Background for Daniel 7?" In *The Book of Daniel: Composition and Reception,* edited by John J. Collins and Peter W. Flint, 1:69–89. Supplements to Vetus Testamentum 83. Leiden: Brill, 2001.

———. "The Decree of Darius the Mede in Daniel 6." *Journal of the Evangelical Theological Society* 29 (1986): 279–86.

———. "The Four Kingdoms of Daniel." *Journal of the Evangelical Theological Society* 29 (1986): 25–36.

Walton, John H., Victor H. Matthews, and Mark W. Chavalas. *The IVP Bible Background Commentary: Old Testament.* Downers Grove, IL: InterVarsity, 2000.

Walton, John H., and Kim E. Walton. *The Bible Story Handbook: A Resource for Teaching 175 Stories from the Bible.* Wheaton: Crossway, 2010.

Walvoord, John F. *Daniel: The Key to Prophetic Revelation.* Chicago: Moody, 1971.

Ware, Bruce A. *God's Lesser Glory: The Diminished God of Open Theism.* Wheaton: Crossway, 2000.

Wenham, David. "The Kingdom of God and Daniel." *Expository Times* 98 (1986–87): 132–34.

Whitcomb, John C. *Darius the Mede: A Study in Historical Identification.* Grand Rapids: Eerdmans, 1959.

Wilkinson, Paul R. *For Zion's Sake: Christian Zionism and the Role of John Nelson Darby.* Studies in Evangelical History and Christian Thought. Milton Keynes, UK: Paternoster, 2007.

Wiseman, D. J. "The Last Days of Babylon." *Christianity Today* 2/4 (November 25, 1957): 7–10.

———. "Some Historical Problems in the Book of Daniel." In *Notes on Some Problems in the Book of Daniel,* edited by D. J. Wiseman, 9–18. London: Tyndale, 1965.

Wolters, Albert M. "The Riddle of the Scales in Daniel 5." *Hebrew Union College Annual* 62 (1991): 155–77.

Wong, G. C. I. "Faithful to the End: A Pastoral Reading of Daniel 10–12." *Expository Times* 110 (1999): 109–13.

Woodard, Branson L., Jr. "Literary Strategies and Authorship in the Book of Daniel." *Journal of the Evangelical Theological Society* 37 (1994): 39–53.

Woude, Adam S. van der. "Prophetic Prediction, Political Prognostication, and Firm Belief: Reflections on Daniel 11:40–12:3." In *The Quest for Context and Meaning: Studies in Biblical Intertextuality in Honor of James A. Sanders,* edited by Craig A. Evans and Shemaryahu Talmon, 63–73. Leiden: Brill, 1997.

Yamauchi, Edwin M. "Daniel and Contacts between the Aegean and the Near East before Alexander." *Evangelical Quarterly* 53 (1981): 37–47.

———. "Hermeneutical Issues in the Book of Daniel." *Journal of the Evangelical Theological Society* 23 (1980): 13–21.

———. *Persia and the Bible.* Grand Rapids: Baker, 1996.

Zimmermann, Frank. "The Writing on the Wall: Dan. 5:25 f." *Jewish Quarterly Review* n.s. 55 (1965): 201–7.

Image Credits

Unless otherwise indicated, photos are copyright © Baker Publishing Group and Dr. James C. Martin. Unless otherwise indicated, illustrations and maps are copyright © Baker Publishing Group.

Photo on page 8 © Kim Walton. Courtesy of the Byzantine and Christian Museum, Athens.

Photo on page 191 © Kim Walton. Courtesy of the Chora Museum, Istanbul.

Photo on page 52 © Kim Walton. Courtesy of the Eretz Museum, Tel Aviv, Israel.

Photo on page 40 © Kim Walton. Courtesy of the Musée du Louvre; Autorisation de photographer et de filmer. Louvre, Paris, France.

Photo on page 72 © Kim Walton. Courtesy of the Pergamon Museum, Berlin.

Photo on page 60 © Kim Walton. Courtesy of the Vatican Museum.

Photo on page 147 © Library of Congress Prints & Photographs Division, [reproduction number, LC-DIG-matpc-03493].

Photo on page 138 © Marie-Lan Nguyen / Wikimedia Commons, CC-by-2.5, courtesy of the Louvre.

Photo on page 49 © Matteo Gabrieli / Shutterstock.com.

Photo on page 103 © M R / Shutterstock.com.

Photos on pages 87, 150 © Rembrandt Harmensz. van Rijn / National Gallery, London, UK / Bridgeman Images.

Photo on page 169 © Private Collection / © Richard and Kailas Icons, London, UK / Bridgeman Images.

Photo on page 126 © Ted Larson.

Photo on page 30 © Valentin de Boulogne / The Louvre, Paris, France / Bridgeman Images.

Photo on page 186 © Werner Forman Archive / Bridgeman Images.

Photo on page 81 © William Blake / Minneapolis Institute of Arts, MN, USA / Bridgeman Images.

Photo on page 34 © Yauhen Novikau / Shutterstock.com.

Photos on pages 59, 149 © The Yorck Project / Wikimedia Commons.

Photo on page 189 © Zev Radovan / Bridgeman Images.

Contributors

General Editors
Mark. L. Strauss
John H. Walton

Associate Editors, Illustrating the Text
Kevin and Sherry Harney

Contributing Author, Illustrating the Text
Donald C. Porter

Series Development
Jack Kuhatschek
Brian Vos

Project Editor
James Korsmo

Interior Design
Brian Brunsting
William Overbeeke

Visual Content
Kim Walton

Cover Direction
Paula Gibson
Michael Cook

Index

Testament of Levi, 158
theocentric poems, 35
Theodotion, 68, 103, 160
theophany, 142, 167
Thermopylae, 175, 179
Thrace, 4, 136, 175, 178–79
Tigris, 167
torah, 19, 23, 137, 149–50, 153–54, 182
transgression, 152, 160, 188. *See also* sin; wickedness
trust, 14, 16, 18–19, 38, 59–60, 63, 106, 108, 110, 114, 118–19, 150, 162

Ugaritic Baal cycle, 60
Ulai Canal, 135, 140–41, 167
unfaithfulness, 130, 143, 152

watchers, 61, 67–69
wickedness, 30, 63, 75–76, 91, 97, 104, 117, 121, 132, 142–44, 149, 150, 156, 159–60, 162, 186–87, 189, 191. *See also* sin; transgression; wickedness

wisdom
  instructional/proverbial, 19, 22, 23, 25, 36
  mantic/prophetic, 22–24, 36
wise men, 24, 28–32, 36–38, 43–44, 51, 87. *See also* astrologers; Chaldeans; enchanters; magicians; sorcerers
worship, 37–38, 48, 50–51, 55, 57, 80, 86, 105, 108, 111–13, 119–20, 125, 131, 157, 184

Xenophon, 84, 97

Zeus, 137, 161, 182–83
ziggurat, 78
zoanthropy, 69, 78
Zoroastrianism, 35, 105, 110, 187